LETTERS FROM THE HEART

The Timeless Teaching
of the Apostle Paul

*"For me to live is Christ
and to die is gain"*

(Philippians 1:21)

ROBERT GRIFFITH

GRACE AND TRUTH PUBLISHING
PO Box 338, Gunnedah NSW 2380 Australia
www.graceandtruthpublishing.com.au

All Bible quotes are from the New International Version (NIV) expect where
otherwise stated.

NEW INTERNATIONAL VERSION (NIV), Copyright 1973, 1978 and 1984 by
international Bible Society. Used by permission of Zondervan Publishing House.
All rights reserved.

Other version quotes are from:

AMPLIFIED BIBLE (AMP), Copyright © 1954, 1958, 1962, 1964, 1965, 1987 by
The Lockman Foundation. Used by permission.

ENGLISH STANDARD VERSION (ESV), Copyright © 2001 by Crossway Bibles,
a division of Good News Publishers. Used by permission. All rights reserved.

NEW AMERICAN STANDARD BIBLE (NASB), Copyright © 1960, 1962, 1963, 1968,
1971, 1972, 1973, 1975, 1977, by The Lockman Foundation. Used by permission.

NEW KING JAMES VERSION (NKJV), Copyright © 1979, 1980, 1982, by Thomas
Nelson Inc. Used by permission. All rights reserved.

THE MESSAGE (MSG), by Eugene Peterson, Copyright © 1993, 1994, 1995, 1996,
and 2000. Used by permission of NavPress Publishing Group. All rights reserved.

REVISED STANDARD VERSION (RSV), Copyright © 1973, by Thomas Nelson Inc.
Used by permission. All rights reserved.

Quotes in square brackets are the author's comment.

ISBN 978-0-6486439-9-9

TABLE OF CONTENTS

~ INTRODUCTION ~

The Apostle Paul, originally named Saul, was most probably born between 5 B.C. and 5 A.D. in Tarsus, in modern-day Turkey. He came from a devout Jewish family and was a Roman citizen.

His family belonged to the tribe of Benjamin, and he was well-educated in Jewish law. Saul was fluent in Hebrew, Greek, and possibly even Aramaic, which enabled him to communicate effectively across a number of different cultures.

Tarsus was a cultural and intellectual centre which was in many ways comparable to Athens and Alexandria. That meant Paul was most likely exposed to various cultural and philosophical influences from a reasonably early age.

Despite this Hellenistic environment, Paul's family maintained strong Jewish beliefs and practices. His Roman citizenship which was inherited from his father, was quite unusual for a Jew and that ended up becoming a rather significant advantage in his later travels and legal trials.

Paul was sent to Jerusalem to be educated under Gamaliel, one of the most notable teachers of Jewish law at that time. Under Gamaliel's tutelage, Paul received an extensive education in the Scriptures and in Jewish traditions.

This background not only provided him with the tools necessary for his future ministry but also instilled in him a fervent devotion to the Jewish law and customs.

Conversion to Christianity

Saul's conversion on the road to Damascus is one of the most significant and dramatic moments in the whole New Testament. Intending to arrest Christians and bring them back to Jerusalem for trial, Saul encountered a blinding light and heard the voice of Jesus Christ himself asking, *"Saul, Saul, why do you persecute me?"* This profound experience led to Paul's conversion, a pivotal moment not only in his life but in the history of Christianity.

Temporarily blinded, Saul was led into the city of Damascus, where Ananias, a Christian disciple, healed him. After Saul's recovery, he was baptized and began to use the name Paul. He then retreated to Arabia for a lengthy period of reflection and preparation.

Approximately three years later, Paul returned to Damascus to commence his ministry.

Paul's Missionary Journeys

There is no doubt that Paul's three missionary journeys were fundamental in spreading the gospel of Jesus Christ far and wide and expanding the Christian faith beyond Jewish communities and deep into the Gentile world.

Paul's First Missionary Journey (around 48-49 A.D.)

With Barnabas and John Mark by his side, Paul travelled across Cyprus and into southern Asia Minor. They faced Jewish opposition but successfully established Christian communities. This journey was marked by Paul's sermon in Antioch of Pisidia, where he outlined the history of Israel and presented Jesus as the promised Messiah.

Paul's Second Missionary Journey (around 50-52 A.D.)

This time with Silas, and later joined by Timothy and Luke, Paul ventured further, crossing into Europe. His work in cities like Philippi, where he and Silas were imprisoned and subsequently released following an earthquake, and also in Athens, where he delivered his very famous Areopagus sermon, highlighted the expansion of Christianity into the Greco-Roman world.

Paul's Third Missionary Journey (around 53-57 A.D.)

Paul revisited Asia Minor and Greece, strengthening the various Christian communities there. His lengthy stay in Ephesus was notable for the "riot of the silversmiths," who were angered by the economic threat Paul's teachings posed to their trade in Artemis worship.

Paul's Journey to Rome (around 60-62 A.D.)

Under arrest, Paul was sent to Rome to stand trial before Caesar. Although this journey was fraught with peril, including a shipwreck on the island of Malta, Paul used the time to preach and teach, further spreading the Christian message.

Paul's writings and Theological Contributions

The Apostle Paul is traditionally credited with writing thirteen books of the New Testament, known as the Pauline epistles. These letters are among the oldest Christian documents in our possession, and they were originally written to a variety of early Christian communities and individuals to address theological issues, moral issues, and personal relationships in the church. Here is a very brief overview of each of Paul's letters:

Romans: Written to the believers in Rome, this epistle lays out Paul's theological framework, emphasizing salvation by grace through faith in Jesus Christ, the role of the law, and the relationship between Jews and Gentiles within the Christian community.

1 Corinthians: Addressed to the church in Corinth, this letter deals with divisions, moral issues, and questions about worship and the resurrection, reflecting the challenges of a diverse and growing church.

2 Corinthians: A follow-up to 1 Corinthians, this letter is more personal and it boldly defends Paul's authority and ministry, addressing the challenges and persecutions he faced.

Galatians: Addressed to the churches in Galatia, this epistle confronts the issue of whether Gentile Christians need to observe Jewish law. Paul argues for justification by grace through faith rather than by the law.

Ephesians: Although its direct recipient is debated, Ephesians is believed to be a circular letter for various churches. It discusses the cosmic significance of Christ and the unity and conduct of the church as the body of Christ.

Philippians: Written from prison, likely in Rome, this letter to the Philippian believers is warm and personal, as it expresses Paul's gratitude and joy. It emphasizes Christ's humility and obedience as a model for Christian life.

Colossians: Addressed to the church in Colossae, this letter counters false teachings and emphasizes the supremacy of Christ and the completeness of the believers in Christ.

1 Thessalonians: This is certainly one of Paul's earliest letters, it offers encouragement and instructions to the young church in Thessalonica, addressing some concerns he heard regarding the second coming of Christ.

2 Thessalonians: Following 1 Thessalonians, this letter further clarifies issues regarding the second coming of Christ, as Paul encourages the church to remain steadfast and disciplined.

1 Timothy: A personal letter to Timothy, a young leader in the church, offering advice on church leadership, false teachings, and personal conduct.

2 Timothy: Believed to be Paul's last letter, written from prison in Rome before his death, it encourages Timothy to be faithful and endure hardships for the gospel.

Titus: Similar to the Timothy letters, this letter is addressed to Titus, guiding him on organizing the church in Crete and teaching sound doctrine.

Philemon: A private letter to Philemon, a leader in the Colossian church, appealing for the reconciliation and kind treatment of Onesimus, a runaway slave who had become a Christian.

These letters collectively form a substantial part of Christian New Testament doctrine and provide tremendous insight into the development of early Christian communities, their practices, challenges, and the theological foundations laid by Paul.

Paul's Death and Legacy

Though the exact details of Paul's death are not really unclear, it is traditionally believed that he was martyred in Rome sometime during 64-68 A.D. during Nero's persecution of the Christians. He is thought to have been beheaded, a form of execution reserved for Roman citizens.

Paul's legacy is monumental. He is considered one of the most important figures in the history of the Western world for his tireless work in spreading Christianity throughout the Roman Empire and for his contributions to Christian theology. Paul's teaching and ministry literally shook the world to the core and upended so many of the deeply engrained religious beliefs.

His writings and teachings continue to influence all Christian thought and practice, making him a central figure in both theological studies and the life of the global church. The Apostle Paul's life and writings show a man committed to spreading the message of Christ, establishing a lasting spiritual community, and addressing complex theological issues within the early church.

The following brief commentaries of Paul's first seven letters will provide a good summary and overview of this unique and highly influential body of work. Each chapter will take you through these ancient texts and provide some important insight and a clear theological framework for the church and the entire Christian faith.

I really encourage you to read all the Biblical text I have included and not just the commentary. You may even use this book as a daily devotion over a period of time. I can assure you it will be worth your time to work through all of Paul's teaching.

When you have finished Romans, 1 & 2 Corinthians, Galatians, Ephesians, Philippians, Colossians, 1 & 2 Thessalonians, 1 & 2 Timothy, Titus and Philemon you will be left with no doubt as to why this man had such an enormous impact on the church and the whole world and why his teaching is indeed, timeless.

~ ROMANS ~

The Book of Romans, one of the letters in the New Testament attributed to the Apostle Paul, is a foundational text for Christian theology, especially concerning Christian doctrine and ethics. It was written to the Christian community in Rome, whom Paul planned to visit on his journey to Spain. The comprehensive presentation of Paul's understanding of the Christian faith in the letter to the Romans, serves as a superb systematic theological guide. Here is a brief chapter by chapter summary by way of introduction:

Chapter 1: Paul opens with a greeting to the Roman Christians, introducing himself and expressing his desire to visit Rome. At the heart of this first chapter is the clear revelation of God's righteousness in the gospel, and the unrighteousness of humanity. Paul argues that the Gentile world has fallen into sinful practices and idolatry, ignoring the truth of God revealed in creation, resulting in God's wrath.

Chapter 2: Paul turns his critique towards the Jews, arguing that they are equally guilty before God despite possessing the law. He introduces the concept of the "true Jew" as one who is inwardly righteous and observes the law in spirit, not merely in letter.

Chapter 3: This chapter highlights the universality of sin: both Jews and Gentiles are under sin and cannot be justified by their own deeds. However, God's righteousness is revealed through faith in Jesus Christ, available to all who believe, without distinction. This establishes the foundational doctrine of justification by grace through faith.

Chapter 4: Paul uses the example of Abraham to demonstrate that justification by grace through faith is not a new concept but is rooted in the Jewish tradition. Abraham's faith was credited to him as righteousness before the law was given, showing that faith, not works, is the basis for righteousness.

Chapter 5: Here, Paul explores the results of justification by grace through faith: peace with God, grace, and the hope of glory. He contrasts Adam, through whom sin entered the world, with Christ, through whom grace and life abound to many.

Chapter 6: Paul addresses the potential misunderstanding that grace encourages sin. He explains that Christians, united with Christ in his death and resurrection, are called to live in newness of life, not continuing in sin.

Chapter 7: This chapter discusses the law's role in relation to sin. Paul describes his own experience with the law, illustrating how it brings awareness of sin but does not empower him to overcome sin. This highlights the struggle between the "inner man" and the flesh.

Chapter 8: This is one of the most encouraging chapters in the Bible. It reassures believers of their status as children of God, led by the Spirit. There is no condemnation for those in Christ. Paul speaks of the hope of future glory, the intercession of the Spirit, and the assurance of God's love.

Chapter 9: Paul expresses his sorrow for Israel's unbelief and discusses God's sovereign choice. He differentiates between physical and spiritual Israel and explains that God's election is based on His mercy and calling, not on human desire or effort.

Chapter 10: The apostle reiterates that righteousness comes by grace, through faith in Christ, not from law-keeping. He emphasizes the importance of confessing Christ as Lord and believing in the resurrection. Paul also expresses his desire for Israel's salvation and points out that faith comes from hearing the message of Christ.

Chapter 11: Paul explains that God has not rejected His people entirely; there is a remnant chosen by grace. The temporary hardening of Israel leads to the inclusion of Gentiles, which in turn will eventually lead to the salvation of all Israel.

Chapter 12: Paul transitions from doctrinal teaching to practical application, urging believers to offer their bodies as living sacrifices and to be transformed by the renewal of their minds. He discusses living in love, serving in the church Jesus birthed, and behaving ethically in the world.

Chapter 13: This chapter deals with the Christian's responsibility to government authorities, emphasizing that all authority comes from God. Paul also calls for love as the fulfillment of the law and urges believers to live honourably.

Chapter 14: Paul addresses the issue of disputable matters in the church, advising believers not to judge one another over issues that are not central to Christian faith. Instead, they should act in love and not cause others to stumble.

Chapter 15: The apostle encourages the strong in faith to bear with the weak and to seek to please their neighbours for their good. Paul expresses his ministry's goal and his travel plans, including his desire to visit Rome.

Chapter 16: Paul concludes with greetings to various individuals in the Roman church, warnings about divisive people, and a final doxology. This chapter highlights the personal and communal aspects of Paul's ministry.

Throughout Romans, Paul presents a comprehensive theological vision that encompasses so many foundational issues, including sin, salvation, grace, faith, righteousness, sanctification, and eschatology, all grounded in the person and work of Jesus Christ. It is a cornerstone for understanding all Christian doctrine and it provides practical guidance for living out the Christian faith.

Now I will unpack each of the sixteen chapters of Romans in more detail as we encounter and wrestle with this amazing letter.

~ ROMANS 1 ~

Introduction:

In Romans 1, Paul unfolds the righteousness of God revealed through the Gospel, contrasted starkly against the backdrop of our unrighteousness. Paul sets the stage here for understanding our desperate need for the gospel and the transformative power it holds.

Greetings and Thanksgiving (1:1-7)

> *"Paul, a servant of Christ Jesus, called to be an apostle and set apart for the gospel of God — the gospel he promised beforehand through his prophets in the Holy Scriptures regarding his Son, who as to his earthly life was a descendant of David, and who through the Spirit of holiness was appointed the Son of God in power by his resurrection from the dead: Jesus Christ our Lord. Through him we received grace and apostleship to call all the Gentiles to the obedience that comes from faith for his name's sake. And you also are among those Gentiles who are called to belong to Jesus Christ. To all in Rome who are loved by God and called to be his holy people: Grace and peace to you from God our Father and from the Lord Jesus Christ." (Romans 1:1-7)*

Paul begins by introducing himself as a servant of Christ Jesus, called to be an apostle, set apart for the gospel of God. Notice how Paul's identity is wrapped up in his relationship to Christ and the gospel. He is not boasting of personal achievements but is humbled by the calling he has received.

This introduction teaches us that our true identity lies not in our achievements, titles, or social status, but in our relationship with Christ. We, like Paul, are called to be servants of the gospel, set apart for God's purposes.

Paul continues by greeting the Roman believers, calling them "loved by God" and *"called to be saints."* This is a reminder to us of our identity in Christ: loved by God and called to holiness.

The Power of the Gospel (1:8-17)

"First, I thank my God through Jesus Christ for all of you, because your faith is being reported all over the world. God, whom I serve in my spirit in preaching the gospel of his Son, is my witness how constantly I remember you in my prayers at all times; and I pray that now at last by God's will, the way may be opened for me to come to you.

I long to see you so that I may impart to you some spiritual gift to make you strong – that is, that you and I may be mutually encouraged by each other's faith. I do not want you to be unaware, brothers and sisters, that I planned many times to come to you (but have been prevented from doing so until now) in order that I might have a harvest among you, just as I have had among the other Gentiles.

I am obligated both to Greeks and non-Greeks, both to the wise and the foolish. That is why I am so eager to preach the gospel also to you who are in Rome.

For I am not ashamed of the gospel, because it is the power of God that brings salvation to everyone who believes: first to the Jew, then to the Gentile. For in the gospel the righteousness of God is revealed – a righteousness that is by faith from first to last, just as it is written: "The righteous will live by faith." (Romans 1:8-17)

Paul now expresses his eagerness to visit Rome to impart some spiritual gift to strengthen the believers. His life is consumed with the service of the gospel – it is his utmost priority. Paul is not ashamed of the gospel; he sees it as the power of God for salvation to everyone who believes.

This leads us to ask ourselves: How do we view the Gospel? Is it merely a set of beliefs we affirm, or is it the power of God that transforms our lives?

The gospel is not just good news; it's dynamic, life-changing news. It's the revelation of God's righteousness imparted to us in Christ. Our response should be like Paul's - not of shame, but of bold proclamation and complete reliance.

The Wrath of God Against Sin (1:18-32)

"First, I thank my God through Jesus Christ for all of you, because your faith is being reported all over the world. God, whom I serve in my spirit in preaching the gospel of his Son, is my witness how constantly I remember you in my prayers at all times; and I pray that now at last by God's will, the way may be opened for me to come to you.

I long to see you so that I may impart to you some spiritual gift to make you strong — that is, that you and I may be mutually encouraged by each other's faith. I do not want you to be unaware, brothers and sisters, that I planned many times to come to you (but have been prevented from doing so until now) in order that I might have a harvest among you, just as I have had among the other Gentiles.

I am obligated both to Greeks and non-Greeks, both to the wise and the foolish. That is why I am so eager to preach the gospel also to you who are in Rome.

For I am not ashamed of the gospel, because it is the power of God that brings salvation to everyone who believes: first to the Jew, then to the Gentile. For in the gospel the righteousness of God is revealed — a righteousness that is by faith from first to last, just as it is written: "The righteous will live by faith." (Romans 1:18-32)

In this section, Paul turns to a darker theme, the reality of God's wrath against human wickedness. He paints a picture of humanity in rebellion against God, suppressing the truth and turning to idolatry. Despite knowing God, they neither glorified Him nor gave thanks. Their foolish hearts were darkened, leading to a downward spiral of sin.

Paul lists a series of vices that characterize a godless society, showing how rejecting the truth about God leads to moral decay and a plethora of sinful behaviours. It's a grim picture, but it's crucial for understanding the depth of human sin and the necessity of God's righteous judgment.

The sobering truth here is that sin is not merely a series of bad choices but a condition that affects every aspect of human existence. It distorts our thinking, desensitizes our hearts, and leads us away from our Creator. But it also highlights the beauty and necessity of the gospel. In a world marred by sin, the gospel is the beacon of hope and the only path to restoration.

As we reflect on Romans 1, we are faced with several challenging questions: How do we view the gospel? Is it the central force in our lives, or have we become ashamed of it? Have we recognized the depth of our sin and the righteousness of God that meets us in the gospel?

Paul's letter challenges us to embrace the gospel fully - not just as a one-time event in our lives but as the ongoing source of our salvation, transformation, and hope. It calls us to examine our hearts, turn away from our idols, and worship the true God.

Let us carry the power of the gospel into every area of our lives. May we each live unashamed of the good news of Jesus Christ, holding it out as the true solution to the sin and brokenness around us.

Conclusion

In Romans chapter 1, Paul lays a foundational understanding for the entire Christian life. It confronts us with our sin, drives us to the foot of the cross, and calls us to live in the light of the gospel.

May we go forth with the courage of Paul, proclaiming the gospel boldly and living out its implications in our daily lives. May the Lord bless us with deeper understanding and stronger faith as we continue to study His Word.

~ ROMANS 2 ~

Introduction:

As we journey further into Paul's epistle to the Romans, we arrive at a chapter that acts as a mirror to our souls. Romans Chapter 2 continues Paul's discourse on the righteousness of God, the sinfulness of man, and the impartial judgment of God. It is a chapter that challenges the self-righteous and calls for a heartfelt obedience to God.

The Impartial Judgment of God (2:1-11)

"You, therefore, have no excuse, you who pass judgment on someone else, for at whatever point you judge another, you are condemning yourself, because you who pass judgment do the same things. Now we know that God's judgment against those who do such things is based on truth.

So when you, a mere human being, pass judgment on them and yet do the same things, do you think you will escape God's judgment? Or do you show contempt for the riches of his kindness, forbearance and patience, not realizing that God's kindness is intended to lead you to repentance?

But because of your stubbornness and your unrepentant heart, you are storing up wrath against yourself for the day of God's wrath, when his righteous judgment will be revealed. God "will repay each person according to what they have done."

To those who by persistence in doing good seek glory, honour and immortality, he will give eternal life. But for those who are self-seeking and who reject the truth and follow evil, there will be wrath and anger.

There will be trouble and distress for every human being who does evil: first for the Jew, then for the Gentile; but glory, honour and peace for everyone who does good: first for the Jew, then for the Gentile. For God does not show favouritism." (Romans 2:1-11)

Paul begins this chapter by addressing the moralist - those who judge others while doing the same things. This is a powerful reminder that when we choose to judge others, we are essentially condemning ourselves because we are all guilty of sin. Paul is dismantling the false security found in moral superiority and religious identity.

This passage calls us to self-examination and humility. It's easy to see the faults in others while being blind to our own. But the truth is, God's judgment is based on truth and is impartial. He does not show favouritism. This truth should humble us and lead us to repentance rather than self-righteous judgment.

Paul emphasizes that it is the kindness, tolerance, and patience of God that leads us to repentance. Often, we think of God's kindness in light terms, but here, it is meant to lead us to a deep, life-changing repentance. God's kindness is not an excuse for complacency but a call to turn from our sinful ways.

This kindness is meant to draw us into a deeper relationship with Him, rooted in gratitude and respect, not in taking Him for granted.

How often do we misinterpret God's patience as approval of our actions? Let this be a wake-up call to recognize God's kindness for what it truly is: an opportunity to change.

The Law and the Heart (2:12-29)

"All who sin apart from the law will also perish apart from the law, and all who sin under the law will be judged by the law. For it is not those who hear the law who are righteous in God's sight, but it is those who obey the law who will be declared righteous. (Indeed, when Gentiles, who do not have the law, do by nature things required by the law, they are a law for themselves, even though they do not have the law. They show that the requirements of the law are written on their hearts, their consciences also bearing witness, and their thoughts sometimes accusing them and at other times even defending them.)"

"This will take place on the day when God judges people's secrets through Jesus Christ, as my gospel declares.

Now you, if you call yourself a Jew; if you rely on the law and boast in God; if you know his will and approve of what is superior because you are instructed by the law; if you are convinced that you are a guide for the blind, a light for those who are in the dark, an instructor of the foolish, a teacher of little children, because you have in the law the embodiment of knowledge and truth — you, then, who teach others, do you not teach yourself? You who preach against stealing, do you steal? You who say that people should not commit adultery, do you commit adultery? You who abhor idols, do you rob temples? You who boast in the law, do you dishonour God by breaking the law? As it is written: "God's name is blasphemed among the Gentiles because of you.

Circumcision has value if you observe the law, but if you break the law, you have become as though you had not been circumcised So then, if those who are not circumcised keep the law's requirements, will they not be regarded as though they were circumcised? The one who is not circumcised physically and yet obeys the law will condemn you who, even though you have the written code and circumcision, are a lawbreaker.

A person is not a Jew who is one only outwardly, nor is circumcision merely outward and physical. No, a person is a Jew who is one inwardly; and circumcision is circumcision of the heart, by the Spirit, not by the written code. Such a person's praise is not from other people, but from God." (Romans 2:12-29)

In this longer section, Paul addresses both Jews and Gentiles, emphasizing that it is not the hearers of the Law who are righteous before God, but the doers of the Law.

This is a crucial point: external adherence to religious practices means nothing without internal transformation. The true Jew, according to Paul, is not one outwardly; true circumcision is a matter of the heart, by the Spirit, not by the letter. This teaches us that true spirituality is not ever about external observance but about inner transformation.

It challenges us to examine our hearts: Are we merely going through the motions, or has our faith genuinely transformed us from the inside out? There are three main areas of application we can discern from this second chapter of Romans:

Self-Examination: Let us examine our own lives afresh. Are there areas where we have been judging others while ignoring our own faults? Let us ask God to reveal these areas to us and to lead us to genuine repentance.

Appreciating God's Kindness: Reflect on the kindness of God in your life. How has His kindness led you to change? Let us respond to His kindness not with complacency, but with a deep, sincere desire to turn from our sinful ways and to live lives that are pleasing to Him.

Heart Transformation: Consider whether your relationship with God is merely about external observance or if it's about a genuine transformation of the heart. Pray for the Holy Spirit to work within you, transforming your heart to reflect God's heart.

Conclusion

Romans Chapter 2 confronts us with the truth of God's impartial judgment and the necessity of a heart transformed by His Spirit. It challenges us to move beyond superficial religion to a genuine relationship with God marked by heartfelt obedience.
Let us not be hearers of the Word only, but doers also. Let our lives be a testament to the transforming power of the gospel, reflecting the righteousness of God not just in our words, but in our actions and our hearts.

As we on now, let's do so with a renewed commitment to live out the truths we have learned, allowing God's kindness to lead us to repentance, and His Spirit to transform our hearts from the inside out.

May God grant us the grace to live the kind of lives which are pleasing to Him, lives that reflect His truth, His love, and His righteousness.

~ ROMANS 3 ~

Introduction

This passage is central to understanding the human condition and the magnificent breadth of God's redemption. In Romans 3, Paul brings to a head the argument he has been building: all have sinned and are in need of God's righteousness.

This chapter contains some of the most essential truths of the Christian faith.

The Universality of Sin (3:1-20)

"What advantage, then, is there in being a Jew, or what value is there in circumcision? Much in every way! First of all, the Jews have been entrusted with the very words of God.

What if some were unfaithful? Will their unfaithfulness nullify God's faithfulness? Not at all! Let God be true, and every human being a liar. As it is written:

"So that you may be proved right when you speak and prevail when you judge." But if our unrighteousness brings out God's righteousness more clearly, what shall we say?

That God is unjust in bringing his wrath on us? (I am using a human argument.) Certainly not! If that were so, how could God judge the world?

Someone might argue, "If my falsehood enhances God's truthfulness and so increases his glory, why am I still condemned as a sinner?" Why not say – as some slanderously claim that we say – "Let us do evil that good may result"? Their condemnation is just!

What shall we conclude then? Do we have any advantage? Not at all! For we have already made the charge that Jews and Gentiles alike are all under the power of sin. As it is written:

"There is no one righteous, not even one; there is no one who understands; there is no one who seeks God. All have turned away, they have together become worthless; there is no one who does good, not even one."

> *"Their throats are open graves; their tongues practice deceit."*
> *"The poison of vipers is on their lips."*
>
> *"Their mouths are full of cursing and bitterness."*
>
> *"Their feet are swift to shed blood; ruin and misery mark their ways, and the way of peace they do not know."*
>
> *"There is no fear of God before their eyes."*
>
> *Now we know that whatever the law says, it says to those who are under the law, so that every mouth may be silenced and the whole world held accountable to God. Therefore no one will be declared righteous in God's sight by the works of the law; rather, through the law we become conscious of our sin." (Romans 3:1-20)*

Paul has already addressed both Gentiles and Jews, showing that all are under sin. Now, he brings his argument to a climax: *"There is no one righteous, not even one; there is no one who understands; there is no one who seeks God. All have turned away..."* (Romans 3:10-12). This is a stark picture of humanity, stripped of any illusion of self-righteousness.

Paul's message here is clear: no one can claim superiority; no one can be justified by their own deeds. This universality of sin is crucial because it levels the playing field and shows that we are all equally in need of God's grace.

As we reflect on this, let us consider our own lives. Are there areas where we have felt superior to others, or believed that we could achieve righteousness on our own? Let's confess these before God, acknowledging our total dependence on His grace.

The Righteousness of God Through Faith (3:21-26)

> *"But now apart from the law the righteousness of God has been made known, to which the Law and the Prophets testify. his righteousness is given through faith in Jesus Christ to all who believe. There is no difference between Jew and Gentile, for all have sinned and fall short of the glory of God, and all are justified freely by his grace through the redemption that came by Christ Jesus."*

"God presented Christ as a sacrifice of atonement, through the shedding of his blood — to be received by faith. He did this to demonstrate his righteousness, because in his forbearance he had left the sins committed beforehand unpunished — he did it to demonstrate his righteousness at the present time, so as to be just and the one who justifies those who have faith in Jesus."
(Romans 3:21-26)

The chapter takes a dramatic turn here. This is the heart of the gospel: God's righteousness given to us through faith in Jesus Christ. This is not a righteousness we earn but one that is freely given.

Paul talks about Jesus whom God presented as a sacrifice of atonement, through the shedding of His blood. This is the centre of our Christian faith: Jesus, fully God and fully human, dying for our sins, reconciling us to God.

This should bring us immense comfort and joy. Despite the depth of our sin, God's grace is more profound. Have you accepted this gift of righteousness? Or are you still trying to earn your way to God?

Boasting is Excluded (3:27-31)

"Where, then, is boasting? It is excluded. Because of what law? The law that requires works? No, because of the law that requires faith. For we maintain that a person is justified by faith apart from the works of the law. Or is God the God of Jews only? Is he not the God of Gentiles too? Yes, of Gentiles too, since there is only one God, who will justify the circumcised by faith and the uncircumcised through that same faith. Do we, then, nullify the law by this faith? Not at all! Rather, we uphold the law."
(Romans 3:27-31)

Paul concludes the chapter by addressing boasting, stating it is excluded by the law of faith. This means our boasting is not in our achievements, our moral standing, or our heritage but in Christ alone. This is a call to humility and gratitude.

As we consider this, let's ask ourselves: Where have we placed our confidence? Have we been boasting in things other than Christ? Let us redirect our hearts to boast only in the Lord, in His death and resurrection, which gives us life.

Romans Chapter 3 is a deep well of theological truth, offering us a clear view of our sinfulness and God's magnificent grace. It demolishes any notion of self-righteousness and lifts high the cross of Christ as the only source of our salvation.

We should carry these truths deep in our hearts as we let them transform how we view ourselves, how we view others, and how we live our lives. Let's commit today to being a people who are marked by humility, gratitude, and faith, always pointing to the righteousness that comes from God, in Christ, and is received by faith alone.

~ ROMANS 4 ~

Introduction

In the magnificent unfolding of the Gospel within Paul's letter to the Romans, Chapter 4 stands as a towering testament to the principle of faith. Here, Paul uses the example of Abraham, the patriarch of the Jewish people, to illustrate that righteousness has always been a matter of faith, not works. As we delve into this chapter, we'll uncover the timeless truth that faith is the key to our relationship with God.

Abraham: The Father of Faith (4:1-8)

"What then shall we say that Abraham, our forefather according to the flesh, discovered in this matter? If, in fact, Abraham was justified by works, he had something to boast about – but not before God. What does Scripture say? "Abraham believed God, and it was credited to him as righteousness."

Now to the one who works, wages are not credited as a gift but as an obligation. However, to the one who does not work but trusts God who justifies the ungodly, their faith is credited as righteousness. David says the same thing when he speaks of the blessedness of the one to whom God credits righteousness apart from works:

"Blessed are those whose transgressions are forgiven, whose sins are covered. Blessed is the one whose sin the Lord will never count against them."(Romans 4:1-8)

Paul begins by asking what we can say about Abraham in terms of his faith. He answers this by stating clearly that Abraham was justified by faith, not by works. If Abraham had been justified by works, he would have had something to boast about. But as it stands, before God, Abraham had no grounds for boasting. This is crucial for us to understand. In our own lives, we often strive to earn approval - be it from others or even from God. But Paul reminds us that, like Abraham, our standing with God is not something we can earn; it's given as a free gift through faith.

Faith Credited as Righteousness (4:9-17)

"Is this blessedness only for the circumcised, or also for the uncircumcised? We have been saying that Abraham's faith was credited to him as righteousness. Under what circumstances was it credited? Was it after he was circumcised, or before? It was not after, but before! And he received circumcision as a sign, a seal of the righteousness that he had by faith while he was still uncircumcised. So then, he is the father of all who believe but have not been circumcised, in order that righteousness might be credited to them. And he is then also the father of the circumcised who not only are circumcised but who also follow in the footsteps of the faith that our father Abraham had before he was circumcised.

It was not through the law that Abraham and his offspring received the promise that he would be heir of the world, but through the righteousness that comes by faith. For if those who depend on the law are heirs, faith means nothing and the promise is worthless, because the law brings wrath. And where there is no law there is no transgression.

Therefore, the promise comes by faith, so that it may be by grace and may be guaranteed to all Abraham's offspring – not only to those who are of the law but also to those who have the faith of Abraham. He is the father of us all. As it is written: "I have made you a father of many nations." He is our father in the sight of God, in whom he believed – the God who gives life to the dead and calls into being things that were not." (Romans 4:9-17)

Paul goes on to discuss how this righteousness by faith was credited to Abraham before he was circumcised. This means that Abraham became the father of all who believe, whether they are circumcised or not.

This shatters any walls between Jews and Gentiles in the church; all are one. The promise to Abraham and his offspring that he would be heir of the world was not through the law but through faith in God.

This is key: the promises of God are accessed through faith, not through adherence to the law or cultural identity.

This challenges us to reconsider our own faith journey. Are there areas in our lives where we are relying on our own efforts or cultural identity rather than trusting in God's promises through faith?

The Nature of True Faith (4:18-25)

> *"Against all hope, Abraham in hope believed and so became the father of many nations, just as it had been said to him, "So shall your offspring be." Without weakening in his faith, he faced the fact that his body was as good as dead — since he was about a hundred years old — and that Sarah's womb was also dead.*
>
> *Yet he did not waver through unbelief regarding the promise of God, but was strengthened in his faith and gave glory to God, being fully persuaded that God had power to do what he had promised. This is why "it was credited to him as righteousness."*
>
> *The words "it was credited to him" were written not for him alone, but also for us, to whom God will credit righteousness — for us who believe in him who raised Jesus our Lord from the dead. He was delivered over to death for our sins and was raised to life for our justification." (Romans 4:18-25)*

Paul paints a vivid picture of Abraham's faith. Abraham believed God's promises despite his and Sarah's old age, which was considered as good as dead. He did not waver through unbelief regarding the promise of God but was strengthened in his faith and gave glory to God, fully persuaded that God had the power to do what he had promised.

This is the essence of true faith: trusting in God's promises even when circumstances make them seem impossible. It's not a blind faith, but a faith that acknowledges God's past faithfulness and trusts in His future promises.

We should ask ourselves, are we, like Abraham, fully persuaded that God has the power to do what He has promised? Do our lives reflect this kind of trust in God?

Romans Chapter 4 brings us back to the core of the Gospel: we are justified by faith, not by works. Abraham, the father of faith, sets a precedent for us - a life fully entrusted to God's promises, defying human logic and circumstances.

As we continue our faith journey, let's pray that we will be able to carry the legacy of Abraham's faith into our lives. Let us hold onto God's promises with unwavering faith, giving glory to Him and spreading this message of hope and faith to those around us.

May our faith be credited to us as righteousness, as we walk in the footsteps of Abraham, the father of all who believe.

~ ROMANS 5 ~

Introduction

As we journey through Paul's epistle to the Romans, we come to a pivotal chapter that stands at the crossroads of our theological understanding and practical application. Romans Chapter 5 dives deeply into the practical implications of faith, exploring themes of peace, grace, suffering, and the unparalleled gift of Jesus Christ. This chapter is not merely doctrinal; it's deeply personal and transformative for every believer.

Peace and Grace Through Faith (5:1-2)

> *"Therefore, since we have been justified through faith, we have peace with God through our Lord Jesus Christ, through whom we have gained access by faith into this grace in which we now stand. And we boast in the hope of the glory of God." (Romans 5:1-2)*

This peace is not the world's peace; it's a profound, enduring peace with our Creator, made possible through Christ. It signifies the end of hostility between the believer and God, an end to the spiritual warfare that rages in the hearts of those apart from Christ. But Paul doesn't stop there; he introduces us to the grace in which we now stand. This standing is not shaky or uncertain; it is secure, a firm footing in the undeserved favour of God. And from this position, we boast in the hope of the glory of God.

As we reflect on these truths, let's ask ourselves: Do we live as people at peace with God? How does this peace change our daily lives? And do we truly appreciate the secure standing we have in His grace?

Suffering Producing Perseverance (5:3-5)

> *"Not only so, but we also glory in our sufferings, because we know that suffering produces perseverance; perseverance, character; and character, hope. And hope does not put us to shame, because God's love has been poured out into our hearts through the Holy Spirit, who has been given to us."*
> *(Romans 5:3-5)*

But Paul is a realist. He knows that life in this fallen world is fraught with trials and suffering. Yet, he challenges our natural perspective on suffering, urging us to rejoice in our sufferings. This is not some sort of call to masochism but to understanding that suffering produces perseverance; perseverance, character; and character, hope.

This hope is not a wishful thought but a confident expectation, rooted in God's love, poured into our hearts through the Holy Spirit. In your struggles and trials, are you allowing them to produce perseverance, character, and hope in you?

Christ's Unparalleled Gift (5:6-11)

"You see, at just the right time, when we were still powerless, Christ died for the ungodly. Very rarely will anyone die for a righteous person, though for a good person someone might possibly dare to die. But God demonstrates his own love for us in this: While we were still sinners, Christ died for us.

Since we have now been justified by his blood, how much more shall we be saved from God's wrath through him! For if, while we were God's enemies, we were reconciled to him through the death of his Son, how much more, having been reconciled, shall we be saved through his life!

Not only is this so, but we also boast in God through our Lord Jesus Christ, through whom we have now received reconciliation." (Romans 5:6-11)

Paul then contrasts our weak, ungodly, sinful nature with the timing and nature of Christ's sacrifice for us. Christ died for us not when we were lovable or righteous, but when we were at our worst. This is the measure of God's love for us.

Furthermore, having been reconciled to God through Christ's death, we are saved through His life. Our reconciliation is not based on our own efforts at all, but on what Christ has done and continues to do for us. How does understanding this deepen your appreciation for Christ's sacrifice and ongoing intercession?

Adam and Christ: The Two Representatives (5:12-21)

"Therefore, just as sin entered the world through one man, and death through sin, and in this way death came to all people, because all sinned — To be sure, sin was in the world before the law was given, but sin is not charged against anyone's account where there is no law. Nevertheless, death reigned from the time of Adam to the time of Moses, even over those who did not sin by breaking a command, as did Adam, who is a pattern of the one to come.

But the gift is not like the trespass. For if the many died by the trespass of the one man, how much more did God's grace and the gift that came by the grace of the one man, Jesus Christ, overflow to the many! Nor can the gift of God be compared with the result of one man's sin: The judgment followed one sin and brought condemnation, but the gift followed many trespasses and brought justification.

For if, by the trespass of the one man, death reigned through that one man, how much more will those who receive God's abundant provision of grace and of the gift of righteousness reign in life through the one man, Jesus Christ!

Consequently, just as one trespass resulted in condemnation for all people, so also one righteous act resulted in justification and life for all people. For just as through the disobedience of the one man the many were made sinners, so also through the obedience of the one man the many will be made righteous.

The law was brought in so that the trespass might increase. But where sin increased, grace increased all the more, so that, just as sin reigned in death, so also grace might reign through righteousness to bring eternal life through Jesus Christ our Lord."
(Romans 5:12-21)

Paul concludes with a profound theological comparison between Adam and Christ. Adam's disobedience brought sin and death into the world, affecting all humanity. In contrast, Christ's obedience brings righteousness and life, offering redemption to all humanity.

This section makes it clear: sin and death entered through one man, and in a similar but far more powerful way, grace and life come through one Man, Jesus Christ. This is the core of the gospel message.

In light of this, consider your own life. In which lineage do you live? Are you living in the legacy of Adam's sin or in the freedom and life of Christ?

Romans Chapter 5 brings us face to face with the profound truths of our faith. We've been given peace with God, access to His grace, a new perspective on suffering, and a new identity in Christ, contrasting the despair of Adam's legacy.

Let's pray that we will walk in the fullness of these truths, living as people transformed by the grace of God, bearing the image of our Lord Jesus Christ in a broken world, and spreading the hope that does not disappoint because God's love has been poured out into our hearts through the Holy Spirit.

~ ROMANS 6 ~

Introduction

In the progression of Paul's letter to the Romans, we transition from the grand themes of justification and reconciliation to the practical implications of those truths in our lives. Chapter 6 is a pivotal moment where theology meets real life, and where belief intersects with behaviour. Paul addresses a crucial question: If grace abounds where sin increases, should we continue in sin that grace may abound? His emphatic answer is very clear! This chapter calls us to a deeper understanding of our identity in Christ and the implications for our daily living.

Dying and Living with Christ (6:1-11)

"What shall we say, then? Shall we go on sinning so that grace may increase? By no means! We are those who have died to sin; how can we live in it any longer? Or don't you know that all of us who were baptized into Christ Jesus were baptized into his death? We were therefore buried with him through baptism into death in order that, just as Christ was raised from the dead through the glory of the Father, we too may live a new life.

For if we have been united with him in a death like his, we will certainly also be united with him in a resurrection like his. 6 For we know that our old self was crucified with him so that the body ruled by sin might be done away with, that we should no longer be slaves to sin — because anyone who has died has been set free from sin.

Now if we died with Christ, we believe that we will also live with him. For we know that since Christ was raised from the dead, he cannot die again; death no longer has mastery over him. 10 The death he died, he died to sin once for all; but the life he lives, he lives to God. In the same way, count yourselves dead to sin but alive to God in Christ Jesus." (Romans 6:1-11)

Paul begins by connecting our daily experience to that of Christ's death and resurrection. He uses the powerful symbol of baptism to illustrate this.

In baptism, we are united with Christ in his death and raised to walk in newness of life. This is not a mere ritual; it's a profound spiritual reality. Our old self was crucified with Christ, breaking the power of sin and freeing us from its tyranny.

This truth has profound implications for our identity and our lifestyle. As Christians, we are no longer slaves to sin; we have been set free and given a new identity in Christ. Yet, this is not just a theological truth, it's a call to action! We must consider ourselves dead to sin and alive to God in Christ Jesus.

Reflect on your own life: Are you living as someone who has been raised to new life with Christ? Or are you still enslaved to old patterns and sins?

Instruments of Righteousness (6:12-14)

> *"Therefore, do not let sin reign in your mortal body so that you obey its evil desires. Do not offer any part of yourself to sin as an instrument of wickedness, but rather offer yourselves to God as those who have been brought from death to life; and offer every part of yourself to him as an instrument of righteousness. For sin shall no longer be your master, because you are not under the law, but under grace." (Romans 6:12-14)*

Paul moves from our position in Christ to our practice in life. He exhorts us to not let sin reign in our mortal bodies or obey its evil desires. Instead, we are to offer ourselves to God as those who have been brought from death to life, and our body parts as instruments of righteousness.

The imagery here is vivid and compelling. Just as instruments can be used to create beautiful music or cause destruction, our bodies can be used for righteousness or for sin. The choice lies with us, empowered by the grace which God has lavished on us in Christ.

Consider your own actions and choices: Are you offering your body parts as instruments of righteousness or are they being used in service to sin?

Slaves to Righteousness (6:15-22)

"What then? Shall we sin because we are not under the law but under grace? By no means! Don't you know that when you offer yourselves to someone as obedient slaves, you are slaves of the one you obey – whether you are slaves to sin, which leads to death, or to obedience, which leads to righteousness? But thanks be to God that, though you used to be slaves to sin, you have come to obey from your heart the pattern of teaching that has now claimed your allegiance. You have been set free from sin and have become slaves to righteousness.

I am using an example from everyday life because of your human limitations. Just as you used to offer yourselves as slaves to impurity and to ever-increasing wickedness, so now offer yourselves as slaves to righteousness leading to holiness. When you were slaves to sin, you were free from the control of righteousness.

What benefit did you reap at that time from the things you are now ashamed of? Those things result in death! But now that you have been set free from sin and have become slaves of God, the benefit you reap leads to holiness, and the result is eternal life."
(Romans 6:15-22)

Paul anticipates another question: If we're not under law but under grace, can we sin freely? Again, his answer is a resounding "No!" He explains using the metaphor of slavery: just as we once offered ourselves as slaves to impurity and to ever-increasing wickedness, now we should be offering ourselves as slaves to righteousness leading to holiness.

The stark contrast between being slaves to sin and slaves to righteousness highlights the transformative power of the gospel of Jesus Christ. Being a slave to righteousness is not a burdensome obligation but a joyful expression of our new identity in Christ, leading to holiness and eternal life.

Let us reflect deeply here and ask ourselves, in what areas of our life do we still feel we are enslaved to sin? How can we instead become more fully a servant to righteousness?

The Free Gift of God (6:23)

"For the wages of sin is death, but the gift of God is eternal life in Christ Jesus our Lord." (Romans 6:23)

Paul concludes the chapter with this powerful summary of the gospel. This is the ultimate contrast between the outcomes of a life enslaved to sin versus a life given over to God.

This verse encapsulates the entire message of Romans 6: our actions have consequences, and the ultimate outcome of sin is death. But, thanks to God's amazing grace, we have been offered a different path, a free gift – eternal life through Christ Jesus.

How does this reality impact your understanding of sin, grace, and obedience? How does it shape the way you live your daily life?

Romans Chapter 6 challenges us to live out the truths of the gospel in our daily lives. It reminds us that our union with Christ has profound ethical implications. We are no longer who we once were; we have been transformed and called to live in accordance with our new identity.

My prayer is that we may embrace this new life with enthusiasm and commitment. May we recognize the weight of the grace that has been bestowed upon us and respond not with a casual attitude towards sin, but with a fervent desire to live lives that are pleasing to God.

In our daily walk, let us remember that we have been buried with Christ through baptism into death, so that, just as Christ was raised from the dead through the glory of the Father, we too may live a new life. This new life is not a burden but a gift - an opportunity to reflect the love, holiness, and righteousness of God in a world that desperately needs His touch.

May we stand firm against the temptations that once held us captive, armed with the knowledge that we have been set free from the power of sin.

Let us walk in that freedom, not as a license to do whatever we please, but as a sacred calling to become more like Christ every day.

As we reflect on the depth of our sin and the height of God's grace, we should be motivated to offer ourselves completely to Him - not as people who have it all figured out, but as redeemed sinners who are deeply grateful for the chance to start anew.

Let's engage with our communities, not as judges or outsiders, but as ambassadors of Christ's love and grace, demonstrating the transformative power of the Gospel through our words and actions.

And finally, may we never forget the ultimate outcome that Paul lays before us: the wages of sin is death, but the free gift of God is eternal life in Christ Jesus our Lord. Let this truth anchor our souls and propel our lives. Let it be the reason we rejoice, the primary motivation behind our obedience, and the hope that lights our path each and every day.

~ ROMANS 7 ~

Introduction

Paul's exploration of the many complexities of the Christian life continues in Romans Chapter 7. Here Paul speaks to the struggle between the law and sin, the conflict within the human heart, and the believer's relationship to the law. It's a chapter rich with theological depth and personal application. It reveals the tension between our old selves and our new identity in Christ.

The Law and the Believer (7:1-6)

> *"Do you not know, brothers and sisters - for I am speaking to those who know the law - that the law has authority over someone only as long as that person lives? For example, by law a married woman is bound to her husband as long as he is alive, but if her husband dies, she is released from the law that binds her to him. So then, if she has sexual relations with another man while her husband is still alive, she is called an adulteress. But if her husband dies, she is released from that law and is not an adulteress if she marries another man.*
>
> *So, my brothers and sisters, you also died to the law through the body of Christ, that you might belong to another, to him who was raised from the dead, in order that we might bear fruit for God. For when we were in the realm of the flesh, the sinful passions aroused by the law were at work in us, so that we bore fruit for death. But now, by dying to what once bound us, we have been released from the law so that we serve in the new way of the Spirit, and not in the old way of the written code."* (Romans 7:1-6)

Paul begins this chapter with an analogy from marriage to explain how believers relate to the law. Just as a woman is bound by law to her husband as long as he lives, we were bound to the law before Christ. But through Christ's death, we died to the law's hold on us, enabling us to belong to Him and bear fruit for God. This is crucial in understanding our new identity in Christ.

We are no longer slaves to the law's demands and penalties; instead, we are united with Christ and serve in the new way of the Spirit.

Reflect on your own life: Are you living as if you are still under the law's condemnation, or are you embracing the freedom and new life offered through the Spirit?

The Purpose and Problem of the Law (7:7-13)

"What shall we say, then? Is the law sinful? Certainly not! Nevertheless, I would not have known what sin was had it not been for the law. For I would not have known what coveting really was if the law had not said, "You shall not covet." But sin, seizing the opportunity afforded by the commandment, produced in me every kind of coveting.

For apart from the law, sin was dead. Once I was alive apart from the law; but when the commandment came, sin sprang to life and I died. I found that the very commandment that was intended to bring life actually brought death. For sin, seizing the opportunity afforded by the commandment, deceived me, and through the commandment put me to death.

So then, the law is holy, and the commandment is holy, righteous and good. Did that which is good, then, become death to me? By no means! Nevertheless, in order that sin might be recognized as sin, it used what is good to bring about my death, so that through the commandment sin might become utterly sinful."
(Romans 7:7-13)

Paul anticipates a misunderstanding here: Is the law sinful? He clarifies that the law is holy and righteous, but it exposes sin in our lives. The law itself is not the problem; sin is. The law reveals sin's true nature and utterly sinful character, leading to death.

These verses challenge us to reconsider our view of God's law. It is not an enemy but a mirror, reflecting our sinful nature and our desperate need for a saviour. How does this understanding change your perception of God's commandments and your own sinfulness?

The Inner Conflict (7:14-23)

"We know that the law is spiritual; but I am unspiritual, sold as a slave to sin. I do not understand what I do. For what I want to do I do not do, but what I hate I do. And if I do what I do not want to do, I agree that the law is good. As it is, it is no longer I myself who do it, but it is sin living in me.

For I know that good itself does not dwell in me, that is, in my sinful nature. For I have the desire to do what is good, but I cannot carry it out. For I do not do the good I want to do, but the evil I do not want to do - this I keep on doing. Now if I do what I do not want to do, it is no longer I who do it, but it is sin living in me that does it.

So I find this law at work: Although I want to do good, evil is right there with me. For in my inner being I delight in God's law; but I see another law at work in me, waging war against the law of my mind and making me a prisoner of the law of sin at work within me. What a wretched man I am! Who will rescue me from this body that is subject to death? Thanks be to God, who delivers me through Jesus Christ our Lord!

So then, I myself in my mind am a slave to God's law, but in my sinful nature a slave to the law of sin." (Romans 7:14-23)

Here, Paul describes a profound internal struggle: the desire to do good, which is at war with the sin living within him. This passage is a vivid portrayal of the tension between the "inner man" and the flesh, highlighting the believer's struggle with sin even after coming to Christ.

Paul's transparent confession, *"For what I want to do I do not do, but what I hate I do ..."* resonates with all of us. It's a reminder that the Christian life is a battleground, not a playground.

Reflect on your own experiences: Where do you see this battle playing out in your life? How does acknowledging this inner conflict help you rely more on the Holy Spirit rather than your strength?

Thanks be to God Through Jesus Christ (7:24-25)

"Thanks be to God, who delivers me through Jesus Christ our Lord! So then, I myself in my mind am a slave to God's law, but in my sinful nature a slave to the law of sin." (Romans 7:24-25)

Paul ends this chapter on a note of hope: Despite the ongoing struggle, there is rescue and deliverance through Jesus Christ. This is not a declaration of defeat but an acknowledgment of our constant need for Christ's saving power.

This conclusion shifts our focus from the struggle to the Saviour. It reminds us that while the battle with sin is very real, victory is assured through Jesus Christ. How does this truth encourage you in your daily struggles against sin?

Romans Chapter 7 offers a profound insight into the Christian experience, marked by struggle yet surrounded by grace. As we navigate the tension between the old self and the new, let us keep our eyes fixed on Jesus, the author and perfecter of our faith.

May we live not under the shadow of the law but in the light of the Gospel, empowered by the Spirit, and grateful for the unending grace that sustains us each day.

Let us confidently embrace whatever the future holds for us, not as those who are perfect, but as those who are being perfected, clinging to the hope and the victory found in our Saviour, Jesus Christ.

~ ROMANS 8 ~

Introduction

Romans Chapter 8 is often regarded as one of the most profound and comforting chapters in the entire Bible. It transitions from the struggle and despair depicted in Romans 7 into the glorious liberty and hope found in life through the Spirit.

This chapter showcases the magnificent reality of our life in Jesus Christ: no condemnation; the indwelling of the Spirit; our adoption as God's children, the hope of glory; and the daily assurance of God's love.

No Condemnation in Christ (8:1-4)

"Therefore, there is now no condemnation for those who are in Christ Jesus, because through Christ Jesus the law of the Spirit who gives life has set you free from the law of sin and death. For what the law was powerless to do because it was weakened by the flesh, God did by sending his own Son in the likeness of sinful flesh to be a sin offering.

And so he condemned sin in the flesh, in order that the righteous requirement of the law might be fully met in us, who do not live according to the flesh but according to the Spirit."
(Romans 8:1-4)

Paul begins this chapter with a powerful declaration: *"Therefore, there is now no condemnation for those who are in Christ Jesus."* This is the triumphant answer to the dilemma of sin and the failure presented in Chapter 7. In Christ, we are never condemned; instead, we are set free from the law of sin and death by the law of the Spirit of life.

Reflect on your life in light of this truth. Are you living as someone who has been freed from condemnation, or are you still ensnared by guilt and shame? Remember, in Christ, you are set free; you are no longer defined by your past failures but by Christ's righteousness.

The Life-Giving Spirit (8:5-11)

"Those who live according to the flesh have their minds set on what the flesh desires; but those who live in accordance with the Spirit have their minds set on what the Spirit desires. The mind governed by the flesh is death, but the mind governed by the Spirit is life and peace. The mind governed by the flesh is hostile to God; it does not submit to God's law, nor can it do so. Those who are in the realm of the flesh cannot please God.

You, however, are not in the realm of the flesh but are in the realm of the Spirit, if indeed the Spirit of God lives in you. And if anyone does not have the Spirit of Christ, they do not belong to Christ. But if Christ is in you, then even though your body is subject to death because of sin, the Spirit gives life because of righteousness.

And if the Spirit of him who raised Jesus from the dead is living in you, he who raised Christ from the dead will also give life to your mortal bodies because of his Spirit who lives in you."
(Romans 8:5-11)

Paul contrasts life lived according to the flesh with life lived according to the Spirit. Those who live according to the flesh have their minds set on what the flesh desires; but those who live in accordance with the Spirit have their minds set on what the Spirit desires. This is not merely a change of behaviour but a transformation of our very mindset and identity.

Examine your own life: Where is your mind set? Are you living in accordance with the flesh or the Spirit? Remember, the Spirit of God, who raised Jesus from the dead, lives in you. He empowers you to live a life that pleases God.

Our Adoption as God's Children (8:12-17)

"Therefore, brothers and sisters, we have an obligation — but it is not to the flesh, to live according to it. For if you live according to the flesh, you will die; but if by the Spirit you put to death the misdeeds of the body, you will live. For those who are led by the Spirit of God are the children of God. "

> *"The Spirit you received does not make you slaves, so that you
> live in fear again; rather, the Spirit you received brought about
> your adoption to sonship. And by him we cry, "Abba, Father."*
>
> *The Spirit himself testifies with our spirit that we are God's
> children. Now if we are children, then we are heirs - heirs of God
> and co-heirs with Christ, if indeed we share in his sufferings in
> order that we may also share in his glory." (Romans 8:12-17)*

In these verses, Paul speaks of the glorious truth of our adoption
as children of God. The Spirit you received does not make you
slaves, so that you live in fear again; rather, the Spirit you
received brought about your adoption to as sons and daughters.
This adoption changes everything; it means intimacy, access,
inheritance, and identity. We are not mere servants; we are
beloved children.

Consider what this means for your relationship with God. Do
you approach Him as a distant judge, or as your loving Father?
Remember, as His child, you are loved, accepted, and cherished.

Suffering and Glory (8:18-30)

> *"I consider that our present sufferings are not worth comparing
> with the glory that will be revealed in us. For the creation waits in
> eager expectation for the children of God to be revealed.*
>
> *For the creation was subjected to frustration, not by its own
> choice, but by the will of the one who subjected it, in hope that the
> creation itself will be liberated from its bondage to decay and
> brought into the freedom and glory of the children of God.*
>
> *We know that the whole creation has been groaning as in the
> pains of childbirth right up to the present time. Not only so, but
> we ourselves, who have the first fruits of the Spirit, groan
> inwardly as we wait eagerly for our adoption to sonship, the
> redemption of our bodies.*
>
> *For in this hope we were saved. But hope that is seen is no hope at
> all. Who hopes for what they already have? But if we hope for
> what we do not yet have, we wait for it patiently."*

"In the same way, the Spirit helps us in our weakness. We do not know what we ought to pray for, but the Spirit himself intercedes for us through wordless groans. And he who searches our hearts knows the mind of the Spirit, because the Spirit intercedes for God's people in accordance with the will of God.

And we know that in all things God works for the good of those who love him, who have been called according to his purpose. For those God foreknew he also predestined to be conformed to the image of his Son, that he might be the firstborn among many brothers and sisters. And those he predestined, he also called; those he called, he also justified; those he justified, he also glorified." (Romans 8:18-30)

Paul does not shy away from the reality of suffering in the Christian life. However, he places it within the larger context of future glory. The sufferings of this present time are not worth comparing with the glory that will be revealed in us. Moreover, we have the promise that all things work together for good for those who love God, who are called according to His purpose. In times of suffering or confusion, cling to this hope. Remember that your current trials are not the final word; God is at work, shaping you for eternal glory.

More Than Conquerors (8:31-39)

"What, then, shall we say in response to these things? If God is for us, who can be against us? He who did not spare his own Son, but gave him up for us all - how will he not also, along with him, graciously give us all things? Who will bring any charge against those whom God has chosen? It is God who justifies.

Who then is the one who condemns? No one. Christ Jesus who died - more than that, who was raised to life - is at the right hand of God and is also interceding for us. Who shall separate us from the love of Christ? Shall trouble or hardship or persecution or famine or nakedness or danger or sword?

As it is written: "For your sake we face death all day long; we are considered as sheep to be slaughtered."

"No, in all these things we are more than conquerors through him who loved us. For I am convinced that neither death nor life, neither angels nor demons, neither the present nor the future, nor any powers, neither height nor depth, nor anything else in all creation, will be able to separate us from the love of God that is in Christ Jesus our Lord." (Romans 8:31-39)

Paul concludes the chapter with this triumphant affirmation of God's love and our security in Christ. *"If God is for us, who can be against us? Neither death nor life, angels nor demons, the present nor the future, nor any powers, can separate us from the love of God that is in Christ Jesus our Lord."* Those words have given millions of people hope to carry on against the odds and trust God to bring a new day and a new sense of peace in the midst of the storms.

As you face the challenges and uncertainties of life, hold fast to this assurance. You are more than a conqueror through Him who loved you. No circumstance, no adversary, and no trial can separate you from the love of God in Christ Jesus.

Romans Chapter 8 is a beautiful declaration of the Christian life lived in the power of the Spirit. It moves from no condemnation to no separation, bookending the chapter with the security we have in Christ. As we step forward into the reality of our lives, our challenges, our joys, and our trials, may we carry these truths with us.

~ ROMANS 9 ~

Introduction

In Romans Chapter 9, we pivot from the heights of assurance and hope detailed in Chapter 8 to a deep, sobering reflection on God's sovereignty and mercy. This chapter is part of Paul's broader theological argument, addressing Israel's role and status in God's redemptive plan.

Paul expresses his profound sorrow for his fellow Israelites and delves into the difficult topics of election, God's promises, and human response. This chapter challenges us to grapple with the complexities of God's justice and grace.

Paul's Anguish Over Israel (9:1-5)

"I speak the truth in Christ - I am not lying, my conscience confirms it through the Holy Spirit - I have great sorrow and unceasing anguish in my heart.

For I could wish that I myself were cursed and cut off from Christ for the sake of my people, those of my own race, the people of Israel. Theirs is the adoption to sonship; theirs the divine glory, the covenants, the receiving of the law, the temple worship and the promises.

Theirs are the patriarchs, and from them is traced the human ancestry of the Messiah, who is God over all, forever praised! Amen." (Romans 9:1-5)

Paul begins with a heartfelt expression of grief for his fellow Jews, who are not part of the Christian faith. His anguish is profound, wishing himself *"cursed and cut off from Christ"* for their sake. He lists the many privileges of Israel: adoption, covenants, glory, law-giving, worship, promises, the patriarchs - emphasizing the tragedy of their unbelief.

Reflect on Paul's love and burden for his people. Do we share a similar burden for those around us who do not know Christ? Are we moved to sorrow and prayer for the lost?

God's Sovereign Choice (9:6-13)

"It is not as though God's word had failed. For not all who are descended from Israel are Israel. Nor because they are his descendants are they all Abraham's children. On the contrary, "It is through Isaac that your offspring will be reckoned."

In other words, it is not the children by physical descent who are God's children, but it is the children of the promise who are regarded as Abraham's offspring. For this was how the promise was stated: "At the appointed time I will return, and Sarah will have a son."

Not only that, but Rebekah's children were conceived at the same time by our father Isaac. Yet, before the twins were born or had done anything good or bad — in order that God's purpose in election might stand: not by works but by him who calls — she was told, "The older will serve the younger." Just as it is written: "Jacob I loved, but Esau I hated." (Romans 9:6-13)

Paul addresses a critical issue: Has God's word failed because Israel, as a whole, did not believe? He answers emphatically, "Not at all!" He explains that not all who are descended from Israel are true Israel, nor are all Abraham's children his true heirs. Instead, the children of the promise are regarded as Abraham's offspring.

This section introduces the somewhat difficult doctrine of divine election. Paul uses the examples of Isaac over Ishmael and Jacob over Esau to illustrate that God's choice is not based on human merit but on His own purposes and promises.

How does this truth sit with us? Are we willing to trust God's sovereign choices, even when we don't understand? Can we rest in the assurance that the Judge of all the earth will do right?

God's Purpose in Election (9:14-23)

What then shall we say? Is God unjust? Not at all! For he says to Moses, "I will have mercy on whom I have mercy, and I will have compassion on whom I have compassion."

"It does not, therefore, depend on human desire or effort, but on God's mercy. For Scripture says to Pharaoh: "I raised you up for this very purpose, that I might display my power in you and that my name might be proclaimed in all the earth." Therefore, God has mercy on whom he wants to have mercy, and he hardens whom he wants to harden.

One of you will say to me: "Then why does God still blame us? For who is able to resist his will?" But who are you, a human being, to talk back to God? "Shall what is formed say to the one who formed it, 'Why did you make me like this?'" "Does not the potter have the right to make out of the same lump of clay some pottery for special purposes and some for common use?

What if God, although choosing to show his wrath and make his power known, bore with great patience the objects of his wrath — prepared for destruction? What if he did this to make the riches of his glory known to the objects of his mercy, whom he prepared in advance for glory." (Romans 9:14-23)

Paul anticipates the question: 'Is God unjust?' He responds with a resounding 'No!' He illustrates God's sovereignty with the example of Pharaoh, showing that God's mercy and hardening served His purposes in history and reveal His glory. Yet, this does not make God unjust; instead, it highlights His sovereign freedom to show mercy to whom He chooses. This is a very challenging teaching that requires humility and faith. It calls us all to recognize our limitations and submit to God's mysterious, yet perfectly just, ways. How do we reconcile God's sovereignty with human responsibility? While we may not fully understand, we can trust in God's good character and His ultimate plan.

The Remnant and the Gentiles (9:24-29)

" ... even us, whom he also called, not only from the Jews but also from the Gentiles? As he says in Hosea: "I will call them 'my people' who are not my people; and I will call her 'my loved one' who is not my loved one,"and,"In the very place where it was said to them, 'You are not my people, there they will be called 'children of the living God.'"

"Isaiah cries out concerning Israel: "Though the number of the Israelites be like the sand by the sea, only the remnant will be saved. For the Lord will carry out his sentence on earth with speed and finality."

It is just as Isaiah said previously: "Unless the Lord Almighty had left us descendants, we would have become like Sodom, we would have been like Gomorrah." (Romans 9:24-29)

Paul explains that not only Jews but also Gentiles are called by God. This was prophesied in the Old Testament and shows that God's plan of salvation extends far beyond ethnic Israel to all nations on earth. The concept of the remnant shows that God always preserves a faithful group who respond to His call.

This should fill us with hope and a sense of mission. God's saving grace reaches out across all human barriers. Are we embracing God's global vision? Are we grateful for His mercy extended to us as Gentiles?

Israel's Unbelief (9:30-33)

"What then shall we say? That the Gentiles, who did not pursue righteousness, have obtained it, a righteousness that is by faith; but the people of Israel, who pursued the law as the way of righteousness, have not attained their goal. Why not? Because they pursued it not by faith but as if it were by works. They stumbled over the stumbling stone.

As it is written: "See, I lay in Zion a stone that causes people to stumble and a rock that makes them fall, and the one who believes in him will never be put to shame." (Romans 9:30-33)

Paul concludes the chapter by reflecting on the irony of the situation: Gentiles, who did not pursue righteousness, have obtained it by faith, while Israel, who pursued God's law of righteousness, has not attained it. The reason? Because they sought it not by faith but as if it were by works. This brings us to the heart of the gospel: salvation is by faith, not by works. It is a gift, not a reward.

This truth should humble us and fill us with gratitude. How does this affect our understanding of God's grace? Are we trying to earn what has been freely given? Are we stumbling over the "rock of offense" by relying on our righteousness?

Romans Chapter 9 is a complex and emotionally charged part of Paul's letter to the Romans, where he delves into the sovereignty of God, especially regarding His choices and purposes. Here, Paul reflects on the plight of Israel, expressing his deep sorrow and unceasing anguish for his fellow Jews, who, despite being God's chosen people, have not universally embraced Christ.

In this chapter, Paul grapples with the tension between God's promises to Israel and the current reality of their unbelief. He defends the integrity of God's word by asserting that the children of the promise, rather than the children of the flesh, are regarded as Abraham's offspring. This distinction underscores the idea that it is not simply ethnic lineage but God's promise that determines the true people of God.

Furthermore, Paul explores the theme of divine sovereignty versus human responsibility. He illustrates this by referring to the stories of Abraham's descendants and the choices of Jacob over Esau, highlighting that God's mercy and compassion are not obligated by human desires or efforts but are instead a matter of divine choice. This raises challenging questions about justice and fairness, which Paul addresses by affirming God's right to demonstrate mercy or harden hearts according to His own will.

Despite these heavy themes, the underlying message is not one of despair, but of hope and trust in God's plan and justice. Paul leads to the conclusion that while humans might not fully understand God's ways, they are called to trust in His wisdom and sovereign plans. We are urged to reflect on the depth of God's sovereignty, the complexity of His purposes, and the inscrutable nature of His choices, whilst also affirming the faithfulness of God to His promises and the call for believers to live in alignment with His divine will.

Introduction

As we continue our journey through Paul's letter to the Romans, we arrive at Chapter 10, a passage that resonates with heartfelt longing and divine clarity. Here, Paul continues his discourse on the salvation of Israel and extends his argument to encompass the righteousness that comes from faith, contrasting it with the righteousness based on the law.

This chapter is a powerful exposition of the gospel's simplicity and universality, calling us to understand and embrace the true path to righteousness and salvation.

The Righteousness of Faith (10:1-4)

"Brothers and sisters, my heart's desire and prayer to God for the Israelites is that they may be saved. For I can testify about them that they are zealous for God, but their zeal is not based on knowledge. Since they did not know the righteousness of God and sought to establish their own, they did not submit to God's righteousness. Christ is the culmination of the law so that there may be righteousness for everyone who believes."
(Romans 10:1-4)

Paul starts with an expression of his deep desire and prayer for Israel's salvation. He acknowledges their zeal for God but laments that it is not based on knowledge, particularly the knowledge of Christ's righteousness, which fulfills the law's demands.

This leads to a profound truth: Christ is the culmination of the law so that there may be righteousness for everyone who believes.

Reflect on your own understanding and desire for righteousness. Are you relying on your efforts or on the righteousness that comes through faith in Christ? Paul's heart aches for those who miss the essence of the gospel; does ours?

The Message of Salvation for All (10:5-13)

> *"Moses writes this about the righteousness that is by the law:*
> *"The person who does these things will live by them." But the*
> *righteousness that is by faith says: "Do not say in your heart,*
> *'Who will ascend into heaven?'" (that is, to bring Christ down)*
> *"or 'Who will descend into the deep?'" (that is, to bring Christ up*
> *from the dead). But what does it say? "The word is near you;*
> *it is in your mouth and in your heart," that is, the message*
> *concerning faith that we proclaim:*
>
> *If you declare with your mouth, "Jesus is Lord," and believe in*
> *your heart that God raised him from the dead, you will be saved.*
> *For it is with your heart that you believe and are justified, and it*
> *is with your mouth that you profess your faith and are saved. As*
> *Scripture says, "Anyone who believes in him will never be put to*
> *shame." For there is no difference between Jew and Gentile - the*
> *same Lord is Lord of all and richly blesses all who call on him, for,*
> *"Everyone who calls on the name of the Lord will be saved."*
> *(Romans 10:5-13)*

Paul contrasts the righteousness which is based on the law with righteousness based on faith, quoting from the Old Testament to highlight the accessibility and simplicity of the gospel. It's not about performing extraordinary feats, but about confessing with your mouth that Jesus is Lord and believing in your heart that God raised Him from the dead.

This passage underscores the universal offer of salvation: *"Everyone who calls on the name of the Lord will be saved."* This is an inclusive, all-encompassing invitation. Consider the implications of this truth. How does it impact your view of evangelism, your prayer life, and your daily interactions with people?

How Will They Hear? (10:14-17)

> *"How, then, can they call on the one they have not believed in?*
> *And how can they believe in the one of whom they have not*
> *heard? And how can they hear without someone preaching to*
> *them? And how can anyone preach unless they are sent? "*

"As it is written: "How beautiful are the feet of those who bring good news!" But not all the Israelites accepted the good news. For Isaiah says, "Lord, who has believed our message?" Consequently, faith comes from hearing the message, and the message is heard through the word about Christ." (Romans 10:14-17)

Paul now transitions to the necessity of preaching the gospel. He outlines a sequence of rhetorical questions emphasizing the importance of sending and preaching for people to hear, believe, and call on the name of the Lord. This section highlights the divine strategy for salvation — it involves human messengers.

Reflect on your role in this divine strategy. Are you actively participating in sharing the gospel? Paul emphasizes that faith comes from hearing the message, and the message is heard through the word about Christ. How committed are you now to spreading this message?

Israel's Rejection and God's Sovereignty (10:18-21)

"But I ask: Did they not hear? Of course they did: "Their voice has gone out into all the earth, their words to the ends of the world." Again I ask: Did Israel not understand? First, Moses says, "I will make you envious by those who are not a nation; I will make you angry by a nation that has no understanding."

And Isaiah boldly says, "I was found by those who did not seek me; I revealed myself to those who did not ask for me." But concerning Israel he says, "All day long I have held out my hands to a disobedient and obstinate people." (Romans 10:18-21)

Paul concludes the chapter by addressing Israel's rejection of the gospel. He uses Old Testament quotes to show that Israel had indeed heard but did not understand; while the Gentiles, who were not seeking God, found Him. This brings us back to the themes of God's sovereignty and human responsibility. Consider how this reflects on our understanding of God's grace and judgment. How do we reconcile Israel's rejection with our call to evangelism?

Paul's use of scripture reminds us that God's plans and purposes, though mysterious, are always just and ultimately aimed at salvation.

Romans Chapter 10 calls us back to the heart of the gospel - a righteousness based on faith, accessible to all who believe. It challenges us to examine our hearts, recommit to the mission of the gospel, and trust in the sovereignty and goodness of God.

As we embrace what the Lord has in store for us today, let us carry this message of salvation, grounded in faith and propelled by love, knowing that *"everyone who calls on the name of the Lord will be saved."* May our lives reflect the beauty and simplicity of this truth, and may we be instruments in God's hands, bringing the message of life to those around us.

~ ROMANS 11 ~

Introduction

In Romans Chapter 11, Paul delves deeper into the mystery of Israel's salvation and the profound wisdom of God's plan for both Jews and Gentiles. This chapter is a continuation and culmination of Paul's argument about God's faithfulness to His covenant people and His overarching plan for redemption.

It is a rich tapestry that weaves together themes of grace, election, partial hardening, and the eventual restoration of Israel, all within the grand narrative of God's redemptive history.

God Has Not Rejected His People (11:1-10)

"I ask then: Did God reject his people? By no means! I am an Israelite myself, a descendant of Abraham, from the tribe of Benjamin. God did not reject his people, whom he foreknew. Don't you know what Scripture says in the passage about Elijah - how he appealed to God against Israel: "Lord, they have killed your prophets and torn down your altars; I am the only one left, and they are trying to kill me"

And what was God's answer to him? "I have reserved for myself seven thousand who have not bowed the knee to Baal." So too, at the present time there is a remnant chosen by grace. And if by grace, then it cannot be based on works; if it were, grace would no longer be grace.

What then? What the people of Israel sought so earnestly they did not obtain. The elect among them did, but the others were hardened, as it is written: "God gave them a spirit of stupor, eyes that could not see and ears that could not hear, to this very day."

And David says: "May their table become a snare and a trap, a stumbling block and a retribution for them. May their eyes be darkened so they cannot see, and their backs be bent forever." (Romans 11:1-10)

Paul begins by addressing a critical question: Has God rejected His people? He answers emphatically, "By no means!" Paul himself is an Israelite, a testament to God's ongoing faithfulness to His covenant people. He introduces the concept of a remnant chosen by grace, underscoring that even in times of widespread unbelief, God preserves a faithful remnant.

This introduces us to the theme of God's sovereign grace. Reflect on your own life: Are there times when you've felt abandoned by God, only to realize later that He had been working behind the scenes, preserving you all along?

The Gentiles' inclusion and Israel's hardening (11:11-24)

"Again I ask: Did they stumble so as to fall beyond recovery? Not at all! Rather, because of their transgression, salvation has come to the Gentiles to make Israel envious. But if their transgression means riches for the world, and their loss means riches for the Gentiles, how much greater riches will their full inclusion bring!

I am talking to you Gentiles. Inasmuch as I am the apostle to the Gentiles, I take pride in my ministry in the hope that I may somehow arouse my own people to envy and save some of them. For if their rejection brought reconciliation to the world, what will their acceptance be but life from the dead? If the part of the dough offered as first fruits is holy, then the whole batch is holy; if the root is holy, so are the branches.

If some of the branches have been broken off, and you, though a wild olive shoot, have been grafted in among the others and now share in the nourishing sap from the olive root, do not consider yourself to be superior to those other branches. If you do, consider this: You do not support the root, but the root supports you.

You will say then, "Branches were broken off so that I could be grafted in." Granted. But they were broken off because of unbelief, and you stand by faith. Do not be arrogant, but tremble. For if God did not spare the natural branches, he will not spare you either."

"Consider therefore the kindness and sternness of God: sternness to those who fell, but kindness to you, provided that you continue in his kindness. Otherwise, you also will be cut off. And if they do not persist in unbelief, they will be grafted in, for God is able to graft them in again.

After all, if you were cut out of an olive tree that is wild by nature, and contrary to nature were grafted into a cultivated olive tree, how much more readily will these, the natural branches, be grafted into their own olive tree!" (Romans 11:11-24)

Paul explains that Israel's stumbling is neither final nor fatal; it serves the purpose of bringing salvation to the Gentiles. But this is not the end of the story. The salvation of the Gentiles, in turn, is meant to provoke Israel to envy and save some of them. This reciprocal dynamic showcases the depth of God's wisdom and the breadth of His redemptive plan.

Paul uses the olive tree metaphor to illustrate this relationship between Jews and Gentiles in the economy of God's kingdom. The Gentiles, wild olive shoots, have been grafted in among the natural branches (Israel) to share in the nourishing sap from the olive root.

This metaphor prompts us to think about our place in God's family. How do we, as Gentiles, honour our connection to the historical people of God? How do we live in humility, recognizing that we are grafted into a story much larger than ourselves?

The Mystery of Israel's Salvation (11:25-32)

"I do not want you to be ignorant of this mystery, brothers and sisters, so that you may not be conceited: Israel has experienced a hardening in part until the full number of the Gentiles has come in, and in this way all Israel will be saved.

As it is written: "The deliverer will come from Zion; he will turn godlessness away from Jacob. And this is my covenant with them when I take away their sins."

"As far as the gospel is concerned, they are enemies for your sake; but as far as election is concerned, they are loved on account of the patriarchs, for God's gifts and his call are irrevocable. Just as you who were at one time disobedient to God have now received mercy as a result of their disobedience, so they too have now become disobedient in order that they too may now receive mercy as a result of God's mercy to you. For God has bound everyone over to disobedience so that he may have mercy on them all." (Romans 11:25-32)

Paul unveils a mystery here: a partial hardening has come upon Israel until the full number of the Gentiles has come in, and in this way, all Israel will be saved. This passage has sparked much debate, but at its heart, it reaffirms God's faithfulness and His commitment to saving His people.

These verses call us to marvel at the mystery and wisdom of God. His ways are not our ways; His thoughts are not our thoughts. How does the recognition of God's mysterious plans impact our faith and our interaction with others?

A Doxology of Praise (11:33-36)

"Oh, the depth of the riches of the wisdom and knowledge of God! How unsearchable his judgments, and his paths beyond tracing out! Who has known the mind of the Lord? Or who has been his counsellor? Who has ever given to God, that God should repay them? For from him and through him and for him are all things. To him be the glory forever! Amen." (Romans 11:33-36)

Paul ends this theologically rich and complex chapter with a doxology, a burst of praise to God for His wisdom, knowledge, judgments, and ways. After contemplating the depths of God's wisdom and mercy, Paul is moved to worship, acknowledging that from Him, through Him, and to Him are all things!

This doxology invites us to respond in worship and awe. Do we take time to pause and reflect on the greatness of God's wisdom and grace? Let us be moved, like Paul, to worship our God for the unsearchable richness of His plan and the mercy He extends to us all.

Romans Chapter 11 challenges us to grapple with the mysteries of God's redemptive plan, reminding us of our place within a story much larger than ourselves. It calls us to humility, gratitude, and awe before the wisdom and mercy of God.

As we step forward, may we do so with a renewed sense of trust in God's sovereign plan, a heart full of gratitude for His grace, and lips quick to praise His holy name. Let us never forget: *"For from Him and through Him and to Him are all things. To Him be the glory forever! Amen."*

May this truth resonate in our hearts and reflect in our lives. As we live out our days, let us not lose sight of the grand narrative of God's redemptive history, in which we have been graciously included. Let our lives be a testimony to the faithfulness of God, a beacon of hope to both Jew and Gentile, and a living doxology that honours the God from whom all blessings flow.

Let us move forward in faith, always carrying the message of reconciliation and hope. May we be instruments in the hands of God, used to provoke envy in a holy manner, leading others to seek the richness found in Christ. As we interact with those from different backgrounds, may our attitudes and actions always reflect the love and grace that have been shown to us.

In times of confusion and doubt, when God's plans often seem inscrutable, let us hold fast to the assurance that His ways are perfect, His wisdom unsearchable, and His judgments just. Let us be comforted by the knowledge that in the end, His mercy will triumph, and His purposes will be fulfilled.

As members of the olive tree, grafted in by grace, let us bear fruit that befits our calling. Let us live lives characterized by faith, hope, and love, demonstrating the transformative power of the gospel. In our dealings with others, may we be known for our compassion, our humility, and our unwavering commitment to the truth of the gospel.

~ ROMANS 12 ~

Introduction

In the twelfth chapter of his letter to the Romans, the Apostle Paul transitions from the lofty theological heights of the first eleven chapters into the practical implications of the gospel in the life of a believer. This chapter marks a significant shift, moving from doctrine to duty, from creed to conduct, from what we believe to how we should live. Here, Paul lays out a blueprint for Christian living, a life transformed by the mercy of God.

A Living Sacrifice (12:1-2)

"Therefore, I urge you, brothers and sisters, in view of God's mercy, to offer your bodies as a living sacrifice, holy and pleasing to God - this is your true and proper worship. Do not conform to the pattern of this world but be transformed by the renewing of your mind. Then you will be able to test and approve what God's will is - his good, pleasing and perfect will." (Romans 12:1-2)

Paul begins with a powerful appeal, this call to present ourselves as living sacrifices. This is radical, but it is not about external rituals, it is about the offering of our entire beings to God as an act of worship. This is the response of gratitude for the mercy we have received.

Reflect on your own life: Is it marked by such sacrificial living? Are you holding back any areas from God's altar? We need to know that transformation only begins when we fully surrender to God, allowing Him to use every part of us for His glory.

Paul also challenges us not to conform to the pattern of this world but to be transformed by the renewing of our minds. This transformation is not a one-time event but an ongoing process, a daily renewal of our thoughts and attitudes that aligns us more closely with God's will. Ask yourself: Are there areas in your life where you've conformed to the world's standards? How can you actively seek the transformation and renewal of your mind?

Gifts of Grace (12:3-8)

"For by the grace given me I say to every one of you: Do not think of yourself more highly than you ought, but rather think of yourself with sober judgment, in accordance with the faith God has distributed to each of you. For just as each of us has one body with many members, and these members do not all have the same function, so in Christ we, though many, form one body, and each member belongs to all the others. We have different gifts, according to the grace given to each of us.

If your gift is prophesying, then prophesy in accordance with your faith; if it is serving, then serve; if it is teaching, then teach; if it is to encourage, then give encouragement; if it is giving, then give generously; if it is to lead, do it diligently; if it is to show mercy, do it cheerfully." (Romans 12:3-8)

In these verses, Paul speaks about the gifts of grace given to each believer for the purpose of serving the body of Christ. He emphasizes humility and sober judgment in the assessment of our gifts. Each one is given according to the measure of faith that God has assigned.

Paul lists various gifts: prophecy, serving, teaching, encouraging, giving, leading, and showing mercy. These gifts are not for personal glorification but for serving others, building up the church, and glorifying God.

Consider your own spiritual gifts: Are you aware of them? Are you using them for the benefit of others and the glory of God? Remember, the church thrives when each member functions according to the gifts God has granted them.

Marks of a True Christian (9:9-21)

Love must be sincere. Hate what is evil; cling to what is good. Be devoted to one another in love. Honour one another above yourselves. Never be lacking in zeal, but keep your spiritual fervour, serving the Lord. Be joyful in hope, patient in affliction, faithful in prayer. Share with the Lord's people who are in need. Practice hospitality.

"Bless those who persecute you; bless and do not curse. Rejoice with those who rejoice; mourn with those who mourn. Live in harmony with one another. Do not be proud, but be willing to associate with people of low position. Do not be conceited.

Do not repay anyone evil for evil. Be careful to do what is right in the eyes of everyone. If it is possible, as far as it depends on you, live at peace with everyone. Do not take revenge, my dear friends, but leave room for God's wrath, for it is written: "It is mine to avenge; I will repay," says the Lord.

On the contrary: "If your enemy is hungry, feed him; if he is thirsty, give him something to drink. In doing this, you will heap burning coals on his head." Do not be overcome by evil, but overcome evil with good." (Romans 12:9-21)

This section is a compelling description of the Christian life in action. It's a portrait of love in action: love without hypocrisy, abhorring what is evil, clinging to what is good, showing honour, zeal, and hope, practicing hospitality, and blessing persecutors. Paul calls believers to live in harmony, to be humble, and not to repay evil for evil. He instructs us to live peaceably with all, as far as it depends on us, and to overcome evil with good.

Examine your life in light of these instructions. How does your life measure up to these standards? Are there areas where you need to grow in love, humility, or patience? Remember, this is not about earning salvation but responding to the grace we've received.

Romans Chapter 12 serves as a bridge between the theological foundations laid in the previous 11 chapters and the practical outworking of those truths in our lives. It calls us to a life of sacrifice, transformation, service, and love - a life that is radically different from the patterns of this world.

As we go forth, may we be inspired to live out the mercies of God in every aspect of our lives, transforming every moment into an offering pleasing to Him. May our lives reflect the beauty and holiness of the gospel, drawing others to the Saviour we serve.

~ ROMANS 13 ~

Introduction

Romans Chapter 13 continues Paul's practical instruction on how the transformative power of the gospel should manifest in a believer's life, particularly in relation to the surrounding society and governing authorities.

This passage is both timely and timeless, speaking into the heart of our responsibilities as citizens and as followers of Christ. In this chapter, Paul navigates the complex relationship between the Christian and the state, urging a life marked by love, light, and lawful conduct.

Respect and Submission to Authorities (13:1-7)

"Let everyone be subject to the governing authorities, for there is no authority except that which God has established. The authorities that exist have been established by God. Consequently, whoever rebels against the authority is rebelling against what God has instituted, and those who do so will bring judgment on themselves. For rulers hold no terror for those who do right, but for those who do wrong.

Do you want to be free from fear of the one in authority? Then do what is right and you will be commended. For the one in authority is God's servant for your good. But if you do wrong, be afraid, for rulers do not bear the sword for no reason. They are God's servants, agents of wrath to bring punishment on the wrongdoer.

Therefore, it is necessary to submit to the authorities, not only because of possible punishment but also as a matter of conscience.

This is also why you pay taxes, for the authorities are God's servants, who give their full time to governing. Give to everyone what you owe them: If you owe taxes, pay taxes; if revenue, then revenue; if respect, then respect; if honour, then honour."
(Romans 13:1-7)

Paul begins this chapter with a strong directive that may seem challenging. He grounds this exhortation in the sovereignty of God, asserting that all authorities that exist have been established by God. Thus, resisting authority amounts to opposing God's decree. This teaching raises questions, especially when we consider unjust or oppressive governments.

How do we reconcile this call to submission with the need to stand against injustice? The key is understanding Paul's overarching concern: promoting peace, order, and welfare within the community while living out our ultimate allegiance to Jesus Christ. It's about influencing society positively and reflecting God's kingdom.

Consider your own attitude and actions towards government and authorities. Are they marked by respect and prayerful support, or by disdain and constant opposition? How can you be a constructive Christian citizen while maintaining your primary allegiance to Christ?

The Continuing Debt of Love (13:8-10)

> *"Let no debt remain outstanding, except the continuing debt to love one another, for whoever loves others has fulfilled the law. The commandments, "You shall not commit adultery," "You shall not murder," "You shall not steal," "You shall not covet," and whatever other command there may be, are summed up in this one command: "Love your neighbour as yourself." Love does no harm to a neighbour. Therefore, love is the fulfillment of the law." (Romans 13:8-10)*

Transitioning from the public sphere to personal ethics, Paul encapsulates the Christian's moral obligation in one command: "*Love your neighbour as yourself.*" Love, Paul argues, is the fulfillment of the law. In loving others, we embody the law's true intent. This command to love transcends all cultural, political, and social boundaries. It challenges us to look beyond our personal interests and preferences and to seek the welfare of others. In a world rife with division, the call to love our neighbour is both radical and redemptive.

Reflect on how you express love in your everyday interactions. Are there prejudices or biases that hinder your ability to love others as Christ loves you? How can you more fully embody this debt of love in your community?

Living as Children of Light (13:11-14)

"And do this, understanding the present time: The hour has already come for you to wake up from your slumber, because our salvation is nearer now than when we first believed. The night is nearly over; the day is almost here. So let us put aside the deeds of darkness and put on the armour of light.

Let us behave decently, as in the daytime, not in carousing and drunkenness, not in sexual immorality and debauchery, not in dissension and jealousy. Rather, clothe yourselves with the Lord Jesus Christ, and do not think about how to gratify the desires of the flesh." (Romans 13:11-14)

Paul concludes the chapter with a stirring wake-up call: "The hour has come for you to wake from sleep." He emphasizes the urgency of the Christian mission in light of the approaching salvation. The night is nearly over; the day is almost here. Therefore, believers are to live honourably, casting off deeds of darkness and putting on the armour of light - a metaphor for a life characterized by righteousness and integrity.

This passage calls for a sober self-assessment and also a firm recommitment to living in the light of Christ. It's a reminder that our time on earth is limited and that we should live each day with purpose and intentionality, embodying the values of the kingdom of God. As we examine our lifestyle, we should ask if there are areas shrouded in darkness which may need the light of Christ?

Romans Chapter 13 challenges us to navigate the complexities of life in a fallen world with wisdom, integrity, and love. It also calls us to a much higher standard of living than many around us in the world, one that honours God and serves others.

~ ROMANS 14 ~

Introduction

Romans Chapter 14 addresses a crucial aspect of Christian life and community: how to handle disagreements over disputable matters. These are issues that are not central to the faith, where believers may hold different views. Paul's guidance is timeless, providing principles for maintaining unity and love within the diverse body of Christ. This message is vital for every church community, reminding us how to navigate differences without losing sight of what truly matters.

The Principle of Acceptance (14:1-4)

"Accept the one whose faith is weak, without quarrelling over disputable matters. One person's faith allows them to eat anything, but another, whose faith is weak, eats only vegetables.

The one who eats everything must not treat with contempt the one who does not, and the one who does not eat everything must not judge the one who does, for God has accepted them. Who are you to judge someone else's servant? To their own master, servants stand or fall. And they will stand, for the Lord is able to make them stand." (Romans 14:1-4)

Paul begins by instructing the Roman believers to accept those whose faith is weak, particularly concerning dietary laws and special days. The call to acceptance is not merely tolerance but a warm, welcoming, non-judgmental embrace. It's about receiving one another as Christ received us, despite our differences.

This acceptance does not mean compromising on any essential doctrines but recognizing the vastness of God's family and the diversity within it. Each servant, Paul writes, is accountable to the Lord and we are not their judge.

Reflect on your interactions within your church community. Are there instances where you've passed judgment on others over non-essential issues? How can you better foster a spirit of acceptance and understanding?

The Principle of Conscience (14:5-12)

"One person considers one day more sacred than another; another considers every day alike. Each of them should be fully convinced in their own mind. Whoever regards one day as special does so to the Lord. Whoever eats meat does so to the Lord, for they give thanks to God; and whoever abstains does so to the Lord and gives thanks to God.

For none of us lives for ourselves alone, and none of us dies for ourselves alone. If we live, we live for the Lord; and if we die, we die for the Lord. So, whether we live or die, we belong to the Lord. For this very reason, Christ died and returned to life so that he might be the Lord of both the dead and the living.

You, then, why do you judge your brother or sister? Or why do you treat them with contempt? For we will all stand before God's judgment seat. It is written: 'As surely as I live,' says the Lord, 'every knee will bow before me; every tongue will acknowledge God.' So then, each of us will give an account of ourselves to God." (Romans 14:5-12)

Paul now shifts focus to individual conscience, and particularly concerning the observance of certain days or dietary restrictions. He emphasizes that each person should be fully convinced in their own mind and act according to their faith. The underlying principle is that whatever we do, we do it unto the Lord. Paul teaches us the importance of respecting people's personal convictions born out of a desire to honour God. He challenges us to consider how we handle our freedom in Christ and how we respect the freedoms and convictions of others.

So, you might ask yourself if you look down on others who view certain disputable matters differently … and are you using your freedom in a way that honours God and edifies others?

The Principle of Love (14:13-15)

"Therefore, let us stop passing judgment on one another. Instead, make up your mind not to put any stumbling block or obstacle in the way of a brother or sister."

> *"I am convinced, being fully persuaded in the Lord Jesus, that nothing is unclean in itself. But if anyone regards something as unclean, then for that person it is unclean. If your brother or sister is distressed because of what you eat, you are no longer acting in love. Do not by your eating destroy someone for whom Christ died." (Romans 14:13-15)*

Paul warns against being a stumbling block to others. Our liberty should never lead others into sin. The guiding principle here in exercising our freedom should be love. If something we consider permissible causes another believer to stumble, we are called to forgo our rights for the sake of love. These verses call us to evaluate our actions through the lens of love and the impact they have on others. Christian liberty is not an excuse for selfishness but an opportunity to demonstrate sacrificial love.

Consider your actions and decisions: Are they guided by love? Are you willing to limit your freedom for the sake of a weaker brother or sister in Christ?

The Principle of Peace and Edification (14:16-23)

> *"Therefore, do not let what you know is good be spoken of as evil. For the kingdom of God is not a matter of eating and drinking, but of righteousness, peace and joy in the Holy Spirit, because anyone who serves Christ in this way is pleasing to God and receives human approval.*
>
> *Let us therefore make every effort to do what leads to peace and to mutual edification. Do not destroy the work of God for the sake of food. All food is clean, but it is wrong for a person to eat anything that causes someone else to stumble. It is better not to eat meat or drink wine or to do anything else that will cause your brother or sister to fall.*
>
> *So, whatever you believe about these things keep between yourself and God. Blessed is the one who does not condemn himself by what he approves. But whoever has doubts is condemned if they eat, because their eating is not from faith; and everything that does not come from faith is sin." (Romans 14:16-23)*

Paul emphasizes that the kingdom of God is not about external matters like eating and drinking, but about righteousness, peace, and joy in the Holy Spirit. We should, therefore, make every effort to do what leads to peace and mutual edification, avoiding actions that cause division over non-essential issues.

This reminds us to prioritize the health and unity of the body of Christ over our preferences or opinions. Our goal should be to build each other up, not tear each other down over disputable matters. Reflect on your priorities: Are they aligned with the values of God's kingdom? How can you contribute to peace and edification in your community?

Romans Chapter 14 challenges us to navigate the complexities of Christian freedom with love, wisdom, and a deep commitment to community. It calls us to a higher standard of living, where love overrides liberty, and unity trumps personal opinions.

In the days ahead, let us commit to living in a way that honours God and edifies our brothers and sisters in Christ. May our lives reflect the righteousness, peace, and joy of the kingdom of God, bringing glory to Him in all things.

~ ROMANS 15 ~

Introduction

In Romans Chapter 15, the Apostle Paul continues to guide the church in Rome - and by extension, all of us - on how to live in harmony and selflessness, particularly within the diverse body of Christ.

This chapter builds upon the principles laid out in Chapter 14, focusing on the strong bearing with the weak and the call to emulate Christ in seeking the good of others. Here, Paul moves from the theoretical to the practical, from individual responsibility to communal living, and from present difficulties to our future hope and unity.

The Example of Christ (15:1-3)

> *"We who are strong ought to bear with the failings of the weak and not to please ourselves. Each of us should please our neighbours for their good, to build them up. For even Christ did not please himself but, as it is written: "The insults of those who insult you have fallen on me." (Romans 15:1-3)*

Paul begins this chapter with a powerful appeal. This sets the tone for Christian living, highlighting sacrifice and selflessness. The 'strong' and 'weak' in faith are called to mutual acceptance, mirroring Christ's acceptance of us. This is certainly not about compromising the truth but about prioritizing unity and love over personal liberty.

Reflect on your attitude towards others in the church. Are there ways you can better support, encourage, or bear with fellow believers? How can you put aside personal preferences or freedoms for the sake of unity and peace?

Paul points us to the ultimate example: Christ did not please Himself but bore our reproaches. Following Christ means adopting a mindset that seeks the good of others, prioritizing their spiritual growth and well-being.

Consider this: How does Christ's example challenge your current lifestyle? In what areas of your life are you called to bear the weaknesses of others?

Scripture and Hope (15:4-13)

> *For everything that was written in the past was written to teach us, so that through the endurance taught in the Scriptures and the encouragement they provide we might have hope.*
>
> *May the God who gives endurance and encouragement give you the same attitude of mind toward each other that Christ Jesus had, so that with one mind and one voice you may glorify the God and Father of our Lord Jesus Christ.*
>
> *Accept one another, then, just as Christ accepted you, in order to bring praise to God." (Romans 15:4-13)*

Paul emphasizes the importance of Scripture for endurance, encouragement, and hope. The endurance and encouragement from the Scriptures enable us to maintain harmony and hope within the Christian community.

This passage invites us to delve deeply into God's Word, as we draw strength and hope which transcends circumstances. It's a reminder that the unity and patience we strive for are not rooted in our strength but in the hope and promise found in Scripture.

So, how does your engagement with Scripture reflect in your patience, encouragement, and hope? How can you more effectively use the Scriptures to foster unity and hope in your community?

Paul's Ministry and Ambition (15:14-22)

> *"I myself am convinced, my brothers and sisters, that you yourselves are full of goodness, filled with knowledge and competent to instruct one another. Yet I have written you quite boldly on some points to remind you of them again, because of the grace God gave me to be a minister of Christ Jesus to the Gentiles.*

"He gave me the priestly duty of proclaiming the gospel of God, so that the Gentiles might become an offering acceptable to God, sanctified by the Holy Spirit.

Therefore, I glory in Christ Jesus in my service to God. I will not venture to speak of anything except what Christ has accomplished through me in leading the Gentiles to obey God by what I have said and done - by the power of signs and wonders, through the power of the Spirit of God.

So, from Jerusalem all the way around to Illyricum, I have fully proclaimed the gospel of Christ. It has always been my ambition to preach the gospel where Christ was not known, so that I would not be building on someone else's foundation.

Rather, as it is written: "Those who were not told about him will see, and those who have not heard will understand. This is why I have often been hindered from coming to you."
(Romans 15:14-22)

Paul shares his heart and mission, highlighting his role as a minister to the Gentiles. He speaks of his ambition to preach the gospel wherever Christ is not known, avoiding building on another's foundation. This reflects a profound commitment to the missionary heart of God, seeking to reach the unreached.

This should challenge us to consider our own mission fields. Who are the 'Gentiles' in your life, the people or places untouched by the gospel? How can you extend the reach of God's kingdom beyond your comfort zone?

Paul's Travel Plans and Prayer Request (15:23-33)

"But now that there is no more place for me to work in these regions, and since I have been longing for many years to visit you, I plan to do so when I go to Spain. I hope to see you while passing through and to have you assist me on my journey there, after I have enjoyed your company for a while. Now, however, I am on my way to Jerusalem in the service of the Lord's people there. For Macedonia and Achaia were pleased to make a contribution for the poor among the Lord's people in Jerusalem."

"They were pleased to do it, and indeed they owe it to them. For if the Gentiles have shared in the Jews' spiritual blessings, they owe it to the Jews to share with them their material blessings. So after I have completed this task and have made sure that they have received this contribution, I will go to Spain and visit you on the way. I know that when I come to you, I will come in the full measure of the blessing of Christ.

I urge you, brothers and sisters, by our Lord Jesus Christ and by the love of the Spirit, to join me in my struggle by praying to God for me. Pray that I may be kept safe from the unbelievers in Judea and that the contribution I take to Jerusalem may be favourably received by the Lord's people there, so that I may come to you with joy, by God's will, and in your company be refreshed. The God of peace be with you all. Amen." (Romans 15:23-33)

Finally, Paul shares his travel plans and requests prayers for his journey and his upcoming ministry. This personal touch reveals the interdependence of the body of Christ. Paul, the great apostle, acknowledges his need for the prayers and support of the Roman Christians.

This serves as a reminder of our need for one another and the power of prayer. How are you supporting missionaries or fellow believers through prayer and encouragement? How can you be more intentional in interceding for the work of the gospel globally?

Romans Chapter 15 calls us to a life of harmony, selflessness, and hope. As we strive to live out these principles, let us draw near to Christ, our ultimate example of sacrificial love and service. Let us be united in purpose, grounded in Scripture, and committed to the mission of spreading the gospel. In doing so, we glorify God and live out the true calling of the Christian life.

Let us embrace whatever tomorrow brings, empowered by the Holy Spirit, to live in such harmony with one another, in accord with Christ Jesus.

~ ROMANS 16 ~

Introduction

In the concluding chapter of Paul's letter to the Romans, we now encounter a personal and communal section of Scripture, often completely overlooked because of its seemingly mundane list of greetings.

However, Romans Chapter 16 is far from trivial; it is a treasure trove of insight into the early Christian community's diversity, unity, and mutual support. It provides a glimpse into the heart of Paul and the fabric of the early Church, revealing the importance of relationships, warnings against divisiveness, and the celebration of shared faith.

Commendation and Greetings (16:1-16)

"I commend to you our sister Phoebe, a deacon of the church in Cenchreae. I ask you to receive her in the Lord in a way worthy of his people and to give her any help she may need from you, for she has been the benefactor of many people, including me.

Greet Priscilla and Aquila, my co-workers in Christ Jesus. They risked their lives for me. Not only I but all the churches of the Gentiles are grateful to them.

Greet also the church that meets at their house.

Greet my dear friend Epenetus, who was the first convert to Christ in the province of Asia.

Greet Mary, who worked very hard for you.

Greet Andronicus and Junia, my fellow Jews who have been in prison with me. They are outstanding among[d] the apostles, and they were in Christ before I was.

Greet Ampliatus, my dear friend in the Lord.

Greet Urbanus, our co-worker in Christ, and my dear friend Stachys.

Greet Apelles, whose fidelity to Christ has stood the test."

"Greet those who belong to the household of Aristobulus.

Greet Herodion, my fellow Jew.

Greet those in the household of Narcissus who are in the Lord.

Greet Tryphena and Tryphosa, those women who work hard in the Lord.

Greet my dear friend Persis, another woman who has worked very hard in the Lord.

Greet Rufus, chosen in the Lord, and his mother, who has been a mother to me, too.

Greet Asyncritus, Phlegon, Hermes, Patrobas, Hermas and the other brothers and sisters with them.

Greet Philologus, Julia, Nereus and his sister, and Olympas and all the Lord's people who are with them.

Greet one another with a holy kiss." (Romans 16:1-16)

Paul begins this chapter by commending Phoebe, a servant and benefactor of many, including Paul himself. This commendation highlights the significant roles women played in the early church.

Paul's greeting to various individuals and households serves to underscore the diverse makeup of the Roman church - Jews and Gentiles, men and women, influential leaders, and ordinary believers - all united in Christ.

This passage challenges us to consider our own community dynamics. Are we acknowledging and appreciating the diverse contributions within our own church? How are we fostering an environment where every member, regardless of status or background, feels valued and an integral to the body of Christ?

Reflect on your personal role within your local church. Are you contributing to the community's welfare and encouragement, as Phoebe did? Are you building up others, recognizing their work in the Lord?

Warning Against Divisiveness (16:17-20)

"I urge you, brothers and sisters, to watch out for those who cause divisions and put obstacles in your way that are contrary to the teaching you have learned. Keep away from them. For such people are not serving our Lord Christ, but their own appetites. By smooth talk and flattery, they deceive the minds of naive people. Everyone has heard about your obedience, so I rejoice because of you; but I want you to be wise about what is good, and innocent about what is evil. The God of peace will soon crush Satan under your feet. The grace of our Lord Jesus be with you." (Romans 16:17-20)

Paul now shifts from greetings to a stern warning against those causing divisions and obstacles contrary to the doctrine learned by the believers. This admonition is as relevant today as it was then. The church is continually threatened by teachings and behaviours that seek to divide rather than unite.

Paul's instruction here is clear: be wise about what is good and innocent about what is evil. This calls for serious discernment - a discernment grounded in Scripture and a commitment to unity in the truth of the gospel. Consider your own actions and beliefs: Are they promoting unity, or are they contributing to division and confusion? How can you better equip yourself to be a uniting influence?

Further greetings (16:21-24)

"Timothy, my co-worker, sends his greetings to you, as do Lucius, Jason and Sosipater, my fellow Jews. I, Tertius, who wrote down this letter, greet you in the Lord. Gaius, whose hospitality I and the whole church here enjoy, sends you his greetings. Erastus, who is the city's director of public works, and our brother Quartus send you their greetings. The grace of our Lord Jesus Christ be with you all. Amen." (Romans 16:21-24)

These few serve as a part of Paul's final greetings. He mentions Timothy, his co-worker, and others who are with him, extending their greetings to the Roman church.

This indicates the communal and supportive nature of the early Christian movement, highlighting that Paul's mission was not a solitary endeavour, it was more of a collective effort involving many individuals from diverse backgrounds.

Furthermore, these verses emphasize the bonds of fellowship among Christians, transcending geographical and cultural boundaries. Paul's greetings from his companions serve as a testament to the unity and mutual support that should characterize the Christian community.

The benediction in verse 24, "*The grace of our Lord Jesus Christ be with you all. Amen,*" appears in some ancient manuscripts and it is a common Pauline closing, underscoring the importance of grace in the Christian faith. It's a prayer and a wish for the readers, that they may experience the unmerited favour and love of Jesus Christ, which is central to the gospel message Paul preached.

This section of the letter, while brief, encapsulates themes of fellowship, support, and grace that run throughout Paul's writings and the New Testament.

Doxology (16:25-27)

> *"Now to him who is able to establish you in accordance with my gospel, the message I proclaim about Jesus Christ, in keeping with the revelation of the mystery hidden for long ages past, but now revealed and made known through the prophetic writings by the command of the eternal God, so that all the Gentiles might come to the obedience that comes from faith - to the only wise God be glory forever through Jesus Christ! Amen." (Romans 16:25-27)*

Paul concludes his letter with a glorious doxology, praising God Who is able to strengthen believers according to the gospel. This doxology is a fitting end to a letter so rich in theological depth and practical instruction. It redirects our focus from the challenges and complexities of church life to the ultimate source of our strength and unity: God Himself.

This doxology invites us to worship and trust in God's power to establish and sustain us. It reminds us that the gospel is the foundation of our faith and the source of our strength.

Reflect on the majesty and power of God as revealed throughout Romans. How should this understanding shape your faith and your actions? Are you relying on His strength and living in accordance with the gospel?

Romans Chapter 16 is not merely a conclusion but a call to remember the personal, communal, and spiritual aspects of our faith. It reminds us of the beauty and challenge of the Christian community, the necessity of vigilance against division, and the ultimate source of our strength and unity: the gospel of Christ.

As we close this exploration of Romans, let's carry forward the lessons of faith, love, unity, and vigilance, committing our lives to God's glory and to the service of one another. May our communities reflect the love and diversity of the early church, united in purpose, grounded in truth, and flourishing in grace.

~ 1 CORINTHIANS ~

The book of 1 Corinthians is a profound and multi-faceted letter written by the Apostle Paul to the new Christian community in Corinth. This community was experiencing a variety of moral, doctrinal, and organizational problems, leading Paul to address these issues and provide guidance. Here is a very brief overview of the sixteen chapters in 1 Corinthians:

Chapter 1: Paul begins with a greeting, thanksgiving, then he emphasizes God's grace to the believers in Corinth. He then quickly transitions to the main issue: divisions within the church, with members aligning themselves with different Christian leaders. Paul criticizes this factionalism, stressing that Christ should be the central figure of unity.

He also introduces a recurring theme: the contrast between human wisdom and God's wisdom, arguing that the message of the cross is foolishness to those who are perishing, but the power of God to those who are being saved.

Chapter 2: Paul continues to contrast divine wisdom with human wisdom. He emphasizes that his preaching has not been with eloquent wisdom but with a clear demonstration of the Spirit's power, so faith would rest not on human wisdom but on God's power. He discusses the role of the Holy Spirit in revealing deep truths of God, which are not accessible through human wisdom.

Chapter 3: Paul addresses the issue of immaturity among the Corinthian believers, using the metaphor of milk and solid food to distinguish between the basic and the deeper Christian teachings.

He revisits the issue of divisions, criticizing the Corinthians for their allegiance to different leaders and reminding them that all leaders are mere servants through whom God works. He uses the metaphor of the church as God's field and building to emphasize unity and collective purpose.

Chapter 4: Paul defends his role as an apostle and addresses the issue of arrogance among the Corinthians. He uses irony to challenge their sense of superiority and calls for them to imitate him, as he imitates Christ, reinforcing the theme of humility and servant leadership.

Chapter 5: Paul addresses a case of sexual immorality in the church, criticizing the community for its pride and failure to discipline the offending member. He stresses the importance of moral purity within the church body.

Chapter 6: This chapter deals with lawsuits among believers and the issue of sexual immorality. Paul exhorts the Corinthians to resolve their disputes within the church community and reminds them of their identity in Christ, which should guide their moral and legal decisions.

Chapter 7: Paul answers questions about marriage, singleness, and divorce, providing some guidance that balances cultural practices with Christian principles. He then emphasizes the importance of remaining faithful in one's current situation while living in anticipation of the Lord's return.

Chapter 8: Addressing the issue of food sacrificed to idols, Paul introduces the principle of Christian freedom moderated by love for other believers. He warns against causing others to stumble through one's exercise of freedom.

Chapter 9: Paul defends his apostolic rights, including financial support, but notes that he has not made use of these rights to avoid hindering the gospel. He stresses the importance of self-discipline and adapting to reach different people with the message of Christ.

Chapter 10: Paul then uses Israel's history as a warning to the Corinthians, urging them to learn from past mistakes and avoid idolatry and immorality. He revisits the issue of eating food offered to idols, emphasizing the need for caution and consideration for others' consciences.

Chapter 11: Paul addresses issues related to worship: head coverings for women (a cultural sign of propriety) and abuses of the Lord's Supper. He calls for respect and unity, then emphasizes the significance of the Lord's Supper as a special proclamation of Jesus' death.

Chapter 12: Paul discusses spiritual gifts, emphasizing their diversity and unity within the body of Christ. He argues that all gifts are given by the same Spirit and are meant for the common good.

Chapter 13: Known as the "love chapter," Paul elevates love as the greatest virtue, surpassing all spiritual gifts. He describes love's characteristics and permanence, underscoring its foundational role in Christian life and community.

Chapter 14: Paul addresses the use of spiritual gifts in public worship, specifically speaking in tongues and prophecy. He stresses the importance of edification and order within the church service.

Chapter 15: This chapter focuses on the resurrection of Christ and its implications for believers. Paul defends the reality of the resurrection, outlines its significance for Christian faith, and describes the nature of the resurrected body.

Chapter 16: Paul concludes this first letter to the Corinthians with personal remarks, travel plans, and final exhortations. He stresses the importance of love, vigilance, faith, and strength in Christian living. He also emphasizes the importance of supporting the Jerusalem church, reflecting the unity and mutual care among different Christian communities.

Throughout the letter, Paul addresses specific problems while providing general principles for Christian living. His message revolves around unity, love, moral integrity, and the distinction between worldly wisdom and divine wisdom. 1 Corinthians is a very rich text that deals with real-world issues within the early Christian community, offering insights that remain relevant for contemporary believers.

The core themes woven throughout 1 Corinthians, such as unity, love, and the significance of the resurrection, are really critical to understanding Christian theology and ethics. Paul's approach combines practical guidance with significant theological depth, encouraging a life that mirrors the values of the Gospel.

Paul's first letter to the Corinthians offers a comprehensive guide for Christian communities, addressing doctrinal, ethical, and practical issues. Its teachings continue to challenge and inspire believers to live out their faith authentically in a complex world, emphasizing the centrality of love, the importance of unity, and the transformative hope of the resurrection.

Now I will unpack each of the sixteen chapters in more detail as we encounter and wrestle with this important letter.

~ 1 CORINTHIANS 1 ~

Introduction

This important letter really speaks across ages, directly into our contemporary struggles and joys. The Apostle Paul is addressing a church not unlike our own, filled with vibrant diversity but also challenged by divisions.

As we explore the first chapter of 1 Corinthians, let us open our hearts to the timeless message of unity in Christ. First, let's set the context for this letter.

Corinth, a bustling port city, was a real melting pot of cultures, religions, and philosophies. Into this dynamic and often divisive environment, Paul planted the seeds of the Gospel, cultivating a community bound not by worldly wisdom but by the message of the cross. However, like any family, the church in Corinth faced its share of internal strife. It's from this place of loving concern that Paul writes to them, and to us today.

Greeting and Thanksgiving (1:1-9)

"Paul, called to be an apostle of Christ Jesus by the will of God, and our brother Sosthenes, to the church of God in Corinth, to those sanctified in Christ Jesus and called to be his holy people, together with all those everywhere who call on the name of our Lord Jesus Christ - their Lord and ours: Grace and peace to you from God our Father and the Lord Jesus Christ.

I always thank my God for you because of his grace given you in Christ Jesus. For in him you have been enriched in every way - with all kinds of speech and with all knowledge - God thus confirming our testimony about Christ among you.

Therefore you do not lack any spiritual gift as you eagerly wait for our Lord Jesus Christ to be revealed. He will also keep you firm to the end, so that you will be blameless on the day of our Lord Jesus Christ. God is faithful, who has called you into fellowship with his Son, Jesus Christ our Lord." (1 Corinthians 1:1-9)

Paul introduces himself as an apostle, emphasizing his authority and divine mission. He addresses the letter not only to the church in Corinth but also to all Christians everywhere, highlighting the universal nature of his message.

He then moves into a section of thanksgiving, a common feature in Pauline epistles. Paul gives thanks to God for the grace given to the Corinthians through Christ Jesus. He highlights how they have been enriched in every way, especially in knowledge and speech. This points to the spiritual gifts and understanding they have received through their faith.

Paul assures the Corinthians that the testimony about Christ has been confirmed among them, indicating that they have indeed embraced the gospel and its teachings. This sets a positive tone, acknowledging their spiritual successes before addressing issues and corrections later in the letter.

He also emphasizes the faithfulness of God, who has called them into fellowship with His Son, Jesus Christ. This strong assurance underlines the foundational Christian concept of a personal relationship with Christ and the security of being in God's hands. The passage ends with a note of divine faithfulness, assuring believers that God will sustain them to the end, guiltless in the day of our Lord Jesus Christ.

Unity Amid Division (1:10-13)

> *"I appeal to you, brothers and sisters, in the name of our Lord Jesus Christ, that all of you agree with one another in what you say and that there be no divisions among you, but that you be perfectly united in mind and thought. My brothers and sisters, some from Chloe's household have informed me that there are quarrels among you.*
>
> *What I mean is this: One of you says, "I follow Paul"; another, "I follow Apollos"; another, "I follow Cephas"; still another, "I follow Christ."*
>
> *Is Christ divided? Was Paul crucified for you? Were you baptized in the name of Paul?" (1 Corinthians 1:10-13)*

Paul's opening appeal in verse 10 is both simple and profound: *"... that all of you agree with one another in what you say and that there be no divisions among you, but that you be perfectly united in mind and thought."* How timely is this appeal in our world today? We live in times marked by serious division everywhere: within nations, communities, and even in many churches. Paul's call is a reminder that our unity is in Jesus Christ. This unity isn't uniformity; it allows for diversity of thought, background, and experience, but it demands a common foundation: Jesus Christ himself.

We should not read this text without reflecting on our own reality. Are there divisions within our community? Are they based on personalities, preferences, or perspectives? The Apostle Paul reminds us that Christ is not divided, and neither should His body, the church, be divided.

Paul's calling is to preach (1:14-17)

> *"I thank God that I did not baptize any of you except Crispus and Gaius, so no one can say that you were baptized in my name. (Yes, I also baptized the household of Stephanas; beyond that, I don't remember if I baptized anyone else.) For Christ did not send me to baptize, but to preach the gospel – not with wisdom and eloquence, lest the cross of Christ be emptied of its power."*
> *(1 Corinthians 1:14-17)*

Once again, Paul addresses the of division and allegiance within the Christian community. Paul is grateful that he baptized only a few members of the Corinthian church, to prevent any claims that they were baptized in his name rather than in Christ's. This highlights Paul's concern over divisions within the community, where some claimed allegiance to specific human leaders rather than to Christ himself.

Paul's focus is on the message of the cross, which he views as central to the Christian faith. He underscores that his primary mission is not to baptize but to preach the gospel. However, this preaching should never rely on human wisdom, lest the cross of Christ be emptied of its power.

Here, Paul emphasizes the priority of the content of the message over the eloquence of its delivery, arguing that the power of the gospel lies in its divine origin and message, never in human rhetoric or man's wisdom. These verses reflect early Christian concerns about unity, the nature of ministry, and the central focus of the Christian message.

The Foolishness of the Cross (1:18-25)

"For the message of the cross is foolishness to those who are perishing, but to us who are being saved it is the power of God. For it is written: "I will destroy the wisdom of the wise; the intelligence of the intelligent I will frustrate."

Where is the wise person? Where is the teacher of the law? Where is the philosopher of this age? Has not God made foolish the wisdom of the world? For since in the wisdom of God the world through its wisdom did not know him, God was pleased through the foolishness of what was preached to save those who believe.

Jews demand signs and Greeks look for wisdom, but we preach Christ crucified: a stumbling block to Jews and foolishness to Gentiles, but to those whom God has called, both Jews and Greeks, Christ the power of God and the wisdom of God. For the foolishness of God is wiser than human wisdom, and the weakness of God is stronger than human strength." (1 Corinthians 1:18-25)

Paul contrasts worldly wisdom with the 'foolishness' of the gospel. *"For the message of the cross is foolishness to those who are perishing, but to us who are being saved it is the power of God."* In a society that esteemed rhetorical skill and intellectual prowess, the message of a crucified Messiah was absolutely ludicrous. Yet, it is precisely in this 'foolishness' that the power and wisdom of God are revealed. Our culture also measures success, wisdom, and worth by standards that are starkly different from the values of the kingdom of God. Are we, as a church, tempted to adopt these measures, seeking worldly wisdom over the 'foolishness' of the Gospel? Paul invites us to embrace the counter-cultural message of the cross, where our weakness becomes the conduit for God's power and strength.

The Wisdom and Power of God (1:26-31)

> *"Brothers and sisters, think of what you were when you were called. Not many of you were wise by human standards; not many were influential; not many were of noble birth. But God chose the foolish things of the world to shame the wise; God chose the weak things of the world to shame the strong. God chose the lowly things of this world and the despised things - and the things that are not - to nullify the things that are, so that no one may boast before him. It is because of him that you are in Christ Jesus, who has become for us wisdom from God - that is, our righteousness, holiness and redemption. Therefore, as it is written: "Let the one who boasts boast in the Lord." (1 Corinthians 1:26-31)*

Paul reminds the Corinthians of their own stories: "Not many of you were wise by human standards; not many were influential; not many were of noble birth." It's a call to humility and a reminder of God's grace. God chose the foolish, the weak, the lowly, so that no one may boast before Him.

It is profoundly liberating to know that in God's kingdom, our value doesn't depend on our achievements, our social status, or our intellectual capacity. We are valued because we are loved by God and redeemed by Christ. This truth should dismantle any hierarchy within our community and prompt us to look at each other through God's eyes.

Conclusion

As we reflect on this chapter, let's remember that unity in the body of Christ is not just a nice-to-have; it's foundational. It's not uniformity or the suppression of differences, but a unity forged in the shared recognition of our need for Christ, our commitment to His message, and our dedication to embodying His love.

So, let's challenge ourselves today: How can we contribute to the unity of our community? How can we embrace the 'foolishness' of the cross in a world that glorifies wisdom and power?

~ 1 CORINTHIANS 2 ~

Introduction

In chapter 2, the Apostle Paul emphasizes the power and wisdom of God as opposed to human wisdom and eloquence. Paul outlines the foundation of his preaching and the profound truth of the Gospel.

The Humility of God's Servant (2:1-5)

"And so it was with me, brothers and sisters. When I came to you, I did not come with eloquence or human wisdom as I proclaimed to you the testimony about God.

For I resolved to know nothing while I was with you except Jesus Christ and him crucified. I came to you in weakness with great fear and trembling.

My message and my preaching were not with wise and persuasive words, but with a demonstration of the Spirit's power, so that your faith might not rest on human wisdom, but on God's power." (1 Corinthians 2:1-5)

Paul starts this chapter by reminding the Corinthians of how he came to them: *"not with eloquence or human wisdom."* He did not rely on his persuasive speeches or impressive words. Instead, he came in weakness, fear, and trembling.

This is really significant because Paul wants to emphasize that the power of the Gospel does not lie in human eloquence or wisdom but in the message of Jesus Christ and Him crucified.

This is a crucial lesson for us today. In a world obsessed with appearances, charisma, and eloquence, Paul reminds us that the true power lies not in our abilities but in the message of the Gospel. When we speak of Jesus, our focus should not be on impressing others with our knowledge or oratory skills but on faithfully conveying the truth of Christ crucified and risen.

Godly vs. Worldly Wisdom (2:6-9)

"We do, however, speak a message of wisdom among the mature, but not the wisdom of this age or of the rulers of this age, who are coming to nothing. No, we declare God's wisdom, a mystery that has been hidden and that God destined for our glory before time began. None of the rulers of this age understood it, for if they had, they would not have crucified the Lord of glory.

However, as it is written: "What no eye has seen, what no ear has heard, and what no human mind has conceived" - the things God has prepared for those who love him ..." (1 Corinthians 2:6-9)

Paul distinguishes between two types of wisdom: the wisdom of this age and the wisdom of God. The rulers of this age, he says, are coming to nothing. They did not understand the wisdom of God; if they had, they would not have crucified the Lord of glory. But as it is written: *"What no eye has seen, what no ear has heard, and what no human mind has conceived"* – these are the things God has prepared for those who love Him.

Here, Paul is revealing a profound mystery. The wisdom of God is not something that can be understood through human intellect or the philosophies of this world. It is revealed to us by God through His Spirit. This means our approach to understanding divine truths should be one of humility and reliance on the Spirit, not on our intellectual capabilities.

The Role of the Spirit in Understanding Wisdom (2:10-13)

" ... these are the things God has revealed to us by his Spirit. The Spirit searches all things, even the deep things of God. For who knows a person's thoughts except their own spirit within them? In the same way no one knows the thoughts of God except the Spirit of God. What we have received is not the spirit of the world, but the Spirit who is from God, so that we may understand what God has freely given us. This is what we speak, not in words taught us by human wisdom but in words taught by the Spirit, explaining spiritual realities with Spirit-taught words."
(1 Corinthians 2:10-13)

The Spirit searches all things, even the deep things of God. No one knows the thoughts of God except the Spirit of God. This is why we, who have received the Spirit, can understand the things freely given us by God. We do not speak in words taught by human wisdom but in words taught by the Spirit.

This section is a reminder that the Christian faith is not merely an intellectual exercise. It is a spiritual journey. The Holy Spirit plays a crucial role in our understanding of God's truths. Without the Spirit, we cannot comprehend the depths of God's wisdom. This is why prayer, meditation, and spiritual openness are essential in our walk with God.

The Natural vs. The Spiritual Person (2:14-16)

"The person without the Spirit does not accept the things that come from the Spirit of God but considers them foolishness and cannot understand them because they are discerned only through the Spirit.

The person with the Spirit makes judgments about all things, but such a person is not subject to merely human judgments, for,

"Who has known the mind of the Lord so as to instruct him?"
But we have the mind of Christ." (1 Corinthians 2:14-16)

Paul concludes this chapter by contrasting the natural person with the spiritual person. The natural person does not accept the things that come from the Spirit of God. They are foolishness to him. But the spiritual person makes judgments about all things, yet he himself is not subject to merely human judgments. "*For who has known the mind of the Lord so as to instruct him? But we have the mind of Christ.*"

This is a powerful statement. Having the mind of Christ means that we view the world and make decisions based on Christ's values and teachings. It means being guided by the Holy Spirit in all aspects of our lives. This does not mean we will be free from struggles or doubts, but it does mean that we approach life differently from those who do not know Christ.

Conclusion

In 1 Corinthians Chapter 2, Paul invites us to embrace a profound understanding that the essence of our faith rests not on human wisdom but on the power of God revealed through the Spirit. As we reflect on this message, let us seek to be more reliant on the Holy Spirit, more immersed in the truth of the Gospel, and more aligned with the mind of Christ.

Let the simplicity of the message of the cross be the cornerstone of our faith, and may our lives reflect the depth of the wisdom that comes only from God.

Let us pray for the humility and the spiritual insight to live out this truth in our daily lives.

~ 1 CORINTHIANS 3 ~

Introduction

This chapter speaks directly to the heart of what it means to be a community united in Christ. Here, the Apostle Paul addresses a divided church in Corinth, providing timeless wisdom for us today.

This chapter challenges us to reflect on our spiritual maturity, unity, and foundation in Christ.

Unity in Christ (3:1-4)

> *"Brothers and sisters, I could not address you as people who live by the Spirit but as people who are still worldly — mere infants in Christ.*
>
> *I gave you milk, not solid food, for you were not yet ready for it. Indeed, you are still not ready. You are still worldly. For since there is jealousy and quarrelling among you, are you not worldly?*
>
> *Are you not acting like mere humans? For when one says, "I follow Paul," and another, "I follow Apollos," are you not mere human beings?" (1 Corinthians 3:1-4)*

Paul begins this chapter with a sobering call to the believers in the church in Corinth. He addresses them as *"mere infants in Christ,"* highlighting their low level of spiritual maturity. This immaturity is evident in their jealousy and quarrelling, signs that they are living by the standards of the world, not by the Spirit.

In our lives, just like the Corinthians, we might find ourselves embroiled in petty disputes, envy, and divisions. These are not merely social issues; they are spiritual concerns. They signal our focus on human leaders or ideologies rather than on Jesus Christ Himself.

Let us ask ourselves: Are our actions and attitudes reflective of Christ's love and unity, or do they reflect our worldly influence?

God's Field and Building (3:5-9)

"What, after all, is Apollos? And what is Paul? Only servants, through whom you came to believe — as the Lord has assigned to each his task. I planted the seed, Apollos watered it, but God has been making it grow.

So, neither the one who plants nor the one who waters is anything, but only God, who makes things grow. The one who plants and the one who waters have one purpose, and they will each be rewarded according to their own labour.

For we are co-workers in God's service; you are God's field, God's building." (1 Corinthians 3:5-9)

Paul uses two powerful metaphors to illustrate the Corinthians' relationship with God and each other: a field and a building. He reminds them that while they may have different roles - like Paul planting and Apollos watering - it is God who gives the growth. The focus shifts from human efforts to divine action. In God's field, we are co-workers, united in purpose, contributing to the growth that God alone can provide.

Similarly, in the building of God, we are not disparate bricks, all scattered and independent; we are co-laborers in God's divine construction project, with Christ as the foundation. This imagery challenges us to evaluate our role in the church.

Are we working in harmony, recognizing that every effort is for God's glory and not our own? Are we building upon the solid foundation of Christ, or are we moved by the shifting sands of societal approval and personal gain?

The Foundation of Our Faith (3:10-15)

"By the grace God has given me, I laid a foundation as a wise builder, and someone else is building on it. But each one should build with care. For no one can lay any foundation other than the one already laid, which is Jesus Christ. If anyone builds on this foundation using gold, silver, costly stones, wood, hay or straw, their work will be shown for what it is, because the Day will bring it to light."

"It will be revealed with fire, and the fire will test the quality of each person's work. If what has been built survives, the builder will receive a reward. If it is burned up, the builder will suffer loss but yet will be saved - even though only as one escaping through the flames." (1 Corinthians 3:10-15)

Paul extends the building metaphor, when he emphasises the importance of the foundation upon which we build our lives and ministries. He warns that every person's work will be tested by fire, revealing its true nature.

This is not a call to fear but to introspection and alignment with God's will. Are our teachings, beliefs, and actions built on the enduring foundation of Jesus Christ, or are they mere wood, hay, and straw, vulnerable to the inevitable fires of trial and judgment?

This passage invites us to examine the materials of our spiritual lives. In our personal faith, our community involvement, and our ministry efforts, are we investing in what is eternal and unshakeable?

God's Temple and Holiness (3:16-17)

"Don't you know that you yourselves are God's temple and that God's Spirit dwells in your midst? If anyone destroys God's temple, God will destroy that person; for God's temple is sacred, and you together are that temple." (1 Corinthians 3:16-17)

Paul delivers a profound truth: we are God's temple, and His Spirit dwells within us. This is not just an individual reality but a corporate one. The church, the community of believers, is where God's Spirit resides. This understanding should transform how we view ourselves and one another, how we handle disagreements, and how we approach all ministry.

If we defile God's temple through division, jealousy, or any form of sin, we are opposing God Himself. Let us then pursue holiness, not as a burdensome duty, but as a joyful response to the indwelling Spirit of God.

The Folly of Worldly Wisdom (3:18-23)

"Do not deceive yourselves. If any of you think you are wise by the standards of this age, you should become "fools" so that you may become wise. For the wisdom of this world is foolishness in God's sight. As it is written: "He catches the wise in their craftiness" and again, "The Lord knows that the thoughts of the wise are futile."

So then, no more boasting about human leaders! All things are yours, whether Paul or Apollos or Cephas or the world or life or death or the present or the future - all are yours, and you are of Christ, and Christ is of God." (1 Corinthians 3:18-23)

Paul concludes the chapter by once again addressing the issue of wisdom - this time contrasting the wisdom of the world with the wisdom of God. He calls for humility, urging us to become "fools" in the eyes of the world so that we may truly be wise in God's sight.

In our pursuit of knowledge, success, and recognition, we must be cautious not to be ensnared by the world's definitions of wisdom and success. Our true identity and value lie not in worldly accolades but in belonging to Christ.

Conclusion

Chapter 3 presents a compelling call to self-reflection, unity, and spiritual growth. As God's field, building, and temple, we are called to a higher standard - one that values collaboration, builds on the foundation of Christ, and honours the indwelling of His Holy Spirit.

Let us leave this chapter, committed to examining our hearts and actions, to rooting out divisions, and to building our lives on the solid rock of Jesus Christ. For in Him, and Him alone, we find true wisdom, unity, and purpose.

Introduction

The Apostle Paul now provides profound insights into Christian leadership, stewardship, and the paradox of the Christian life. He calls upon us all to reflect on our attitudes towards leadership, judgment, and how we live out our faith in the face of adversity.

The True Nature of Apostleship (4:1-5)

"This, then, is how you ought to regard us: as servants of Christ and as those entrusted with the mysteries God has revealed. Now it is required that those who have been given a trust must prove faithful.

I care very little if I am judged by you or by any human court; indeed, I do not even judge myself. My conscience is clear, but that does not make me innocent. It is the Lord who judges me.

Therefore, judge nothing before the appointed time; wait until the Lord comes. He will bring to light what is hidden in darkness and will expose the motives of the heart. At that time each will receive their praise from God." (1 Corinthians 4:1-5)

Paul begins this chapter by urging the Corinthians to regard him and other apostles as servants of Christ and stewards of the mysteries of God. The primary requirement of stewards is to be found faithful. Paul is unconcerned with judgment from humans or any human court; his conscience is clear, but he acknowledges that the Lord is his ultimate judge.

This challenges us to reassess our view of Christian leadership and our own roles within the church. Are we serving as faithful stewards of what God has entrusted to us, whether it be our resources, talents, or the gospel itself?

Let us remember that our ultimate accountability is not to human standards but to God alone.

The Apostles' Humility and Suffering (4:6-13)

"Now, brothers and sisters, I have applied these things to myself and Apollos for your benefit, so that you may learn from us the meaning of the saying, "Do not go beyond what is written." Then you will not be puffed up in being a follower of one of us over against the other. For who makes you different from anyone else? What do you have that you did not receive? And if you did receive it, why do you boast as though you did not?

Already you have all you want! Already you have become rich! You have begun to reign - and that without us! How I wish that you really had begun to reign so that we also might reign with you! For it seems to me that God has put us apostles on display at the end of the procession, like those condemned to die in the arena. We have been made a spectacle to the whole universe, to angels as well as to human beings. We are fools for Christ, but you are so wise in Christ! We are weak, but you are strong! You are honoured, we are dishonoured!

To this very hour we go hungry and thirsty, we are in rags, we are brutally treated, we are homeless. We work hard with our own hands. When we are cursed, we bless; when we are persecuted, we endure it; when we are slandered, we answer kindly. We have become the scum of the earth, the garbage of the world - right up to this moment." (1 Corinthians 4:6-13)

Paul gives us this stark contrast between the arrogant attitude some Corinthians have adopted and the humility and suffering experienced by the apostles. He describes the apostles as the *"scum of the earth, the refuse of all things."* This hyperbolic language emphasizes the suffering and dishonour they endure every day for the sake of Jesus Christ.

These verses are a powerful reminder of the cost of discipleship and the humility required to follow Christ. In our own lives, are we prepared to embrace humility and suffer for the sake of the gospel? Let us be inspired by the apostles' example to endure hardships and remain faithful, even when faced with contempt and persecution.

A Fatherly Warning and Call to Imitation (4:14-17)

"I am writing this not to shame you but to warn you as my dear children. Even if you had ten thousand guardians in Christ, you do not have many fathers, for in Christ Jesus I became your father through the gospel.

Therefore, I urge you to imitate me. For this reason, I have sent to you Timothy, my son whom I love, who is faithful in the Lord. He will remind you of my way of life in Christ Jesus, which agrees with what I teach everywhere in every church."
(1 Corinthians 4:14-17)

Paul shifts from harsh rebuke to a tender, fatherly tone. He emphasizes that his admonishment comes from a place of love, not to shame, and he invites the Corinthians to imitate him as he imitates Christ. He then mentions sending Timothy to remind them of his ways in Christ.

Paul's change in tone reminds us of the balance between correction and encouragement in Christian leadership and discipleship. As members of Christ's church, are we open to correction? Do we lead and guide others with love and patience, encouraging them to follow Christ more closely?

The Kingdom of God vs. Empty Boasting (4:18-21)

"Some of you have become arrogant, as if I were not coming to you. But I will come to you very soon, if the Lord is willing, and then I will find out not only how these arrogant people are talking, but what power they have.

For the kingdom of God is not a matter of talk but of power. What do you prefer? Shall I come to you with a rod of discipline, or shall I come in love and with a gentle spirit?" *(1 Corinthians 4:18-21)*

Paul addresses the arrogance of some who have become puffed up in his absence. He contrasts the kingdom of God with mere words, emphasizing that the kingdom is not a matter of talk but of power.

He ends with a question that underscores his authority and the seriousness of his intended visit: *"What do you wish? Shall I come to you with a rod, or with love in a spirit of gentleness?"*

This passage challenges us to examine our own lives: Are we living in a manner which is consistent with the kingdom of God, characterized by power, love, and self-discipline, or are we caught up in empty boasting and outward appearances? Let us seek to embody the values of the kingdom in our actions and relationships.

As we reflect on chapter 4, let us consider our role as stewards of the mysteries of God, the humility required in our service, the importance of fatherly discipline and imitation in the faith, and the true nature of the kingdom of God.

May we walk in faithfulness, humility, and power, always seeking to glorify God in all aspects of our lives.

Introduction

We now confront a challenging yet crucial passage of Scripture, 1 Corinthians Chapter 5. This chapter calls us to a higher standard of moral integrity and community discipline within the body of Christ.

Paul addresses a severe issue within the Corinthian church, one that tests the boundaries of grace, love, and holiness. Let's delve into the wisdom of God's word to understand how it applies to us today.

Immorality in the Church (5:1-2)

"It is actually reported that there is sexual immorality among you, and of a kind that even pagans do not tolerate: A man is sleeping with his father's wife. And you are proud! Shouldn't you rather have gone into mourning and have put out of your fellowship the man who has been doing this?"
(1 Corinthians 5:1-2)

Paul begins with a direct and shocking revelation: there is sexual immorality among the Corinthians, of a kind not even tolerated among pagans. The response of the church to this sin is equally concerning — they are proud and have not mourned the sin that has infiltrated their community.

This calls us to examine our own hearts and communities. Have we become complacent or even boastful about behaviours that grieve the Holy Spirit? Are we courageous enough to address sin in our midst, not out of judgment or pride, but out of a deep concern for the purity and witness of the church?

The Call for Church Discipline (5:3-5)

"For my part, even though I am not physically present, I am with you in spirit. As one who is present with you in this way, I have already passed judgment in the name of our Lord Jesus on the one who has been doing this."

"So when you are assembled and I am with you in spirit, and the power of our Lord Jesus is present, hand this man over to Satan for the destruction of the flesh, so that his spirit may be saved on the day of the Lord." (1 Corinthians 5:3-5)

Paul, though absent in body, is present in spirit and has already passed judgment on the man who committed this act. He instructs the church to do the same — to deliver such a person to Satan for the destruction of the flesh so that his spirit may be saved in the Day of the Lord.

This introduces the difficult concept of church discipline, a practice designed not for vengeance but for restoration. It's a call for the church to act decisively in cases of blatant sin, aiming for the repentance and ultimate salvation of the offender. How do we balance grace and discipline in our community? Are we willing to take hard steps for the sake of purity, love, and restoration?

The Metaphor of Leaven (5:6-8)

"Your boasting is not good. Don't you know that a little yeast leavens the whole batch of dough? Get rid of the old yeast, so that you may be a new unleavened batch - as you really are. For Christ, our Passover lamb, has been sacrificed. Therefore, let us keep the Festival, not with the old bread leavened with malice and wickedness, but with the unleavened bread of sincerity and truth." (1 Corinthians 5:6-8)

Paul uses the metaphor of leaven to illustrate how a little sin can affect the whole community. He urges the Corinthians to cleanse out the old leaven so they might be a new lump, as they are really unleavened, for Christ, our Passover lamb, has been sacrificed.

This metaphor challenges us to consider how unchecked sin can permeate and corrupt the entire church. It's a call to purity and holiness, reminding us that Christ has made us new creations. Are we living as those who have been made new, or are we clinging to the old ways that lead to corruption?

Immoral People Within the Church (5:9-13)

> *"I wrote to you in my letter not to associate with sexually immoral people - not at all meaning the people of this world who are immoral, or the greedy and swindlers, or idolaters. In that case you would have to leave this world. But now I am writing to you that you must not associate with anyone who claims to be a brother or sister but is sexually immoral or greedy, an idolater or slanderer, a drunkard or swindler. Do not even eat with such people. What business is it of mine to judge those outside the church? Are you not to judge those inside? God will judge those outside. "Expel the wicked person from among you."*
> *(1 Corinthians 5:9-13)*

Paul clarifies his earlier advice about associating with immoral people, emphasizing that his warning pertains to those within the church. Christians are not to isolate themselves from the world but are called to be distinct from those who profess Christ yet live in open sin. These verses challenge us to discern how we relate to others within the church and the world. Are we enabling sin by ignoring it within our community? How do we balance engagement with the world while maintaining our call to be a holy and distinct people?

Conclusion

Paul confronts us with the necessity of addressing sin within our community, not out of malice, but out of love and concern for the body of Christ and the individual. He challenges us to uphold God's standards of holiness and purity within our own lives and our church. Let us therefore commit to being a community that lovingly but firmly upholds God's truth, disciplines with the aim of restoration, and lives out the holiness to which we have been called in Christ.

May we do so with humble hearts, seeking God's wisdom and guidance in these challenging aspects of our life together. May our actions always reflect the love and purity of our Lord Jesus Christ, Who has been sacrificed for us.

~ 1 CORINTHIANS 6 ~

Introduction

Chapter 6 of Paul's first epistle to the Corinthians speaks directly to the heart of our Christian walk and our interaction with the world around us. In this chapter, Paul addresses issues of conflict, morality, and identity among the believers in Corinth, issues that are just as relevant for us today. He challenges us to reflect on our understanding of justice, purity, and our bodies as temples of the Holy Spirit.

Settling Disputes Among Believers (6:1-8)

"If any of you has a dispute with another, do you dare to take it before the ungodly for judgment instead of before the Lord's people? Or do you not know that the Lord's people will judge the world? And if you are to judge the world, are you not competent to judge trivial cases? Do you not know that we will judge angels? How much more the things of this life!

Therefore, if you have disputes about such matters, do you ask for a ruling from those whose way of life is scorned in the church? I say this to shame you. Is it possible that there is nobody among you wise enough to judge a dispute between believers? But instead, one brother takes another to court - and this in front of unbelievers!

The very fact that you have lawsuits among you means you have been completely defeated already. Why not rather be wronged? Why not rather be cheated? Instead, you yourselves cheat and do wrong, and you do this to your brothers and sisters."
(1 Corinthians 6:1-8)

Paul starts this chapter by addressing the problem of believers taking their disputes before secular courts rather than resolving them within the church. He is astonished that these Christians are seeking judgment from the unrighteous instead of trusting their own community, which is destined to judge the world and even angels.

Paul prompts us to consider how we handle conflicts within our church and Christian relationships. Are we quick to seek worldly solutions, or do we trust the wisdom and discernment God has placed within His body? This is a call for us to develop a culture of resolving conflicts internally, in a manner that reflects God's justice, mercy, and reconciliation.

The Call to Holiness (6:9-11)

"Or do you not know that wrongdoers will not inherit the kingdom of God? Do not be deceived: Neither the sexually immoral nor idolaters nor adulterers nor men who have sex with men nor thieves nor the greedy nor drunkards nor slanderers nor swindlers will inherit the kingdom of God. And that is what some of you were. But you were washed, you were sanctified, you were justified in the name of the Lord Jesus Christ and by the Spirit of our God." (1 Corinthians 6:9-11)

Paul provides a sobering list of behaviours incompatible with the kingdom of God, reminding the Corinthians of their past and the transformative power of the Gospel. He underscores that such were some of them, but they have been washed, sanctified, and justified in the name of the Lord Jesus Christ and by the Spirit of our God. Here lies a powerful testimony to the transformative work of Christ in our lives. We are challenged to remember our new identity in Christ and live accordingly, not conforming to the sinful patterns of our past or the world around us. Let us examine our lives: Are there areas where we have compromised our call to holiness?

The Body as the Temple of the Holy Spirit (6:12-20)

"I have the right to do anything," you say - but not everything is beneficial. "I have the right to do anything" - but I will not be mastered by anything. You say, "Food for the stomach and the stomach for food, and God will destroy them both." The body, however, is not meant for sexual immorality but for the Lord, and the Lord for the body. By his power God raised the Lord from the dead, and he will raise us also."

"Do you not know that your bodies are members of Christ himself? Shall I then take the members of Christ and unite them with a prostitute? Never! Do you not know that he who unites himself with a prostitute is one with her in body? For it is said, "The two will become one flesh." But whoever is united with the Lord is one with him in spirit. Flee from sexual immorality. All other sins a person commits are outside the body, but whoever sins sexually, sins against their own body.

Do you not know that your bodies are temples of the Holy Spirit, who is in you, whom you have received from God? You are not your own; you were bought at a price. Therefore, honour God with your bodies." (1 Corinthians 6:12-20)

Paul moves on to address the problem of sexual immorality, emphasizing that the believers' bodies are members of Christ himself. He introduces a profound concept: our bodies are temples of the Holy Spirit. Therefore, we are called to glorify God in our bodies, which belong not to us but to God. This is a call to view our bodies and our sexuality through a sacred lens. In a world that often encourages the opposite, we are to honour God with our physical selves, recognizing the high price paid for our redemption. How do we treat our bodies? Are we engaging in behaviours that desecrate the temple of the Holy Spirit, or are we living as those bought with a price, glorifying God in our bodies?

Conclusion

Paul speaks to us about the sanctity of our relationships, our bodies, and our lives before God. It challenges us to live out our faith in practical, everyday decisions, particularly in how we resolve conflicts, how we honour God with our bodies, and how we reflect the transformative power of the Gospel in our lives.

So let us carry with us the weight of our calling as we strive to resolve our disputes with love and wisdom, live out our new identity in Christ with purity and holiness, and honour God with our bodies, remembering that we are not our own; we were bought at a price.

~ 1 CORINTHIANS 7 ~

Introduction

Now we delve into a section rich with guidance for our personal and relational lives. In this chapter the Apostle Paul addresses some questions from the Corinthian church regarding marriage, singleness, and relationships.

This chapter, filled with practical advice and spiritual wisdom, challenges us to consider how we live out our commitments to God and to one another in the context of our current stations in life.

The Sanctity of Marriage (7:1-7)

"Now for the matters you wrote about: "It is good for a man not to have sexual relations with a woman." But since sexual immorality is occurring, each man should have sexual relations with his own wife, and each woman with her own husband.

The husband should fulfill his marital duty to his wife, and likewise the wife to her husband. The wife does not have authority over her own body but yields it to her husband. In the same way, the husband does not have authority over his own body but yields it to his wife.

Do not deprive each other except perhaps by mutual consent and for a time, so that you may devote yourselves to prayer. Then come together again so that Satan will not tempt you because of your lack of self-control. I say this as a concession, not as a command. I wish that all of you were as I am. But each of you has your own gift from God; one has this gift, another has that."
(1 Corinthians 7:1-7)

Paul begins by responding to a statement about marriage and sexual relations, affirming that marriage is good and that spouses should fulfill their marital duties to each other, recognizing that their bodies do not belong solely to themselves but also to their spouses. Yet, Paul also acknowledges the gift of singleness and the different callings God places on each person's life.

This teaches us the importance of respecting and honouring our marital commitments, viewing our relationships through the lens of mutual service and dedication to one another in Christ. For those who are married, how are we honouring and serving our spouses? For those who are single, how are we using our singleness for the service of God?

Remain where you were called (7:8-16)

"Now to the unmarried and the widows I say: It is good for them to stay unmarried, as I do. But if they cannot control themselves, they should marry, for it is better to marry than to burn with passion.

To the married I give this command (not I, but the Lord): A wife must not separate from her husband. But if she does, she must remain unmarried or else be reconciled to her husband. And a husband must not divorce his wife.

To the rest I say this (I, not the Lord): If any brother has a wife who is not a believer and she is willing to live with him, he must not divorce her. And if a woman has a husband who is not a believer and he is willing to live with her, she must not divorce him. For the unbelieving husband has been sanctified through his wife, and the unbelieving wife has been sanctified through her believing husband. Otherwise, your children would be unclean, but as it is, they are holy.

But if the unbeliever leaves, let it be so. The brother or the sister is not bound in such circumstances; God has called us to live in peace. How do you know, wife, whether you will save your husband? Or, how do you know, husband, whether you will save your wife?" (1 Corinthians 7:8-16)

Paul continues by addressing different groups within the church: the unmarried, widows, those married to fellow believers, and those married to unbelievers. He advises each group, essentially encouraging them to remain in the situation in which they were called, unless circumstances change according to God's leading. Importantly, Paul highlights the sanctifying effect of a believing spouse in a mixed marriage and the importance of maintaining such unions if possible.

The key principle here is contentment and faithfulness in our current circumstances. Whether single, married, or somewhere in between, how are we honouring God in our current state? Are we seeking God's will and living out our Christian witness in our relationships?

Living According to One's Calling (7:17-24)

"Nevertheless, each person should live as a believer in whatever situation the Lord has assigned to them, just as God has called them. This is the rule I lay down in all the churches. Was a man already circumcised when he was called? He should not become uncircumcised. Was a man uncircumcised when he was called? He should not be circumcised.

Circumcision is nothing and uncircumcision is nothing. Keeping God's commands is what counts. Each person should remain in the situation they were in when God called them.

Were you a slave when you were called? Don't let it trouble you — - although if you can gain your freedom, do so. For the one who was a slave when called to faith in the Lord is the Lord's freed person; similarly, the one who was free when called is Christ's slave. You were bought at a price; do not become slaves of human beings. Brothers and sisters, each person, as responsible to God, should remain in the situation they were in when God called them." (1 Corinthians 7:17-24)

Paul expands his instruction beyond marriage to encompass all life situations. He emphasizes that it's not our external circumstances that define our relationship with God, but our obedience and commitment to Him. Whether circumcised or uncircumcised, slave or free, we are called to remain in the condition in which we were called, yet live as servants of Christ.

This challenges us to consider our own life situations. Are we constantly seeking change for personal gain or comfort, or are we seeking to live faithfully and fruitfully for God wherever He has placed us? How can we serve God and others more effectively in our current circumstances?

The Time is Short (7:25-31)

"Now about virgins: I have no command from the Lord, but I give a judgment as one who by the Lord's mercy is trustworthy. Because of the present crisis, I think that it is good for a man to remain as he is. Are you pledged to a woman? Do not seek to be released. Are you free from such a commitment? Do not look for a wife. But if you do marry, you have not sinned; and if a virgin marries, she has not sinned. But those who marry will face many troubles in this life, and I want to spare you this.

What I mean, brothers and sisters, is that the time is short. From now on those who have wives should live as if they do not; those who mourn, as if they did not; those who are happy, as if they were not; those who buy something, as if it were not theirs to keep; those who use the things of the world, as if not engrossed in them. For this world in its present form is passing away."
(1 Corinthians 7:25-31)

Paul reflects on the transient nature of the world and advises believers to live with a sense of urgency and detachment from worldly concerns. Those who have wives should live as if they had none, those who weep as if they did not weep, and those who rejoice as if they did not rejoice. This is not a call to neglect our earthly responsibilities, but rather to prioritize our eternal relationship with God above all.

How does this perspective change the way we approach our relationships, possessions, and daily activities? Are we living in a manner that reflects the temporary nature of our earthly lives and the eternal significance of our relationship with God?

Advice on Marriage and Singleness (7:32-40)

"I would like you to be free from concern. An unmarried man is concerned about the Lord's affairs — how he can please the Lord. But a married man is concerned about the affairs of this world - how he can please his wife - and his interests are divided. An unmarried woman or virgin is concerned about the Lord's affairs: Her aim is to be devoted to the Lord in both body and spirit."

"But a married woman is concerned about the affairs of this world - how she can please her husband. I am saying this for your own good, not to restrict you, but that you may live in a right way in undivided devotion to the Lord.

If anyone is worried that he might not be acting honourably toward the virgin he is engaged to, and if his passions are too strong and he feels he ought to marry, he should do as he wants. He is not sinning. They should get married. But the man who has settled the matter in his own mind, who is under no compulsion but has control over his own will, and who has made up his mind not to marry the virgin - this man also does the right thing. So then, he who marries the virgin does right, but he who does not marry her does better.

A woman is bound to her husband as long as he lives. But if her husband dies, she is free to marry anyone she wishes, but he must belong to the Lord. In my judgment, she is happier if she stays as she is - and I think that I too have the Spirit of God. "
(1 Corinthians 7:32-40)

Finally, Paul provides guidance aimed at promoting undivided devotion to the Lord. He lays out the advantages and challenges of both marriage and singleness, leaving the choice to individual conviction and the Lord's calling. He concludes by affirming the goodness of marriage while also praising the benefits of singleness in serving the Lord without distraction. Whether we are single, married, or considering marriage, how can we best use our situation to serve God fully and devote ourselves to Him? Let us seek God's guidance and wisdom in our relationships and life choices, striving for a heart undivided in its devotion to the Lord.

Conclusion

In chapter 7, the Apostle Paul provides with some timeless principles for our relationships, marital status, and engagement with the world. Whether in singleness or marriage, in whatever situation we find ourselves. So, may our relationships and life choices reflect our ultimate commitment to our Lord and Saviour, Jesus Christ.

~ 1 CORINTHIANS 8 ~

Introduction

We now come to a passage that speaks profoundly into our lives, especially in how we interact within our diverse community of faith. In chapter 8, Paul addresses a contentious issue in the Corinthian church: the eating of food sacrificed to idols.

This chapter, though centred on a specific first-century problem, extends timeless principles about Christian freedom, love, and the sensitive navigation of our liberties in light of others' consciences.

Knowledge versus Love (8:1-3)

> *"Now about food sacrificed to idols: We know that "We all possess knowledge." But knowledge puffs up while love builds up. Those who think they know something do not yet know as they ought to know. But whoever loves God is known by God."*
> *(1 Corinthians 8:1-3)*

Paul begins by contrasting two powerful forces within the Christian life: knowledge and love. He acknowledges that while knowledge is important, it can lead to pride if not tempered by love. Love, on the other hand, builds up and strengthens the community.

This then sets the stage for the entire discussion, reminding us that our actions and decisions should be governed by love for our brothers and sisters in Christ, not merely by our understanding or freedom.

So let us reflect on our interactions and beliefs. Are they marked more by a pursuit of being right, or by a desire to build others up in love?

How does love manifest in our everyday decisions, particularly when we know our actions could impact others within our church community?

The Issue of Food Sacrificed to Idols (8:4-6)

"So then, about eating food sacrificed to idols: We know that "An idol is nothing at all in the world" and that "There is no God but one." For even if there are so-called gods, whether in heaven or on earth (as indeed there are many "gods" and many "lords"), yet for us there is but one God, the Father, from whom all things came and for whom we live; and there is but one Lord, Jesus Christ, through whom all things came and through whom we live."
(1 Corinthians 8:4-6)

Paul addresses the issue at hand directly: the eating of food sacrificed to idols. He acknowledges the "knowledge" that there is only one God and that idols are really nothing. However, this knowledge is not shared by all, especially not by those who have turned to Christ from pagan backgrounds. In our context, while we may not deal with food sacrificed to idols, we encounter similar dilemmas where our freedom might become a stumbling block to others. How do we handle our freedom with alcohol consumption, entertainment choices, or cultural practices? Are we sensitive to the backgrounds and weaknesses of others?

The Danger of Causing Others to Stumble (8:7-13)

"But not everyone possesses this knowledge. Some people are still so accustomed to idols that when they eat sacrificial food they think of it as having been sacrificed to a god, and since their conscience is weak, it is defiled. But food does not bring us near to God; we are no worse if we do not eat, and no better if we do.

Be careful, however, that the exercise of your rights does not become a stumbling block to the weak. For if someone with a weak conscience sees you, with all your knowledge, eating in an idol's temple, won't that person be emboldened to eat what is sacrificed to idols? So this weak brother or sister, for whom Christ died, is destroyed by your knowledge. When you sin against them in this way and wound their weak conscience, you sin against Christ. Therefore, if what I eat causes my brother or sister to fall into sin, I will never eat meat again, so that I will not cause them to fall."
(1 Corinthians 8:7-13)

The heart of this chapter lies in Paul's serious concern for the weaker believer. He emphasizes that if someone with a sensitive conscience sees a mature believer eating in an idol's temple, it might embolden them to act against their own conscience, leading them into sin. Paul concludes with a powerful personal resolution: if food causes his brother or sister to stumble, he will never eat meat again, lest he cause them to fall.

The principle here extends far beyond the specific issue of food; it challenges us to consider how our actions, permissible though they may be, might affect the spiritual well-being of others. Are there areas in our lives where we need to exercise restraint for the sake of others? Are we willing to forego our rights to protect our brothers and sisters in Christ?

Conclusion

In 1 Corinthians Chapter 8, Paul calls us to a higher standard of love and sensitivity towards the consciences of our fellow believers. As we walk in our Christian liberty, let us do so with a profound regard for the spiritual health and growth of our church family. Let our freedom be exercised in love, our knowledge tempered with compassion, and our actions directed towards building others up, not causing them to stumble.

As we move on from this challenging part of Paul's letter, may we each commit to loving our brothers and sisters selflessly, recognizing that in the kingdom of God, love truly edifies, and in love, we find the truest expression of our freedom in Christ.

Introduction

Now we turn our hearts and minds to chapter 9 - a passage where the Apostle Paul provides a profound insight into his ministry and the Christian life. Here, Paul delves into the concepts of freedom, rights, and responsibilities as a follower of Christ, and he concludes with a compelling metaphor for the Christian journey. As we unpack this rich text, let us consider how Paul's words speak to our own walk with God and our service to others.

Rights, Freedom, and the Gospel (9:1-18)

"Am I not free? Am I not an apostle? Have I not seen Jesus our Lord? Are you not the result of my work in the Lord? Even though I may not be an apostle to others, surely I am to you! For you are the seal of my apostleship in the Lord.

This is my defence to those who sit in judgment on me. Don't we have the right to food and drink? Don't we have the right to take a believing wife along with us, as do the other apostles and the Lord's brothers and Cephas? Or is it only I and Barnabas who lack the right to not work for a living?

Who serves as a soldier at his own expense? Who plants a vineyard and does not eat its grapes? Who tends a flock and does not drink the milk? Do I say this merely on human authority? Doesn't the Law say the same thing? For it is written in the Law of Moses: "Do not muzzle an ox while it is treading out the grain." Is it about oxen that God is concerned? Surely he says this for us, doesn't he? Yes, this was written for us, because whoever ploughs and threshes should be able to do so in the hope of sharing in the harvest.

If we have sown spiritual seed among you, is it too much if we reap a material harvest from you? If others have this right of support from you, shouldn't we have it all the more?

But we did not use this right. On the contrary, we put up with anything rather than hinder the gospel of Christ."

"Don't you know that those who serve in the temple get their food from the temple, and that those who serve at the altar share in what is offered on the altar? In the same way, the Lord has commanded that those who preach the gospel should receive their living from the gospel.

But I have not used any of these rights. And I am not writing this in the hope that you will do such things for me, for I would rather die than allow anyone to deprive me of this boast. For when I preach the gospel, I cannot boast, since I am compelled to preach.

Woe to me if I do not preach the gospel! If I preach voluntarily, I have a reward; if not voluntarily, I am simply discharging the trust committed to me.

What then is my reward? Just this: that in preaching the gospel I may offer it free of charge, and so not make full use of my rights as a preacher of the gospel." (1 Corinthians 9:1-18)

Paul begins by defending his apostleship and all the rights that come with it, such as the right to material support from the churches he serves. However, he quickly moves to the heart of his message: though he has these rights, he has chosen not to exercise them in order not to hinder the gospel of Christ. Instead, Paul has made himself a servant to all, adapting to the needs and cultures of those he ministers to so that he might save some.

This passage challenges us to consider our personal rights and freedoms in light of the gospel. Are there areas in our lives where we might need to lay down our rights for the sake of others? How can we adapt our approach to better serve and reach those around us with the love and message of Christ?

Becoming All Things to All People (9:19-23)

"Though I am free and belong to no one, I have made myself a slave to everyone, to win as many as possible. To the Jews I became like a Jew, to win the Jews. To those under the law I became like one under the law (though I myself am not under the law), so as to win those under the law."

> *"To those not having the law I became like one not having the*
> *law (though I am not free from God's law but am under Christ's*
> *law), so as to win those not having the law. To the weak I became*
> *weak, to win the weak. I have become all things to all people so*
> *that by all possible means I might save some. I do all this for*
> *the sake of the gospel, that I may share in its blessings."*
> *(1 Corinthians 9:19-23)*

Paul elaborates on his missionary strategy: becoming all things to all people. This does not mean compromising his faith or moral standards but rather setting aside personal preferences and cultural differences to reach others with the gospel. His ultimate goal is clear: to share in the blessings of the gospel with as many as possible.

Paul's approach calls us to reflect on our own evangelistic efforts. Are we willing to step out of our comfort zones to reach others for Christ? How can we more effectively communicate the gospel in a way that resonates with those from different backgrounds or beliefs?

Running the Race to Win (9:24-27)

> *"Do you not know that in a race all the runners run, but only*
> *one gets the prize? Run in such a way as to get the prize.*
> *Everyone who competes in the games goes into strict training.*
> *They do it to get a crown that will not last, but we do it to get a*
> *crown that will last forever.*
>
> *Therefore, I do not run like someone running aimlessly; I do not*
> *fight like a boxer beating the air. No, I strike a blow to my body*
> *and make it my slave so that after I have preached to others, I*
> *myself will not be disqualified for the prize."*
> *(1 Corinthians 9:24-27)*

Paul concludes this chapter with a very powerful metaphor: the Christian life as a race. Just as athletes exercise self-control and train rigorously to win a perishable wreath, Christians are called to run their race with discipline and purpose so they may obtain an imperishable crown.

Paul speaks of disciplining his body and keeping it under control, highlighting the seriousness with which he pursues his calling.

This imagery invites us to examine our own spiritual disciplines and commitment to God's calling. Are we running aimlessly, or are we focused on the prize of eternal life with Christ? What steps do we need to take to run our race more effectively, ensuring that we are not disqualified for the prize?

Conclusion

In 1 Corinthians Chapter 9, the Apostle Paul presents us with a wonderful model of ministry and Christian living, marked by selflessness, adaptability, and discipline. He challenges us to consider how we use our freedoms, how we relate to others, and how we pursue our heavenly calling.

As we reflect on this chapter in the days ahead, may we be inspired by Paul's example to run our race with perseverance, to lay aside every weight and sin that clings so closely, and to fix our eyes on Jesus, the founder and perfecter of our faith. May we live such lives that are not only faithful but also fruitful, and lives which impact the world around us with the transforming power of the gospel.

~ 1 CORINTHIANS 10 ~

Introduction

This chapter is rich with historical reflection, stern warnings, and practical guidance for our Christian walk. The Apostle Paul, with the wisdom and urgency of a seasoned shepherd, calls all the believers in Corinth - and us today - to heed the lessons of Israel's past; to live with awareness and self-discipline; and to seek the glory of God in all things.

As we explore this chapter, let us open our hearts to the timeless truths Paul imparts and consider how they apply to our lives.

The Example of Israel (10:1-11)

"For I do not want you to be ignorant of the fact, brothers and sisters, that our ancestors were all under the cloud and that they all passed through the sea. They were all baptized into Moses in the cloud and in the sea. They all ate the same spiritual food and drank the same spiritual drink; for they drank from the spiritual rock that accompanied them, and that rock was Christ. Nevertheless, God was not pleased with most of them; their bodies were scattered in the wilderness.

Now these things occurred as examples to keep us from setting our hearts on evil things as they did. Do not be idolaters, as some of them were; as it is written: "The people sat down to eat and drink and got up to indulge in revelry." We should not commit sexual immorality, as some of them did - and in one day twenty-three thousand of them died. We should not test Christ, as some of them did – and were killed by snakes. And do not grumble, as some of them did - and were killed by the destroying angel.

These things happened to them as examples and were written down as warnings for us, on whom the culmination of the ages has come." (1 Corinthians 10:1-11)

Paul begins by reminding the Corinthians of the Israelites, who experienced God's mighty deliverance and provision but fell into sin and rebellion.

Despite being under the cloud of God's presence and crossing the sea in a miraculous escape from Egypt, many of them were still disobedient and thus displeased God. Their experiences serve as examples for us, warnings to not crave evil things, to not idolize, to not engage in sexual immorality, to not test Christ, and to not grumble.

This historical reflection serves as a mirror for our own lives. Are there areas where we, despite experiencing God's grace and provision, have fallen into complacency or outright rebellion?

Let us examine our hearts and turn away from any idolatry, immorality, or ingratitude that may distance us from God.

The Call to Vigilance (10:12-13)

> *"So, if you think you are standing firm, be careful that you don't fall! No temptation has overtaken you except what is common to mankind. And God is faithful; he will not let you be tempted beyond what you can bear. But when you are tempted,*
> *he will also provide a way out so that you can endure it."*
> *(1 Corinthians 10:1-13)*

In a sobering warning, Paul reminds us that whoever thinks he stands must be careful lest he fall. Yet, he also offers comfort, affirming that no temptation has overtaken us except what is common to humanity.

God is faithful; He will not let us be tempted beyond what we can bear and will provide a way out so that we can endure it.

In these verses, Paul calls us to humility and vigilance. Are we overconfident in our spiritual standing, or are we watchful, aware of our vulnerabilities? Let us remember that in every temptation, God provides strength and a way of escape.

We are not alone in our struggles; we share them with our brothers and sisters in Christ, and together, we can find the strength to overcome.

Idol Feasts and the Lord's Supper (10:14-22)

"Therefore, my dear friends, flee from idolatry. I speak to sensible people; judge for yourselves what I say. Is not the cup of thanksgiving for which we give thanks a participation in the blood of Christ? And is not the bread that we break a participation in the body of Christ? Because there is one loaf, we, who are many, are one body, for we all share the one loaf.

Consider the people of Israel: Do not those who eat the sacrifices participate in the altar? Do I mean then that food sacrificed to an idol is anything, or that an idol is anything? No, but the sacrifices of pagans are offered to demons, not to God, and I do not want you to be participants with demons.

You cannot drink the cup of the Lord and the cup of demons too; you cannot have a part in both the Lord's table and the table of demons. Are we trying to arouse the Lord's jealousy? Are we stronger than he?" (1 Corinthians 10:14-22)

Paul then contrasts participation in idol feasts with participation in the Lord's Supper. He warns against the incompatibility of communing with Christ while also engaging in activities that honour demons. The cup we bless and the bread we break in communion are a sharing in the body and blood of Christ, and thus, our allegiance must be undivided.

This section prompts us to consider our own allegiances and the consistency of our witness. Are there areas in our lives where we are attempting to partake of both the table of the Lord and the table of demons? Let us recommit ourselves to Christ, ensuring that our actions and choices reflect our devotion to Him alone.

All to the Glory of God (10:23-33)

"I have the right to do anything," you say - but not everything is beneficial. "I have the right to do anything" - but not everything is constructive. No one should seek their own good, but the good of others. Eat anything sold in the meat market without raising questions of conscience, for, "The earth is the Lord's, and everything in it."

" If an unbeliever invites you to a meal and you want to go, eat whatever is put before you without raising questions of conscience. But if someone says to you, "This has been offered in sacrifice," then do not eat it, both for the sake of the one who told you and for the sake of conscience. I am referring to the other person's conscience, not yours. For why is my freedom being judged by another's conscience? If I take part in the meal with thankfulness, why am I denounced because of something I thank God for?

So, whether you eat or drink or whatever you do, do it all for the glory of God. Do not cause anyone to stumble, whether Jews, Greeks or the church of God - even as I try to please everyone in every way. For I am not seeking my own good but the good of many, so that they may be saved." (1 Corinthians 10:23-33)

Paul concludes chapter 10 by revisiting the principle of Christian freedom, reminding the Corinthians that not all things are beneficial or constructive. We are to seek not our own good, but the good of others, so that they may be saved. Whether eating, drinking, or doing anything else, we are to do it all for the glory of God, avoiding anything that might cause another to stumble.

Here lies the heart of Christian living - doing all for the glory of God and the edification of others. In our freedom, are we considering the impact of our actions on our brothers and sisters? Are we living in such a way that others are drawn to Christ through us?

Conclusion

In 1 Corinthians Chapter 10, Paul offers us invaluable lessons from the past, present, and future perspective of Christian living. He invites us to learn from Israel's mistakes, to live with vigilant hearts, to maintain our allegiance to Christ above all, and to do everything for God's glory and the good of others. May we take these lessons to heart today, applying them to our lives, so that we may run our race faithfully, avoid the pitfalls of sin, and shine as lights in a world in need of the saving grace of Christ.

~ 1 CORINTHIANS 11 ~

Introduction

In this section of his letter, Paul addresses issues of decorum, distinction, and devotion within the Christian community, particularly in the context of worship and the Lord's Supper. He speaks to timeless themes of honour, respect, and remembrance that resonate with our faith and practice today.

As we unpack this chapter, let us open our hearts to the transformative power of God's Word and its implications for our lives and our communal worship.

Head Coverings and Honour (11:1-16)

"Follow my example, as I follow the example of Christ. I praise you for remembering me in everything and for holding to the traditions just as I passed them on to you.

But I want you to realize that the head of every man is Christ, and the head of the woman is man, and the head of Christ is God. Every man who prays or prophesies with his head covered dishonours his head. But every woman who prays or prophesies with her head uncovered dishonours her head - it is the same as having her head shaved.

For if a woman does not cover her head, she might as well have her hair cut off; but if it is a disgrace for a woman to have her hair cut off or her head shaved, then she should cover her head.

A man ought not to cover his head, since he is the image and glory of God; but woman is the glory of man. For man did not come from woman, but woman from man; neither was man created for woman, but woman for man. It is for this reason that a woman ought to have authority over her own head, because of the angels. Nevertheless, in the Lord woman is not independent of man, nor is man independent of woman. For as woman came from man, so also man is born of woman. But everything comes from God.

Judge for yourselves: Is it proper for a woman to pray to God with her head uncovered?"

"Does not the very nature of things teach you that if a man has long hair, it is a disgrace to him, but that if a woman has long hair, it is her glory? For long hair is given to her as a covering. If anyone wants to be contentious about this, we have no other practice - nor do the churches of God." (1 Corinthians 11:1-16)

Paul begins by discussing the cultural practice of head coverings, which was prevalent at that time, focusing on the principles of honour and authority within the context of worship. He speaks of the distinctions between men and women in the expression of their devotion and the recognition of authority structures as they relate to Christ and the church. This is one of the passages in the Bible which have caused a great deal of conflict over the years and still, to this day, there are churches who ignore the cultural reality behind this passage and continue oppressing woman in the church, denying them their God-given freedom in Christ.

We must understand that when Paul wrote these words, women has been silent, covered and denied any place in the spiritual life of God's people for generations. When Jesus changed all that and set them gloriously free, the reality of the kingdom of God was unleashed on our world. So now, in Christ, there was *"neither male nor female."* (Galatians 3:28). However, Paul recognised that in a male dominated society, it was going to take a long time for women to be completely liberated in their day to day lives and so in a number of places in his letters, he appears to be saying to women that they need to remain in those cultural chains. That is not the case at all and even Paul himself, had women leaders in his group of close companions.

There are many today who cannot believe that women were once denied their rightful place among God's people and they rejoice that cultural norms have now changed, at least in many places. However, the underlying principles of this passage remain relevant: recognizing and respecting the cultural realities within which we exercise our freedom in Christ. So, let us always consider how we express honour and respect within our community and before God. Are our actions in worship reflective of a heart that seeks to glorify God and respect others?

The Lord's Supper: A Call to Self-Examination (11:17-22)

"In the following directives I have no praise for you, for your meetings do more harm than good. In the first place, I hear that when you come together as a church, there are divisions among you, and to some extent I believe it. No doubt there have to be differences among you to show which of you have God's approval.

So then, when you come together, it is not the Lord's Supper you eat, for when you are eating, some of you go ahead with your own private suppers. As a result, one person remains hungry and another gets drunk. Don't you have homes to eat and drink in? Or do you despise the church of God by humiliating those who have nothing? What shall I say to you? Shall I praise you? Certainly not in this matter!" (1 Corinthians 11:17-22)

Paul transitions to address the manner in which the Corinthian believers were observing the Lord's Supper. Instead of a time of humble reflection and unity, it had become an occasion for division, selfishness, and disregard for others, particularly the poor among them. Paul rebukes this behaviour, calling the church back to the true meaning and solemnity of this sacrament.

This section invites us to examine our own approach to the Lord's Supper and, more broadly, our own attitudes toward community and fellowship. Do we come to the table of the Lord with humility and respect for our fellow believers? Are we mindful of the unity and equality that should characterize our gatherings, especially in the presence of Christ's sacrifice for us?

Proper Observance of the Lord's Supper (11:23-26)

"For I received from the Lord what I also passed on to you: The Lord Jesus, on the night he was betrayed, took bread, and when he had given thanks, he broke it and said, "This is my body, which is for you; do this in remembrance of me." In the same way, after supper he took the cup, saying, "This cup is the new covenant in my blood; do this, whenever you drink it, in remembrance of me." For whenever you eat this bread and drink this cup, you proclaim the Lord's death until he comes." (1 Corinthians 11:23-26)

Paul reminds the Corinthians of the tradition he received and passed on to them concerning the Lord's Supper. He recounts the words of Jesus Himself during the Last Supper, emphasizing the significance of the bread and cup as symbols of Jesus' body and blood, given for us. This sacrament is a profound declaration of the Lord's death until He comes again, calling for solemn reflection and sincere worship.

As we partake in the Lord's Supper, let us do so with reverence and deep gratitude for the sacrifice of Christ. Let this time be one of reflection, confession, and commitment, as we remember what Jesus has done for us and proclaim His death and resurrection. Let us also look forward with hope to His return.

Self-Examination and Mutual Respect (11:27-34)

"So then, whoever eats the bread or drinks the cup of the Lord in an unworthy manner will be guilty of sinning against the body and blood of the Lord.

Everyone ought to examine themselves before they eat of the bread and drink from the cup. For those who eat and drink without discerning the body of Christ eat and drink judgment on themselves.

That is why many among you are weak and sick, and a number of you have fallen asleep. But if we were more discerning with regard to ourselves, we would not come under such judgment.

Nevertheless, when we are judged in this way by the Lord, we are being disciplined so that we will not be finally condemned with the world.

So then, my brothers and sisters, when you gather to eat, you should all eat together. Anyone who is hungry should eat something at home, so that when you meet together it may not result in judgment." (1 Corinthians 11:27-34)

Paul concludes with a stern warning against partaking in the Lord's Supper in an unworthy manner, which leads to judgment upon oneself.

He instructs the believers to examine themselves before eating the bread and drinking the cup, ensuring that their hearts and motives are pure, and to recognize the body of Christ in one another, thus avoiding judgment and division.

This final section of chapter 11 calls for some introspection and community-mindedness in our approach to worship and the Lord's Supper. Are we examining our hearts, confessing our sins, and seeking reconciliation with one another? Are we mindful of the unity and significance of the body of Christ as we gather together?

Conclusion

Paul challenges us in this chapter to honour God in our worship and conduct, to approach the Lord's Supper with reverence and self-examination, and to live out the implications of Christ's sacrifice in our relationships and community life.

May our worship be pleasing to God, reflective of the respect and love due to Him and to one another, as we remember the sacrifice of our Lord Jesus Christ and anticipate His glorious return.

~ 1 CORINTHIANS 12 ~

Introduction

In chapter 12, the Apostle Paul addresses the issue of spiritual gifts and the metaphor of the church as the body of Christ. In this passage, Paul talks about the diversity and unity that should characterize our Christian community.

As we explore these important verses, let us open our hearts to the teachings of the Holy Spirit and consider how these principles apply to our lives and our fellowship together.

The Variety of Spiritual Gifts (12:1-11)

"Now about the gifts of the Spirit, brothers and sisters, I do not want you to be uninformed. You know that when you were pagans, somehow or other you were influenced and led astray to mute idols.

Therefore, I want you to know that no one who is speaking by the Spirit of God says, "Jesus be cursed," and no one can say, "Jesus is Lord," except by the Holy Spirit.

There are different kinds of gifts, but the same Spirit distributes them. There are different kinds of service, but the same Lord. There are different kinds of working, but in all of them and in everyone it is the same God at work.

Now to each one the manifestation of the Spirit is given for the common good. To one there is given through the Spirit a message of wisdom, to another a message of knowledge by means of the same Spirit, to another faith by the same Spirit, to another gifts of healing by that one Spirit, to another miraculous powers, to another prophecy, to another distinguishing between spirits, to another speaking in different kinds of tongues, and to still another the interpretation of tongues.

All these are the work of one and the same Spirit, and he distributes them to each one, just as he determines."
(1 Corinthians 12:1-11)

Paul begins by addressing the Corinthians' questions regarding spiritual gifts. He emphasizes that while there are different kinds of gifts, services, and workings, they are all given by the same Spirit, Lord, and God who works all things in all persons. Each believer is given a manifestation of the Spirit for the common good, ranging from wisdom and knowledge to faith, healing, miracles, prophecy, discernment, tongues, and interpretation.

Let us reflect on how we view and use our spiritual gifts. Are we aware of the gifts the Holy Spirit has bestowed upon us? Are we employing these gifts for the common good and the edification of the church, or are we neglecting them, or worse, using them for personal gain or status? Let us also commit to seeking and stewarding these gifts in humility and love, always aiming to build up the body of Christ.

One Body with Many Members (12:12-20)

> *"Just as a body, though one, has many parts, but all its many parts form one body, so it is with Christ. For we were all baptized by one Spirit so as to form one body - whether Jews or Gentiles, slave or free – and we were all given the one Spirit to drink. Even so the body is not made up of one part but of many.*
>
> *Now if the foot should say, "Because I am not a hand, I do not belong to the body," it would not for that reason stop being part of the body. And if the ear should say, "Because I am not an eye, I do not belong to the body," it would not for that reason stop being part of the body. If the whole body were an eye, where would the sense of hearing be? If the whole body were an ear, where would the sense of smell be?*
>
> *But in fact God has placed the parts in the body, every one of them, just as he wanted them to be. If they were all one part, where would the body be? As it is, there are many parts, but one body." (1 Corinthians 12:12-20)*

Paul uses the metaphor of the body to illustrate the unity and diversity of the church. Just as a body is one unit, but with many parts, so it is with Christ's body, the church. We, though many, are one body in Christ, and individually members thereof.

Diversity does not mean division; rather, it enriches the body and contributes to its functionality. This metaphor challenges us to consider our own attitudes toward diversity within our church.

Do we value and honour each member's contributions, or do we foster division and envy? Are we willing to recognize and also celebrate the different gifts and roles within our community, understanding that each one is vital to the health and mission of the church?

Mutual Care and Concern (12:21-26)

"The eye cannot say to the hand, "I don't need you!" And the head cannot say to the feet, "I don't need you!" On the contrary, those parts of the body that seem to be weaker are indispensable, and the parts that we think are less honourable we treat with special honour.

And the parts that are unpresentable are treated with special modesty, while our presentable parts need no special treatment. But God has put the body together, giving greater honour to the parts that lacked it, so that there should be no division in the body, but that its parts should have equal concern for each other. If one part suffers, every part suffers with it; if one part is honoured, every part rejoices with it." (1 Corinthians 12:21-26)

Paul continues to develop the body metaphor, emphasizing that all the members of the body should have equal concern for one another. If one part suffers, every part suffers with it; if one part is honoured, every part rejoices with it. This mutual care reflects the interconnectedness and interdependence of the church members.

Let us ponder how well we practice mutual care and concern in our community. Are we attentive to the needs and struggles of our brothers and sisters? Are we quick to rejoice with those who rejoice and weep with those who weep?

Let us strive to foster a community where every member feels valued, supported, and connected.

The Appointment of Members in the Body (12:27-31)

"Now you are the body of Christ, and each one of you is a part of it. And God has placed in the church first of all apostles, second prophets, third teachers, then miracles, then gifts of healing, of helping, of guidance, and of different kinds of tongues. Are all apostles? Are all prophets? Are all teachers? Do all work miracles? Do all have gifts of healing? Do all speak in tongues? Do all interpret? Now eagerly desire the greater gifts."
(1 Corinthians 12:27-31)

Paul reminds the Corinthians that God has appointed various roles within the church, listing apostles, prophets, teachers, miracles, gifts of healing, helping, administration, and various kinds of tongues. He encourages the pursuit of the greater gifts but hints at a more excellent way, which he will expound in the following chapter.

In our pursuit of spiritual gifts and service, let us remember that our primary goal is not personal fulfillment or recognition but the edification of the church and the glorification of God. Are we content with the roles and tasks God has assigned to us, and are we eager to serve in whatever capacity we are needed? Let us also remember that while we seek to use our gifts, the greatest of all gifts and the guiding principle of all service is love.

Conclusion

Paul calls us here to embrace the diversity of gifts, services, and operations within the church while maintaining the unity of the Spirit. As members of one body, let us value and care for each other, recognizing that each person and gift is crucial to the health and function of the body.

May we commit to using our gifts for the common good, supporting one another in love, and together advancing the mission of Christ in the world.

~ 1 CORINTHIANS 13 ~

Introduction

We now embark on a journey through one of the most profound and celebrated passages in the New Testament. Often recited at weddings and praised for its poetic beauty, this chapter delves deep into the heart of Christian life and faith – which is love.

The Apostle Paul, after discussing spiritual gifts and the functioning of the church body, pivots to something even more foundational and transformative. As we explore this "love chapter," let's open our hearts to the transforming power of God's love and its imperative role in our lives as followers of Jesus Christ.

The Primacy of Love (13:1-3)

> "If I speak in the tongues of men or of angels, but do not have love, I am only a resounding gong or a clanging cymbal. If I have the gift of prophecy and can fathom all mysteries and all knowledge, and if I have a faith that can move mountains, but do not have love, I am nothing. If I give all I possess to the poor and give over my body to hardship that I may boast, but do not have love, I gain nothing." (1 Corinthians 13:1-3)

Paul begins with a powerful assertion: without love, our most impressive gifts and sacrifices are empty and profitless. He uses hyperbolic language to describe speaking in tongues, prophetic powers, understanding mysteries, having all knowledge, faith that moves mountains, giving away all possessions, and even suffering martyrdom. Yet, he states unequivocally that without love, these actions amount to nothing.

This challenges us to examine our motives and actions. Are our endeavours - however noble or spiritual - rooted in love? In our pursuit of spiritual gifts, service, or even personal sacrifice, let us not lose sight of love, the greatest attribute that should underpin every aspect of our Christian walk.

The Characteristics of Love (13:4-7)

"Love is patient, love is kind. It does not envy, it does not boast, it is not proud. It does not dishonour others, it is not self-seeking, it is not easily angered, it keeps no record of wrongs.

Love does not delight in evil but rejoices with the truth. It always protects, always trusts, always hopes, always perseveres."
(1 Corinthians 13:4-7)

In this section, Paul beautifully articulates what love is and what love is not. Love is patient and kind; it does not envy or boast; it is not arrogant or rude. Love does not insist on its own way; it is not irritable or resentful; it does not rejoice at wrongdoing but rejoices with the truth. Love bears all things, believes all things, hopes all things, endures all things.

Each of these characteristics invites self-reflection. How does our love measure up to this divine standard? This portrayal of love serves as a mirror, reflecting our deficiencies and inviting us to grow. Let's ask ourselves: How can we embody this love more fully in our relationships, in our church, and in our daily interactions with others?

The Permanence of Love (13:8-13)

"Love never fails. But where there are prophecies, they will cease; where there are tongues, they will be stilled; where there is knowledge, it will pass away. For we know in part and we prophesy in part, but when completeness comes, what is in part disappears.

When I was a child, I talked like a child, I thought like a child, I reasoned like a child. When I became a man, I put the ways of childhood behind me. For now, we see only a reflection as in a mirror; then we shall see face to face. Now I know in part; then I shall know fully, even as I am fully known.

And now these three remain: faith, hope and love. But the greatest of these is love." *(1 Corinthians 13:8-13)*

Paul contrasts love's enduring nature with the temporary nature of spiritual gifts. Prophecies will cease, tongues will be stilled, knowledge will pass away, for our current understanding and prophesying are partial. But when completeness comes, the partial will disappear. In the end, three things remain: faith, hope, and love, with love being the greatest.

This passage reminds us of the transient nature of our earthly pursuits and gifts compared to the eternal nature of love. Are we investing in what is temporary, or are we cultivating love, the virtue that will endure forever? As we anticipate the day of completeness in Christ, let our lives be marked by the everlasting love of God, poured out upon us by the Holy Spirit.

Conclusion

In this famous 'Love Chapter,' Paul elevates love as the supreme virtue, surpassing all spiritual gifts and achievements. This divine love, agape, is selfless, sacrificial, and unconditional, reflecting the very nature of God Himself.

As we ponder this chapter, may we strive not just to understand love or admire its qualities, but to live it out in our daily lives. Let us remember that to embody Christian love is to reflect the very heart of God to a world in desperate need of His love.

As we go forth, may the love described in these verses become the hallmark of our lives, transforming our relationships, guiding our service, and deepening our faith. In a world of transient things, may we cling to and exemplify the greatest of all - love.

~ 1 CORINTHIANS 14 ~

Introduction

This passage is rich with instruction and insight into the use of spiritual gifts within the life of the church. After emphasizing the supremacy of love in the previous chapter, Paul now turns his attention to the gifts of prophecy and speaking in tongues, setting forth principles for orderly worship and mutual edification. As we explore this chapter, let us seek to understand the Apostle's heart and God's desire for our gatherings and our growth as a body of believers.

The Priority of Prophecy over Speaking in Tongues (14:1-5)

"Follow the way of love and eagerly desire gifts of the Spirit, especially prophecy. For anyone who speaks in a tongue[a] does not speak to people but to God. Indeed, no one understands them; they utter mysteries by the Spirit. But the one who prophesies speaks to people for their strengthening, encouraging and comfort. Anyone who speaks in a tongue edifies themselves, but the one who prophesies edifies the church. I would like every one of you to speak in tongues, but I would rather have you prophesy. The one who prophesies is greater than the one who speaks in tongues, unless someone interprets, so that the church may be edified."
(1 Corinthians 14:1-5)

Paul begins by urging the Corinthian believers to pursue love and earnestly desire spiritual gifts, especially prophecy. Unlike tongues, which primarily benefits the speaker, prophecy edifies, encourages, guides and comforts the entire congregation. While speaking in tongues is a sign for unbelievers, prophecy serves believers, building up the church. Paul's concern here is not to depreciate the gift of tongues but to prioritize the building up of the church community.

In our spiritual pursuits, are we focusing on gifts that build up others or merely on those that enrich ourselves? Let us evaluate our contributions to church life:

Are they aimed at personal status, or do they seek the common good? Let's prioritize gifts and actions that strengthen, encourage, and comfort our brothers and sisters in Christ.

The Necessity of Understanding and Order (14:6-19)

"Now, brothers and sisters, if I come to you and speak in tongues, what good will I be to you, unless I bring you some revelation or knowledge or prophecy or word of instruction? Even in the case of lifeless things that make sounds, such as the pipe or harp, how will anyone know what tune is being played unless there is a distinction in the notes?

Again, if the trumpet does not sound a clear call, who will get ready for battle? So it is with you. Unless you speak intelligible words with your tongue, how will anyone know what you are saying? You will just be speaking into the air. Undoubtedly there are all sorts of languages in the world, yet none of them is without meaning. If then I do not grasp the meaning of what someone is saying, I am a foreigner to the speaker, and the speaker is a foreigner to me. So it is with you. Since you are eager for gifts of the Spirit, try to excel in those that build up the church.

For this reason, the one who speaks in a tongue should pray that they may interpret what they say. For if I pray in a tongue, my spirit prays, but my mind is unfruitful. So what shall I do? I will pray with my spirit, but I will also pray with my understanding; I will sing with my spirit, but I will also sing with my understanding. Otherwise, when you are praising God in the Spirit, how can someone else, who is now put in the position of an inquirer, say "Amen" to your thanksgiving, since they do not know what you are saying? You are giving thanks well enough, but no one else is edified. I thank God that I speak in tongues more than all of you. But in the church, I would rather speak five intelligible words to instruct others than ten thousand words in a tongue." (1 Corinthians 14:6-19)

Paul continues by highlighting the importance of intelligibility in worship - whether that is through prophecy, speaking in tongues with interpretation, or the gift of divine knowledge.

Just as musical instruments need to produce distinct notes to be understood, so must our contributions in church be clear and comprehensible to benefit others. Paul values speaking in tongues but stresses that in the church, he would rather speak five intelligible words to instruct others than ten thousand words in a tongue.

This teaches us the value of clarity and understanding in our communication. Whether we're teaching, preaching, praying, or singing, are we doing so in a way that others can understand and be edified? Let our expressions of worship and our use of spiritual gifts, always aim for the edification of the entire body.

The Tongues Dilemma (14:20-25)

"Brothers and sisters, stop thinking like children. In regard to evil be infants, but in your thinking be adults. In the Law it is written: "With other tongues and through the lips of foreigners I will speak to this people, but even then, they will not listen to me, says the Lord."

Tongues, then, are a sign, not for believers but for unbelievers; prophecy, however, is not for unbelievers but for believers. So, if the whole church comes together and everyone speaks in tongues, and inquirers or unbelievers come in, will they not say that you are out of your mind?

But if an unbeliever or an inquirer comes in while everyone is prophesying, they are convicted of sin and are brought under judgment by all, as the secrets of their hearts are laid bare. So, they will fall down and worship God, exclaiming, "God is really among you!" (1 Corinthians 14:20-25)

Orderly Worship for Edification (14:26-33)

"What then shall we say, brothers and sisters? When you come together, each of you has a hymn, or a word of instruction, a revelation, a tongue or an interpretation. Everything must be done so that the church may be built up. If anyone speaks in a tongue, two - or at the most three - should speak, one at a time, and someone must interpret."

"If there is no interpreter, the speaker should keep quiet in the church and speak to himself and to God. Two or three prophets should speak, and the others should weigh carefully what is said. And if a revelation comes to someone who is sitting down, the first speaker should stop. For you can all prophesy in turn so that everyone may be instructed and encouraged. The spirits of prophets are subject to the control of prophets. For God is not a God of disorder but of peace - as in all the congregations of the Lord's people." (1 Corinthians 14:26-33)

Paul provides practical instructions for orderly worship services, where everyone contributes but all things should be done for building up. He sets specific guidelines for speaking in tongues and prophesying within the church assembly, ensuring that everything is done decently and in order. The underlying principle is that God is not a God of confusion but of peace.

How does our corporate worship reflect the principles of order and peace? Are our services marked by a spirit of mutual respect and a desire for communal edification? Let each of us commit to conducting all our gatherings in a manner that reflects God's character and fosters an environment where every member can grow and be encouraged in their faith.

The Role of Women in Church Services (14:34-40)

"Women should remain silent in the churches. They are not allowed to speak, but must be in submission, as the law says. If they want to inquire about something, they should ask their own husbands at home; for it is disgraceful for a woman to speak in the church. Or did the word of God originate with you? Or are you the only people it has reached?

If anyone thinks they are a prophet or otherwise gifted by the Spirit, let them acknowledge that what I am writing to you is the Lord's command. But if anyone ignores this, they will themselves be ignored.

Therefore, my brothers and sisters, be eager to prophesy, and do not forbid speaking in tongues. But everything should be done in a fitting and orderly way." (1 Corinthians 14:34-40)

In the closing verses, Paul addresses the role of women in the Corinthian church, urging silence in the assemblies and directing them to ask their husbands at home if they have questions. This instruction, controversial and often misunderstood, relates to the specific cultural and situational context of the Corinthian church. It is crucial to interpret this passage considering the whole counsel of Scripture and the cultural context of the time.

As I discussed earlier (p.125), this is one a few passages in the Bible which have caused a great deal of conflict over the years and still, to this day, there are churches who ignore the cultural reality behind this passage and continue oppressing woman in the church and deny them their God-given freedom in Christ.

We must understand that when Paul wrote these words, women has been silent, covered and denied any place in the spiritual life of God's people. When Jesus changed all that and set them gloriously free, the reality of the kingdom of God was unleashed on our world. So now, in Christ, there was *"neither male nor female."* (Galatians 3:28).

However, Paul recognised that in a male dominated society, it was going to take a long time for women to be completely liberated in their day to day lives and so in a number of places in his letters, he appears to be saying to women that they need to remain in those cultural chains. That is not the case at all and even Paul himself, had women leaders in his group of close companions.

There are many today who cannot believe that women were once denied their rightful place in among God's people and they rejoice that cultural norms have now changed, at least in many places. However, the underlying principles of this passage remain relevant: recognizing and respecting the cultural realities within which we exercise our freedom in Christ.

In dealing with complex and culturally bound instructions, let us seek wisdom and guidance from the Holy Spirit, balancing scriptural truths with the cultural context of our times.

Let us foster environments where all members, regardless of gender, can grow, contribute, and flourish according to their spiritual gifts, under the order and authority established by God.

Conclusion

In 1 Corinthians Chapter 14, Paul calls us to pursue spiritual gifts that edify the church, to value clarity and order in our gatherings, and to maintain peace and understanding within our spiritual family.

As we reflect on this chapter, may we commit to using our gifts for the common good, to communicating clearly and effectively, and to contributing to orderly and uplifting worship that honours God and edifies His people.

~ 1 CORINTHIANS 15 ~

Introduction

We now come to one of the most profound and essential chapters in all of Scripture: 1 Corinthians Chapter 15. In this passage, the Apostle Paul provides us with a comprehensive treatise on the resurrection of Christ and its implications for believers. As we explore this cornerstone of our faith, let us be reminded of the hope and victory we possess through our risen Lord and Saviour, Jesus Christ.

The Importance of the Resurrection (15:1-11)

"Now, brothers and sisters, I want to remind you of the gospel I preached to you, which you received and on which you have taken your stand. By this gospel you are saved, if you hold firmly to the word I preached to you. Otherwise, you have believed in vain. For what I received I passed on to you as of first importance: that Christ died for our sins according to the Scriptures, that he was buried, that he was raised on the third day according to the Scriptures, and that he appeared to Cephas, and then to the Twelve.

After that, he appeared to more than five hundred of the brothers and sisters at the same time, most of whom are still living, though some have fallen asleep. Then he appeared to James, then to all the apostles, and last of all he appeared to me also, as to one abnormally born. For I am the least of the apostles and do not even deserve to be called an apostle, because I persecuted the church of God.

But by the grace of God I am what I am, and his grace to me was not without effect. No, I worked harder than all of them - yet not I, but the grace of God that was with me.

Whether, then, it is I or they, this is what we preach, and this is what you believed." (1 Corinthians 15:1-11)

Paul begins by reminding the Corinthian believers of the gospel he preached to them, which is of first importance: that Christ died for our sins according to the Scriptures, that He was buried, and was raised on the third day according to the Scriptures.

The great Apostle emphasizes the historicity and witness of Christ's resurrection, noting that He appeared to Cephas, then the Twelve, and then to more than five hundred brethren at once.

The resurrection of Christ is not a peripheral doctrine; it is central to our faith and salvation. It is the evidence of God's power over death and the assurance of our forgiveness and justification. Let us hold firmly to this truth, for in believing and proclaiming Christ's resurrection, we stand on the solid ground of historical fact and divine revelation.

The Consequences of Denying the Resurrection (15:12-19)

"But if it is preached that Christ has been raised from the dead, how can some of you say that there is no resurrection of the dead? If there is no resurrection of the dead, then not even Christ has been raised. And if Christ has not been raised, our preaching is useless and so is your faith. More than that, we are then found to be false witnesses about God, for we have testified about God that he raised Christ from the dead. But he did not raise him if in fact the dead are not raised.

For if the dead are not raised, then Christ has not been raised either. And if Christ has not been raised, your faith is futile; you are still in your sins. Then those also who have fallen asleep in Christ are lost. If only for this life we have hope in Christ, we are of all people most to be pitied." (1 Corinthians 15:12-19)

Paul confronts the logical consequences of anyone denying the resurrection, a view held by some in Corinth. If Christ has not been raised, our preaching is in vain, our faith is futile, we are still in our sins, and those who have fallen asleep in Christ are lost. The resurrection is not an optional belief; it is foundational to the Christian hope and future resurrection.

Let us examine our own understanding and embrace of the resurrection. Do we live as people of hope, or as those without assurance? The resurrection empowers us to face life and death with confidence, knowing that in Christ, our future is secure and death has lost its sting.

The Order of the Resurrection (15:20-28)

> *"But Christ has indeed been raised from the dead, the first fruits of those who have fallen asleep. For since death came through a man, the resurrection of the dead comes also through a man. For as in Adam all die, so in Christ all will be made alive. But each in turn: Christ, the first fruits; then, when he comes, those who belong to him. Then the end will come, when he hands over the kingdom to God the Father after he has destroyed all dominion, authority and power.*
>
> *For he must reign until he has put all his enemies under his feet. The last enemy to be destroyed is death. For he "has put everything under his feet." Now when it says that "everything" has been put under him, it is clear that this does not include God himself, who put everything under Christ. When he has done this, then the Son himself will be made subject to him who put everything under him, so that God may be all in all."*
> *(1 Corinthians 15:20-28)*

Paul affirms that Christ has indeed been raised from the dead, the first fruits of those who have fallen asleep. He outlines the order of the resurrection: Christ, the first fruits; then, at His coming, those who belong to Him. Finally, the end will come when He hands over the kingdom to God the Father, having destroyed all dominion, authority, and power.

This passage provides a glorious picture of God's unfolding plan of redemption. We live in the time between Christ's resurrection and His return. Are we living as citizens of His kingdom, actively participating in His victory over sin and death, and looking forward to His triumphant return?

Implications of the Resurrection (15:29-34)

> *"Now if there is no resurrection, what will those do who are baptized for the dead? If the dead are not raised at all, why are people baptized for them? And as for us, why do we endanger ourselves every hour? I face death every day - yes, just as surely as I boast about you in Christ Jesus our Lord."*

"If I fought wild beasts in Ephesus with no more than human hopes, what have I gained? If the dead are not raised, "Let us eat and drink, for tomorrow we die." Do not be misled: "Bad company corrupts good character." Come back to your senses as you ought, and stop sinning; for there are some who are ignorant of God — I say this to your shame." (1 Corinthians 15:29-34)

This passage deals with the implications of the resurrection for Christian life and belief. Paul uses a series of arguments to emphasize the importance of the resurrection, starting with a cryptic reference to baptism for the dead, a practice mentioned nowhere else in the Bible, which suggests a form of vicarious baptism on behalf of those who have died. This reference is used to underline the absurdity of denying the resurrection, given that certain practices within the community presuppose it.

Interpreting verse 29, particularly the reference to 'baptism for the dead,' is a complex task, given its unique mention in the Bible and apparent tension with the broader theological concepts of individual faith and salvation. Scholars and theologians have proposed various interpretations, acknowledging the challenge this verse presents due to the lack of explicit contextual explanation from Paul or elsewhere in Scripture.

In interpreting any isolated verse like this, it's crucial to consider the broader theological context of Paul's writings and the New Testament. The predominant message is one of personal faith in Christ as the basis for salvation, which seems to stand in tension with the idea of vicarious baptism for salvation.

Therefore, most interpretations seek to reconcile this verse with the overarching themes of individual faith, the finality of Christ's work on the cross, and the resurrection. Given the very obvious lack of clarity, verse 29 continues to be a subject of theological exploration.

Paul then moves to personal reflections on the dangers he faces as a consequence of his faith, arguing that such risks are only justified by the hope of resurrection. His mention of fighting with beasts in Ephesus is metaphorical, highlighting the struggles faced by believers.

Finally, Paul warns against bad company and moral laxity, emphasizing that the denial of resurrection leads to moral decay. He calls for vigilance and righteousness, grounding ethical behaviour in the hope of resurrection.

This segment underscores the centrality of the resurrection in Christian doctrine and its practical implications for living a life in accordance with faith.

The Nature of the Resurrected Body (15:35-49)

"But someone will ask, "How are the dead raised? With what kind of body will they come?" How foolish! What you sow does not come to life unless it dies. When you sow, you do not plant the body that will be, but just a seed, perhaps of wheat or of something else. But God gives it a body as he has determined, and to each kind of seed he gives its own body. Not all flesh is the same: People have one kind of flesh, animals have another, birds another and fish another.

There are also heavenly bodies and there are earthly bodies; but the splendour of the heavenly bodies is one kind, and the splendour of the earthly bodies is another. The sun has one kind of splendour, the moon another and the stars another; and star differs from star in splendour.

So will it be with the resurrection of the dead. The body that is sown is perishable, it is raised imperishable; it is sown in dishonour, it is raised in glory; it is sown in weakness, it is raised in power; it is sown a natural body, it is raised a spiritual body. If there is a natural body, there is also a spiritual body.

So, it is written: "The first man Adam became a living being;" the last Adam, a life-giving spirit. The spiritual did not come first, but the natural, and after that the spiritual. The first man was of the dust of the earth; the second man is of heaven. As was the earthly man, so are those who are of the earth; and as is the heavenly man, so also are those who are of heaven. And just as we have borne the image of the earthly man, so shall we bear the image of the heavenly man." (1 Corinthians 15:35-49)

Paul addresses questions about the nature of the resurrection body. He uses the analogy of a seed dying in order to produce a new life, illustrating the transformation from the perishable, dishonourable, and weak to the imperishable, glorious, and powerful. Just as we have borne the image of the man of dust, we shall also bear the image of the man of heaven.

In a world preoccupied with physical appearance and strength, this is a powerful reminder of our ultimate transformation. Our current physical struggles and limitations are temporary. Let us live with the hope of our future glorification, allowing this hope to shape our values and actions today.

The Victory through Our Lord Jesus Christ (15:50-58)

> *"I declare to you, brothers and sisters, that flesh and blood cannot inherit the kingdom of God, nor does the perishable inherit the imperishable. Listen, I tell you a mystery: We will not all sleep, but we will all be changed - in a flash, in the twinkling of an eye, at the last trumpet. For the trumpet will sound, the dead will be raised imperishable, and we will be changed. For the perishable must clothe itself with the imperishable, and the mortal with immortality. When the perishable has been clothed with the imperishable, and the mortal with immortality, then the saying that is written will come true: "Death has been swallowed up in victory."*
>
> *"Where, O death, is your victory? Where, O death, is your sting?" The sting of death is sin, and the power of sin is the law. But thanks be to God! He gives us the victory through our Lord Jesus Christ.*
>
> *Therefore, my dear brothers and sisters, stand firm. Let nothing move you. Always give yourselves fully to the work of the Lord, because you know that your labour in the Lord is not in vain."*
> (1 Corinthians 15:50-58)

Paul concludes with a triumphant proclamation of victory over death and sin through Jesus Christ. He encourages us all to stand firm and immovable, always abounding in the work of the Lord, knowing that their labour is not in vain in the Lord.

The resurrection assures us that our faith, our hope, and our labour in the Lord are not futile but are leading to an eternal, glorious reality. Let this assurance motivate us to faithful, diligent service and moral courage, even amidst challenges and uncertainties.

In 1 Corinthians Chapter 15, we are reminded of the pivotal truth of our faith: Christ is risen! He has conquered death, and in Him, we too shall be raised. May this truth fill us with unshakeable hope, guide our lives, and empower our witness to a world in need of this glorious gospel.

Let us live and serve in the light of the resurrection, anticipating the day when we will fully experience the victory we have in our Lord Jesus Christ.

~ 1 CORINTHIANS 16 ~

Introduction

This final chapter of Paul's first letter to the Corinthians, beckons us with practical instructions and heartfelt exhortations. While seemingly straightforward, this chapter encapsulates essential themes for our whole Christian walk: stewardship, brotherhood, vigilance, and love.

Let us delve into these final words from Paul, allowing them to challenge and shape our lives as members of God's family.

The Collection for the Saints (16:1-4)

"Now about the collection for the Lord's people: Do what I told the Galatian churches to do. On the first day of every week, each one of you should set aside a sum of money in keeping with your income, saving it up, so that when I come no collections will have to be made. Then, when I arrive, I will give letters of introduction to the men you approve and send them with your gift to Jerusalem. If it seems advisable for me to go also, they will accompany me." (1 Corinthians 16:1-4)

Paul begins here with instructions regarding the collection for the saints in Jerusalem. He emphasizes the principle of regular, proportionate giving, urging each person to set aside a sum of money on the first day of every week, according to their ability. This systematic and intentional approach to giving highlights the importance of planned generosity in the life of a believer.

How do we view and practice giving within our own lives? Are we giving systematically and generously to the work of God and the needs of His people?

Let this be a reminder that our stewardship of resources is an integral part of our worship and service to the Lord. May we give not grudgingly or out of compulsion, but cheerfully and abundantly, reflecting the heart of our generous God.

Plans and Provision (16:5-9)

"After I go through Macedonia, I will come to you - for I will be going through Macedonia. Perhaps I will stay with you for a while, or even spend the winter, so that you can help me on my journey, wherever I go. For I do not want to see you now and make only a passing visit; I hope to spend some time with you if the Lord permits. But I will stay on at Ephesus until Pentecost, because a great door for effective work has opened to me, and there are many who oppose me." (1 Corinthians 16:5-9)

Paul shares his travel plans and his desire to visit the believers in Corinth, indicating his intention to stay with them for a while if the Lord permits. He speaks of a wide-open door for effective work, despite many adversaries. This shows Paul's submission to God's timing and recognition of divine opportunities amidst challenges.

Are we open to God's leading in our plans and willing to seize the many opportunities He provides, even when faced with opposition? Let us be reminded that God's timing and plans are perfect. As we make our own plans, may we do so with prayer and flexibility, willing to be used by God wherever and however He sees fit.

Exhortations to the Church (16:10-18)

"When Timothy comes, see to it that he has nothing to fear while he is with you, for he is carrying on the work of the Lord, just as I am. No one, then, should treat him with contempt. Send him on his way in peace so that he may return to me. I am expecting him along with the brothers.

Now about our brother Apollos: I strongly urged him to go to you with the brothers. He was quite unwilling to go now, but he will go when he has the opportunity. Be on your guard; stand firm in the faith; be courageous; be strong. Do everything in love. You know that the household of Stephanas were the first converts in Achaia, and they have devoted themselves to the service of the Lord's people."

"I urge you, brothers and sisters, to submit to such people and to everyone who joins in the work and labours at it. I was glad when Stephanas, Fortunatus and Achaicus arrived, because they have supplied what was lacking from you. For they refreshed my spirit and yours also. Such men deserve recognition."
(1 Corinthians 16:10-18)

Paul continues with some personal remarks and exhortations regarding Timothy, Apollos, and some others. He encourages the church to treat Timothy well and to respect those who labour among them. Paul highlights the importance of acknowledging and supporting those who devote themselves to the work of the Lord.

How do we treat our leaders and fellow workers in Christ? Are we supportive, encouraging, and respectful? Let us recognize and appreciate the efforts of those who labour for the Gospel, offering them our support, encouragement, and love. In doing so, we foster a community that honours God and strengthens His servants.

Final Greetings and Exhortations (16:19-24)

"The churches in the province of Asia send you greetings. Aquila and Priscilla greet you warmly in the Lord, and so does the church that meets at their house. All the brothers and sisters here send you greetings. Greet one another with a holy kiss.

I, Paul, write this greeting in my own hand. If anyone does not love the Lord, let that person be cursed! Come, Lord! The grace of the Lord Jesus be with you. My love to all of you in Christ Jesus. Amen." *(1 Corinthians 16:19-24)*

Paul concludes with a series of potent exhortations: to be on guard, stand firm in the faith, be courageous, be strong, and do everything in love. He sends greetings from the churches of Asia, highlighting the interconnectedness of the body of Christ. His final words resonate with grace, love, and a call to faithfulness. These closing commands provide a blueprint for our Christian conduct.

Are we watchful, standing firm in our faith, acting with courage, and strengthened by God's Spirit? Is love the driving force behind our actions? As we interact with one another and face the world, let our lives be marked by these attributes, embodying the love and grace of our Lord Jesus Christ.

As we reflect on 1 Corinthians Chapter 16, let us embrace Paul's practical guidance and heartfelt admonitions. May we be faithful stewards, generous in giving, supportive of one another, steadfast in faith, and abundant in love.

In all things, may our lives honour God and build up His church. And as we go forward, may the grace of our Lord Jesus Christ be with us, the love of God guide us, and the fellowship of the Holy Spirit unite and strengthen us, now and forevermore.

As we conclude our study of Paul's first letter to the Corinthians, we can appreciate that it stands as a pivotal text within the New Testament, offering profound insights into the early Christian community's life, challenges, and theology.

This epistle addresses a wide array of issues, from divisions and moral dilemmas to questions about worship practices, spiritual gifts, and the resurrection of the dead. Through his responses, Paul not only provides specific guidance to the Corinthians but also articulates key aspects of Christian doctrine, including the nature of the church as the body of Christ, the importance of love as the greatest spiritual gift, and the centrality of the resurrection to Christian hope and faith.

The letter's enduring relevance lies in its ability to speak to the complexities of Christian life and faith, emphasizing unity, love, and resurrection hope as foundational to the identity and mission of the Christian community.

~ 2 CORINTHIANS ~

The book of 2 Corinthians is a complex and multifaceted text, rich in theological insights, personal reflections, and apostolic guidance. It is Paul's second letter to the Christian community in Corinth, a city known for its cultural diversity, economic prosperity, and moral challenges.

This letter, more personal and introspective than its predecessor, addresses several key themes and issues within the early Christian community. Here is an overview and brief analysis of all thirteen chapters:

Introduction (1:1-11)

Paul begins with a traditional greeting but quickly moves into a theme that pervades the entire letter: the concept of consolation and suffering. Paul describes his hardships in Asia, emphasizing that these experiences enable believers to comfort others. This section introduces the idea that suffering and comfort are part of the Christian experience, designed to foster dependence on God rather than on oneself.

Paul's Ministry and Defence (1:12-7:16)

This large section can be divided into several parts, each addressing different aspects of Paul's ministry and the challenges he faces. Paul discusses his sincerity and integrity as an apostle, contrasting his own authentic, suffering-infused ministry with the so-called "super-apostles" who boast of strength and worldly success. He speaks of his change in travel plans, addressing accusations of fickleness and defending his apostolic authority and decision-making as guided by God, not human wisdom.

In chapters 3 to 7, Paul elaborates on the nature of Christian ministry. He uses the metaphor of the "new covenant" contrasting it with the old covenant, emphasizing the Spirit's role in transforming believers. A number of themes of reconciliation, transformation, and the transient nature of earthly troubles are highlighted, culminating in a heartfelt appeal for open-hearted reconciliation between him and the Corinthian church.

The Collection for Jerusalem (8:1-9:15)

Paul shifts focus to the practical matter of the collection for the poor in Jerusalem. He encourages generosity, using the example of the Macedonian churches and the model of selflessness of Christ. This section is notable for its insights into early Christian practices regarding mutual aid and the principles of cheerful and willing giving.

Paul's Defence of His Apostolic Authority (10:1-13:10)

Here, Paul confronts his opponents more directly, defending his authority and ministry. He argues against those who judge by appearances and boast about external achievements. Paul asserts that true apostolic authority is rooted in Christ and characterized by humility and suffering, not worldly power or eloquence. He uses irony and sarcasm to undercut his opponents' claims, presenting his weaknesses as the true marks of an apostle.

Conclusion and Final Greetings (13:11-14)

Paul concludes with exhortations to self-examination, joy, maturity, peace, and love. He ends with a Trinitarian blessing, highlighting the grace of Jesus Christ, the love of God, and the fellowship of the Holy Spirit.

Themes and Theological Insights:

Strength in Weakness: One of the most profound themes in 2 Corinthians is the concept of finding strength in weakness. Paul illustrates how his own vulnerabilities and sufferings are not signs of failure but of Christ's power working through him. This counterintuitive principle is central to our understanding Christian leadership and discipleship.

Reconciliation and Ministry: The letter emphasizes the ministry of reconciliation, entrusted to believers by God. This includes reconciliation between individuals, within communities, and most importantly, between humans and God through Jesus Christ.

Generosity and Stewardship: Paul's discussion of the collection for Jerusalem provides insights into the early church's views on financial generosity, communal support, and the principles governing the use of resources for the common good.

The Nature of True Apostleship: Contrasting with the many false apostles, Paul presents a model of Christian leadership that is service-oriented, marked by suffering, and authenticated by signs of the Spirit's work.

The New Covenant: The letter contrasts the glory of the new covenant in the Spirit with the old covenant of the letter (law), highlighting the transformative power of the Spirit in the lives of believers.

2 Corinthians, therefore, offers a deep dive into the heart and mind of Paul as an apostle, pastor, and theologian. It addresses practical, theological, and ethical issues within the early Christian community, providing timeless insights into Christian life and ministry.

Now I will unpack each of the thirteen chapters in more detail as we embrace the importance teaching of the Apostle Paul in this important letter.

Introduction

The first chapter of Paul's second letter to the Corinthians is a passage rich in comfort, challenge, and profound spiritual insight. As we examine this important text, let's open our hearts to the lessons God has for us, especially how to find comfort in affliction and extend that comfort to others.

Affliction and God's Comfort (1:1-7)

"Paul, an apostle of Christ Jesus by the will of God, and Timothy our brother, to the church of God in Corinth, together with all his holy people throughout Achaia: Grace and peace to you from God our Father and the Lord Jesus Christ.

Praise be to the God and Father of our Lord Jesus Christ, the Father of compassion and the God of all comfort, who comforts us in all our troubles, so that we can comfort those in any trouble with the comfort we ourselves receive from God. For just as we share abundantly in the sufferings of Christ, so also our comfort abounds through Christ.

If we are distressed, it is for your comfort and salvation; if we are comforted, it is for your comfort, which produces in you, patient endurance of the same sufferings we suffer. And our hope for you is firm, because we know that just as you share in our sufferings, so also you share in our comfort." (2 Corinthians 1:1-7)

Paul begins his letter with a greeting that is both traditional and deeply personal. He introduces himself along with Timothy, not merely as apostles of Christ Jesus by the will of God, but as brothers in Christ to the church in Corinth. This sets the stage for a letter not just of instruction, but of heartfelt connection.

Immediately, Paul dives into the heart of his message: the relationship between affliction and comfort. He praises the God of all comfort, who comforts us in all our troubles.

Notice, Paul does not say some troubles, but all. This is the God who meets us in every dark valley, every moment of despair. Why does God comfort us? Paul says it's so we can comfort those in any trouble with the comfort we ourselves receive from God.

This is a profound principle of the Kingdom: the comfort we receive is not meant to end with us. It's designed to flow through us. In our suffering, we are united with Christ, and in our comfort, we share that union with others.

The Purpose of Suffering (1:8-11)

"We do not want you to be uninformed, brothers and sisters, about the troubles we experienced in the province of Asia. We were under great pressure, far beyond our ability to endure, so that we despaired of life itself.

Indeed, we felt we had received the sentence of death. But this happened that we might not rely on ourselves but on God, who raises the dead. He has delivered us from such a deadly peril, and he will deliver us again.

On him we have set our hope that he will continue to deliver us, as you help us by your prayers. Then many will give thanks on our behalf for the gracious favour granted us in answer to the prayers of many." (2 Corinthians 1:8-11)

Paul doesn't shy away from sharing his own experiences. He speaks of hardships in Asia, of being under great pressure, far beyond his ability to endure, to the point where he despaired of life itself. Yet, he identifies the purpose in this despair: it was to teach him not to rely on himself but on God, who raises the dead.

Here, Paul touches on a mystery: suffering can lead to greater life and reliance on God. He's honest about his weakness, modelling for us what it means to be transparent in our struggles.

His trust in God, amidst severe trials, serves as a profound example for us. It encourages us to rely not on our strength but on the resurrection power of God.

Participating in the Suffering and Comfort of Christ (1:12-22)

"Now this is our boast: Our conscience testifies that we have conducted ourselves in the world, and especially in our relations with you, with integrity and godly sincerity. We have done so, relying not on worldly wisdom but on God's grace. For we do not write you anything you cannot read or understand. And I hope that, as you have understood us in part, you will come to understand fully that you can boast of us just as we will boast of you in the day of the Lord Jesus.

Because I was confident of this, I wanted to visit you first so that you might benefit twice. I wanted to visit you on my way to Macedonia and to come back to you from Macedonia, and then to have you send me on my way to Judea. Was I fickle when I intended to do this? Or do I make my plans in a worldly manner so that in the same breath I say both "Yes, yes" and "No, no"?

But as surely as God is faithful, our message to you is not "Yes" and "No." For the Son of God, Jesus Christ, who was preached among you by us — by me and Silas and Timothy — was not "Yes" and "No," but in him it has always been "Yes." For no matter how many promises God has made, they are "Yes" in Christ. And so, through him the "Amen" is spoken by us to the glory of God.

Now it is God who makes both us and you stand firm in Christ. He anointed us, set his seal of ownership on us, and put his Spirit in our hearts as a deposit, guaranteeing what is to come. "
(2 Corinthians 1:12-22)

Paul continues by discussing the integrity of his actions and decisions, grounding them in simplicity and godly sincerity. This is not a worldly boast but a testament to the grace of God working in him.

He speaks here about the promises of God, reminding us that no matter how many promises God has made, they are "Yes" in Christ. And so, through Christ, the "Amen" is spoken by us to the glory of God. What a beautiful image! Our lives, lived in faith, become a continuous affirmation of God's promises.

Paul also reminds us that it is God who makes us stand firm in Christ. He has anointed us, set his seal of ownership on us, and put his Spirit in our hearts. This is not just theology; it's identity. We are owned, sealed, and indwelt by the living God!

Affliction and God's Comfort (1:23-24)

"I call God as my witness — and I stake my life on it - that it was in order to spare you that I did not return to Corinth. Not that we lord it over your faith, but we work with you for your joy, because it is by faith you stand firm." (2 Corinthians 1:23-24)

These last two verses serve as a poignant testament to the nature of spiritual leadership and mutual faith. Here, the Apostle Paul emphasizes his earnest desire to not be a burden or cause of sorrow to the Corinthians, reflecting a deep pastoral care and respect for their spiritual autonomy. He underscores that his authority as an apostle is not for dominating their faith, but for working alongside them to foster their joy.

This mutual joy is deeply rooted in faith, highlighting that the essence of Christian leadership is not about exerting power over others, but about empowering them in their journey of faith. Thus, Paul's words encapsulate a model of leadership that is characterized by empathy, support, and a shared commitment to the growth of faith.

Conclusion

As we reflect on this chapter, let's consider how we experience God's comfort in our afflictions. Are we transparent with our struggles, allowing others to minister to us, just as Paul was? Are we diligent in extending the comfort we've received to those around us? Remember, our sufferings and comforts are not merely individual experiences; they are communal. They tie us to the body of Christ, enabling us to participate in the sufferings and consolations of Christ himself. May we be conduits of comfort, recognizing that our afflictions, endured in Christ, can lead to life and comfort for others.

Introduction

In this second chapter, the Apostle Paul delves into the themes of forgiveness, ministry, and the presence of Christ in the midst of His people. As we unpack these sacred verses, let's open our hearts to the transformative power of God's Word, seeking to understand and embody the aroma of Christ in our lives.

The Ministry of Reconciliation (2:1-4)

"So, I made up my mind that I would not make another painful visit to you. For if I grieve you, who is left to make me glad but you whom I have grieved? I wrote as I did, so that when I came, I would not be distressed by those who should have made me rejoice. I had confidence in all of you, that you would all share my joy. For I wrote you out of great distress and anguish of heart and with many tears, not to grieve you but to let you know the depth of my love for you." (2 Corinthians 2:1-4)

Paul starts this chapter with a personal reflection on his decision not to visit Corinth again in sorrow. Behind these words lies a deep pastoral sensitivity; Paul is deeply connected to the Corinthian community's joys and sorrows. He has made a difficult decision out of love, not wanting to cause them pain but to promote joy and healing. This opening sets the stage for understanding the nature of Christian leadership and community life—it's not about wielding authority harshly but about seeking the well-being of others, even when it involves personal sacrifice. Here, Paul models for us a leadership that mirrors the shepherd heart of Jesus.

Forgiveness and Restoration (2:5-11)

"If anyone has caused grief, he has not so much grieved me as he has grieved all of you to some extent - not to put it too severely. The punishment inflicted on him by the majority is sufficient. Now instead, you ought to forgive and comfort him, so that he will not be overwhelmed by excessive sorrow. "

"I urge you, therefore, to reaffirm your love for him. Another reason I wrote you was to see if you would stand the test and be obedient in everything. Anyone you forgive, I also forgive. And what I have forgiven - if there was anything to forgive - I have forgiven in the sight of Christ for your sake, in order that Satan might not outwit us. For we are not unaware of his schemes."
(2 Corinthians 2:5-11)

Paul transitions to address a specific issue in the community: someone has caused pain, not just to Paul but to the entire church. While the details are not specified, it's clear this situation had led to some form of church discipline. Now, Paul advocates for forgiveness and restoration.

The Apostle underscores an essential principle in the life of the church: discipline is aimed at restoration, not punishment. Forgiveness is not optional but a fundamental expression of the love and unity we have in Christ. Paul calls the believers to reaffirm their love for the offender, because unforgiveness can give Satan a foothold in the community. This is a potent reminder for us today about the destructive power of unresolved conflicts and the healing power of forgiveness.

The Triumph of Christ (2:12-17)

"Now when I went to Troas to preach the gospel of Christ and found that the Lord had opened a door for me, I still had no peace of mind, because I did not find my brother Titus there. So, I said goodbye to them and went on to Macedonia.

But thanks be to God, who always leads us as captives in Christ's triumphal procession and uses us to spread the aroma of the knowledge of him everywhere. For we are to God the pleasing aroma of Christ among those who are being saved and those who are perishing. To the one we are an aroma that brings death; to the other, an aroma that brings life. And who is equal to such a task?

Unlike so many, we do not peddle the word of God for profit. On the contrary, in Christ we speak before God with sincerity, as those sent from God." (2 Corinthians 2:12-17)

In one of the most moving metaphors in all his letters, Paul describes his ministry and, by extension, the Christian life, as a "*triumphal procession*" in Christ. In the Roman world, such a procession was a display of victory and celebration. But Paul flips the script: he sees himself not as the triumphant general but as a captive in Christ's victory march, spreading the "*aroma of the knowledge of Him.*"

This passage invites us to reflect on our own lives and ministries: Are we spreading the fragrance of Christ in our environments? Paul acknowledges that this aroma is received differently by those who are being saved and those who are perishing - one as the fragrance of life, the other as the smell of death. This dual reaction underscores the powerful and often divisive nature of the Gospel message.

Moreover, Paul defends his sincerity and the integrity of his ministry, contrasting it with those who "*peddle the word of God for profit.*" In today's context, this challenges us to examine the authenticity and purity of our ministry motives.

Conclusion

As we conclude this chapter, let us consider: What does it mean to be the aroma of Christ in our communities? It means to walk in forgiveness and reconciliation, to seek the well-being of our brothers and sisters, and to live out the Gospel with sincerity and love, even when faced with personal cost or misunderstanding.

Let's not shy away from the ministry of reconciliation entrusted to us, for through it, we participate in the triumph of Christ. May we be agents of healing, bearers of forgiveness, and carriers of the life-giving aroma of Christ in a world that desperately needs the hope and love of the Gospel.

Let us pray for the grace to live out these truths, for the strength to forgive as we have been forgiven, and for the courage to carry the sweet aroma of Christ into every area of our lives. Amen.

~ 2 CORINTHIANS 3 ~

Introduction

Paul now invites us into a deeper reflection on the nature of the New Covenant and the transformation it brings into our lives. This is about identity, transformation, and the surpassing glory of life in the Spirit.

Let us approach this word with open hearts, eager to be changed by the truths God has for us today.

The New Covenant: Written on Hearts (3:1-3)

> *"Are we beginning to commend ourselves again? Or do we need, like some people, letters of recommendation to you or from you? You yourselves are our letter, written on our hearts, known and read by everyone. You show that you are a letter from Christ, the result of our ministry, written not with ink but with the Spirit of the living God, not on tablets of stone but on tablets of human hearts." (2 Corinthians 3:1-3)*

Paul begins by addressing the important question of legitimacy and authority. Unlike other teachers who relied on letters of recommendation, Paul declares that the Corinthians themselves are his letter of recommendation, written not on tablets of stone but on human hearts.

This imagery sets the stage for one of the central themes of this chapter: the contrast between the Old Covenant, symbolized by the law inscribed on stone, and the New Covenant, marked by the Spirit writing on human hearts.

In our lives, this raises significant questions: What is written on our hearts? Are our lives a letter that reflects the love and grace of Christ to the world around us?

The New Covenant invites us into a living, dynamic relationship with God, where His laws and love are not external requirements but internal realities shaping our very being.

The Ministry of the Spirit vs. the Letter (3:4-6)

"Such confidence we have through Christ before God. Not that we are competent in ourselves to claim anything for ourselves, but our competence comes from God. He has made us competent as ministers of a new covenant - not of the letter but of the Spirit; for the letter kills, but the Spirit gives life." (2 Corinthians 3:4-6)

Paul contrasts the ministry of the Spirit with the ministry of the letter. The letter, representing the Old Covenant Law, brings death because it condemns; it sets standards humans cannot fulfill on their own. In stark contrast, the Spirit gives life, empowering us to live in ways we never could under the law's rigid demands.

This section invites us to reflect on the source of our confidence and competence. Are we trying to serve God in our strength, following a set of rules and regulations? Or are we allowing the Spirit to lead us, relying on His power and guidance? The New Covenant offers us not a new set of rules but a new way to live, led and empowered by the Spirit of God.

The Glory of the New Covenant (3:7-11)

"Now if the ministry that brought death, which was engraved in letters on stone, came with glory, so that the Israelites could not look steadily at the face of Moses because of its glory, transitory though it was, will not the ministry of the Spirit be even more glorious? If the ministry that brought condemnation was glorious, how much more glorious is the ministry that brings righteousness! For what was glorious has no glory now in comparison with the surpassing glory. And if what was transitory came with glory, how much greater is the glory of that which lasts!" (2 Corinthians 3:7-11)

Here, Paul delves deeper into the contrast between the Old and New Covenants, using the story of Moses and the veil as a powerful illustration. Under the Old Covenant, Moses' face shone with a fading glory after meeting with God, a glory so intense he had to veil his face.

However, this glory was temporary and fading, just like the covenant it represented. In contrast, the New Covenant comes with a surpassing and lasting glory. Under this covenant, we have unfettered access to God's presence, and unlike Moses, we have no need for a veil. This speaks to the openness and transparency we can have before God and each other because of Christ's work on the cross. We are invited into a relationship marked by freedom, not fear; transformation, not condemnation.

Reflecting and Transforming (3:12-18)

> *"Therefore, since we have such a hope, we are very bold. We are not like Moses, who would put a veil over his face to prevent the Israelites from seeing the end of what was passing away. But their minds were made dull, for to this day the same veil remains when the old covenant is read. It has not been removed, because only in Christ is it taken away.*
>
> *Even to this day when Moses is read, a veil covers their hearts. But whenever anyone turns to the Lord, the veil is taken away. Now the Lord is the Spirit, and where the Spirit of the Lord is, there is freedom.*
>
> *And we all, who with unveiled faces contemplate the Lord's glory, are being transformed into his image with ever-increasing glory, which comes from the Lord, who is the Spirit."*
> (2 Corinthians 3:12-18)

Paul concludes this chapter with one of the most beautiful promises in Scripture: As we behold the glory of the Lord, we are transformed into His image with ever-increasing glory. This is the climax of the New Covenant – not just a new set of laws, but a transformational relationship with God.

This is not a passive transformation. It requires us to turn to the Lord, to gaze upon His glory. In our context, this could mean soaking in His presence through prayer, engaging deeply with His Word, and living in conscious awareness of His love and grace. As we do, the Holy Spirit works within us, changing us from the inside out.

Conclusion

As we reflect on this profound chapter, let us ask ourselves: Are we living under the freedom and transformation of the New Covenant? Are our lives reflecting the glory of the Lord to the world around us?

Let this be our prayer today: that we would be true letters of Christ, known and read by everyone; that we would not minister by the letter that brings death, but by the Spirit that gives life; and that, as we behold His glory, we would be transformed into His likeness with ever-increasing glory.

May our lives reflect the beauty and the glory of the Lord, as we live not under the old written code but in the freedom and power of the Spirit.

~ 2 CORINTHIANS 4 ~

Introduction

We now come to another really important part of Paul's second letter to the Church at Corinth. Chapter 4 speaks powerfully to the paradoxes of Christian ministry and the Christian life: power in weakness; life in death; and the treasure of the gospel held in jars of clay. In this chapter, the Apostle Paul opens his heart, sharing the realities of his struggles and the sustaining power of God's grace. Let's embark on this journey, seeking to understand and apply these timeless truths in our own lives.

The Light of the Gospel (4:1-6)

> *"Therefore, since through God's mercy we have this ministry, we do not lose heart. Rather, we have renounced secret and shameful ways; we do not use deception, nor do we distort the word of God. On the contrary, by setting forth the truth plainly we commend ourselves to everyone's conscience in the sight of God. And even if our gospel is veiled, it is veiled to those who are perishing.*
>
> *The god of this age has blinded the minds of unbelievers, so that they cannot see the light of the gospel that displays the glory of Christ, who is the image of God. For what we preach is not ourselves, but Jesus Christ as Lord, and ourselves as your servants for Jesus' sake.*
>
> *For God, who said, "Let light shine out of darkness," made his light shine in our hearts to give us the light of the knowledge of God's glory displayed in the face of Christ."*
> *(2 Corinthians 4:1-6)*

Paul starts the chapter by affirming the nature of his ministry. He has renounced secret and shameful ways, not using deception or distorting the word of God.

This commitment to transparency and truth is foundational for all Christian ministry. Paul knows the power of the gospel he carries; it is not his own message, but the revelation of Christ.

In verses 3-4, Paul addresses the issue of the gospel being veiled to those who are perishing, blinded by the god of this age. This introduces a sobering truth: not all will receive the light of the gospel. Yet, this does not deter Paul at all; instead, it fuels his commitment to preach not himself but Jesus Christ as Lord.

In our own lives, how do we approach the sharing of the gospel? Are we discouraged when people do not respond, or do we continue to shine the light of Christ, knowing that some veils are only removed through persistent prayer and faithful witness?

Treasure in Jars of Clay (4:7-12)

> *"But we have this treasure in jars of clay to show that this all-surpassing power is from God and not from us. We are hard pressed on every side, but not crushed; perplexed, but not in despair; persecuted, but not abandoned; struck down, but not destroyed. We always carry around in our body the death of Jesus, so that the life of Jesus may also be revealed in our body.*
>
> *For we who are alive are always being given over to death for Jesus' sake, so that his life may also be revealed in our mortal body. So then, death is at work in us, but life is at work in you."* (2 Corinthians 4:7-12)

This section contains yet another powerful metaphor. We have this treasure (the light of the knowledge of God's glory displayed in Christ) in jars of clay (our frail, human bodies) to show that this all-surpassing power is from God and not from us.

Paul vividly describes the afflictions he faces: hard-pressed, perplexed, persecuted, struck down. Yet, in each instance, he is not crushed, driven to despair, abandoned, or destroyed.

This passage challenges us to view our weaknesses and hardships differently. They are not signs of God's disfavour or abandonment; rather, they are the backdrop against which God's power is most clearly seen. In what areas of your life do you feel weak or afflicted? How can you allow God's power to be displayed in those areas?

Life Through Death (4:13-15)

"It is written: "I believed; therefore, I have spoken." Since we have that same spirit of[c] faith, we also believe and therefore speak, because we know that the one who raised the Lord Jesus from the dead will also raise us with Jesus and present us with you to himself. All this is for your benefit, so that the grace that is reaching more and more people may cause thanksgiving to overflow to the glory of God." (2 Corinthians 4:13-15)

Paul continues with the theme of resurrection life springing from death. He quotes Psalm 116:10, identifying with the psalmist's trust in God despite affliction. Paul's reliance on God who raises the dead is the source of his resilience. He speaks of carrying around in his body the death of Jesus so that the life of Jesus may also be revealed.

This is a profound truth for us: our sufferings, when united with Christ, can lead to life for ourselves and others. Our trials are not pointless; they can serve to advance the gospel and bring grace to many. How does this perspective change the way you view your current struggles or pains?

Fixing Our Eyes on What Is Unseen (4:16-18)

"Therefore, we do not lose heart. Though outwardly we are wasting away, yet inwardly we are being renewed day by day. For our light and momentary troubles are achieving for us an eternal glory that far outweighs them all. So, we fix our eyes not on what is seen, but on what is unseen, since what is seen is temporary, but what is unseen is eternal." (2 Corinthians 4:16-18)

Paul concludes the chapter by contrasting the outer and inner self. Though outwardly we are wasting away, inwardly we are being renewed day by day. He encourages us not to lose heart, focusing not on temporary troubles but on eternal glory. The challenges we face now are preparing for us an eternal glory that far outweighs them all. This perspective is not natural; it's supernatural. It requires a shift from the visible to the invisible, from the temporal to the eternal.

What are the temporary troubles that have been weighing you down? How can you begin to view them in light of eternal glory? Conclusion: Carrying the Light of Christ

As we close, let's remember the central message of 2 Corinthians chapter 4. We carry the extraordinary treasure of the gospel in our ordinary, fragile lives. This contrast between the treasure and the clay pots highlights God's power, not our strength.

Let us walk each day in humility, recognizing our weakness but embracing the power of Christ within us. May we be vessels of His light, boldly proclaiming the gospel while relying on His strength in every affliction. And may our eyes remain fixed on the eternal, allowing the temporary trials to shape us into His likeness, preparing us for an eternal weight of glory beyond all comparison.

~ 2 CORINTHIANS 5 ~

Introduction

In this chapter, the Apostle Paul dives deep into the heart of the Christian identity, calling, and hope. He reveals the radical transformation that occurs in us through Christ and challenges us to live as ambassadors for Christ in the world. Let's allow the Holy Spirit to guide our understanding and application of these eternal truths.

The Eternal House and the Earthly Tent (5:1-5)

"For we know that if the earthly tent we live in is destroyed, we have a building from God, an eternal house in heaven, not built by human hands. Meanwhile we groan, longing to be clothed instead with our heavenly dwelling, because when we are clothed, we will not be found naked.

For while we are in this tent, we groan and are burdened, because we do not wish to be unclothed but to be clothed instead with our heavenly dwelling, so that what is mortal may be swallowed up by life.

Now the one who has fashioned us for this very purpose is God, who has given us the Spirit as a deposit, guaranteeing what is to come." (2 Corinthians 5:1-5)

Paul begins this chapter with a powerful metaphor contrasting our earthly bodies (our 'earthly tent') with our future resurrection bodies (our 'eternal house in heaven'). This imagery speaks to our transient state in this world and our eternal destiny with God. Our current suffering and "groaning" are not pointless; they are the birth pangs of a greater reality, our eternal home with God.

This perspective shifts how we view our lives and sufferings. Instead of clinging desperately to the temporary, we are called to live with eternity in mind. How does this eternal perspective change the way you approach your challenges, hopes, and fears?

Living by Faith, Not by Sight (5:6-10)

"Therefore, we are always confident and know that as long as we are at home in the body, we are away from the Lord For we live by faith, not by sight. We are confident, I say, and would prefer to be away from the body and at home with the Lord.

So, we make it our goal to please him, whether we are at home in the body or away from it. For we must all appear before the judgment seat of Christ, so that each of us may receive what is due us for the things done while in the body, whether good or bad." (2 Corinthians 5:6-10)

Paul continues by affirming that while we are at home in the body, we are away from the Lord, and thus, we live by faith, not by sight. This statement is a call to trust in the unseen realities of God's kingdom, even as we navigate the seen world. Our ultimate goal is to please Him, whether we are here in the body or away from it, knowing we must all appear before the judgment seat of Christ.

This passage challenges us to examine our priorities and actions: Are we living to please God, or are our efforts directed towards pleasing ourselves or others? How can we cultivate a life of faith that seeks to please God in all things?

The Ministry of Reconciliation (5:11-21)

"Since then, we know what it is to fear the Lord, we try to persuade others. What we are is plain to God, and I hope it is also plain to your conscience. We are not trying to commend ourselves to you again but are giving you an opportunity to take pride in us, so that you can answer those who take pride in what is seen rather than in what is in the heart. If we are "out of our mind," as some say, it is for God; if we are in our right mind, it is for you.

For Christ's love compels us, because we are convinced that one died for all, and therefore all died. And he died for all, that those who live should no longer live for themselves but for him who died for them and was raised again."

"So, from now on we regard no one from a worldly point of view. Though we once regarded Christ in this way, we do so no longer. Therefore, if anyone is in Christ, the new creation has come: The old has gone, the new is here!

All this is from God, who reconciled us to himself through Christ and gave us the ministry of reconciliation: that God was reconciling the world to himself in Christ, not counting people's sins against them. And he has committed to us the message of reconciliation.

We are therefore Christ's ambassadors, as though God were making his appeal through us. We implore you on Christ's behalf: Be reconciled to God. God made him who had no sin to be sin for us, so that in him we might become the righteousness of God."
(2 Corinthians 5:11-21)

Here lies the heart of this whole chapter: Paul's exposition on the ministry of reconciliation. Through Christ, God was reconciling the world to Himself, not counting people's sins against them. And He has committed to us the message of reconciliation. We are therefore Christ's ambassadors, as though God were making His appeal through us.

This is a profound calling! As believers, we are not merely saved from something (sin and death) but for something – participating in God's redemptive work in the world. This ministry of reconciliation goes beyond personal peace to include the calling to bring others into this peace with God.

Reflect on your role as an ambassador for Christ. How are you participating in this ministry of reconciliation in your daily life? How does understanding yourself as an ambassador for Christ change how you interact with those around you?

Verse 17 is monumental: *"Therefore, if anyone is in Christ, the new creation has come: The old has gone, the new is here!"* This is the essence of our identity as followers of Christ. We are not merely improved versions of our old selves; we are entirely new creations.

This new identity has significant implications for how we view ourselves and our past. It's not our past failures, our achievements, or even our social status that define us; it is our new identity in Christ. How does embracing your identity as a new creation in Christ change the way you view yourself and your past?

Conclusion

As we conclude, we really should reflect on the profound truths of 2 Corinthians Chapter 5. We are reminded of our hope for an eternal home, our call to live by faith, our ministry of reconciliation, and our new identity as creations in Christ.

May we leave here today not only inspired by these truths but transformed by them. Let us live as ambassadors for Christ, carrying the message of reconciliation to a broken world, and walking confidently as new creations, defined not by our past but by our future in Him.

Let us pray for the courage and strength to live out this high calling, for the wisdom to navigate our earthly tents with eternal perspectives, and for the love and power to be effective ambassadors of Christ's reconciliation.

Introduction

We now approach the incredibly rich and challenging words of 2 Corinthians Chapter 6. In this passage, Apostle Paul delves into the heart of the Christian ministry, detailing the trials, the character, and the urgent call of those who serve God. Let us listen, reflect, and apply these timeless truths, understanding what it means to be God's servants in a world that often stands in opposition to His ways.

The Urgency of Reconciliation (6:1-2)

> *"As God's co-workers we urge you not to receive God's grace in vain. For he says, "In the time of my favour I heard you, and in the day of salvation I helped you." I tell you, now is the time of God's favour, now is the day of salvation." (2 Corinthians 6:1-2)*

Paul begins this chapter with a compelling plea: *"As God's co-workers we urge you not to receive God's grace in vain."* He reminds us that the message of reconciliation we carry with us is urgent, grounded in the 'now' of God's favour and the 'day' of salvation.

This urgency is not born out of panic but out of the recognition of the precious opportunity that each moment presents to live out and spread the gospel.

In your life, how are you responding to this call of urgency? Are you living in a way that reflects the immediate and pressing nature of God's kingdom work?

The Marks of God's Servants (6:3-10)

> *"We put no stumbling block in anyone's path, so that our ministry will not be discredited. Rather, as servants of God we commend ourselves in every way: in great endurance; in troubles, hardships and distresses; in beatings, imprisonments and riots; in hard work, sleepless nights and hunger; in purity, understanding, patience and kindness; in the Holy Spirit and in sincere love."*

"... in truthful speech and in the power of God; with weapons of righteousness in the right hand and in the left; through glory and dishonour, bad report and good report; genuine, yet regarded as impostors; known, yet regarded as unknown; dying, and yet we live on; beaten, and yet not killed; sorrowful, yet always rejoicing; poor, yet making many rich; having nothing, and yet possessing everything." (2 Corinthians 6:3-10)

In this rich passage, Paul outlines the paradoxical nature of the Christian ministry through a series of contrasts: seen as impostors, yet genuine; as unknown, yet well known; dying, and yet we live on; punished, yet not killed; sorrowful, yet always rejoicing; poor, yet making many rich; having nothing, and yet possessing everything.

These contrasts reveal the reality of serving Christ in a fallen world. They show that the external circumstances of our lives do not define our identity or the validity of our ministry. Rather, it is our steadfastness, our faith, and our joy in Christ that shine forth in the darkest of times.

Reflect on your own journey. In what ways have you experienced these paradoxes in your life? How can you continue to serve faithfully amidst the challenges you face?

The Call to Holiness (6:11-18)

"We have spoken freely to you, Corinthians, and opened wide our hearts to you. We are not withholding our affection from you, but you are withholding yours from us. As a fair exchange - I speak as to my children - open wide your hearts also.

Do not be yoked together with unbelievers. For what do righteousness and wickedness have in common? Or what fellowship can light have with darkness? What harmony is there between Christ and Belial?

Or what does a believer have in common with an unbeliever? What agreement is there between the temple of God and idols? For we are the temple of the living God."

"As God has said: 'I will live with them and walk among them, and I will be their God, and they will be my people.' Therefore, "Come out from them and be separate, says the Lord. Touch no unclean thing, and I will receive you. And, "I will be a Father to you, and you will be my sons and daughters, says the Lord Almighty." (2 Corinthians 6:11-18)

Paul shifts his focus to the relationships of the Corinthians, urging them not to be yoked together with unbelievers. This is not a call to isolation but to holiness; it's about ensuring that our deepest alliances and commitments reflect the transformative power of the gospel. The call to come out and be separate is not one of physical removal from the world but a command to be distinct in our values, actions, and relationships.

This section challenges us to examine our lives: Are there areas where we are compromising our commitment to Christ for the sake of comfort, convenience, or acceptance? How can we live as people of God in a way that is true to our calling and distinct from the world around us?

Paul concludes this chapter with the glorious promises of God: "I will live with them and walk among them, and I will be their God, and they will be my people." This is the heart of the gospel – God dwelling with His people. It's a promise that provides us with profound comfort, motivation, and identity.

These promises are not just future hopes; they are present realities. God walks with us, lives in us, and claims us as His own. How does the reality of God's presence and commitment change the way you live? How does it affect the way you view yourself and your call to holiness?

Conclusion

As we close, let's remember the key messages from 2 Corinthians Chapter 6. We are called to grasp the urgency of God's work, to endure hardships as God's servants, to pursue holiness in all our relationships, and to live in the light of God's promises.

Let this chapter not only be a call to reflection but a call to action. May we be inspired to live out the reality of our identity as God's people, embracing the paradoxes of the Christian life, and holding fast to the promises of God's presence and love.

Let us pray for the grace to live as true servants of God, marked by purity, understanding, patience, kindness, the Holy Spirit, and sincere love. May our lives be a testament to the enduring power and presence of our God.

Introduction

Chapter 7 is indeed a profound and moving portion of Scripture. It is here where the Apostle Paul shares his heart and reveals the dynamic of godly sorrow leading to repentance, transformation, and ultimately, joy. As we unpack this chapter, let's open our hearts to the lessons the Holy Spirit wants to teach us about repentance, reconciliation, and the deep, cleansing work of godly sorrow in our lives.

Holiness in the Light of God's Promises (7:1)

"Therefore, since we have these promises, dear friends, let us purify ourselves from everything that contaminates body and spirit, perfecting holiness out of reverence for God." (2 Corinthians 7:1)

Paul begins with a stirring call: "Since we have these promises, dear friends, let us purify ourselves from everything that contaminates body and spirit, perfecting holiness out of reverence for God." The promises Paul refers to are those of God's indwelling presence and fatherly relationship with us. These are not light promises; they carry the weight of divine commitment and love.

This opening verse sets a tone of serious reflection: Are we living in light of God's promises? The call to purify ourselves is not about legalistic self-effort but about a response to the overwhelming grace we've been given. It's a call to examine our lives, to align our actions, thoughts, and desires with the holiness of God, out of reverence, not fear. What does this purification look like in your life today?

Paul's Joy in the Corinthians' Repentance (7:2-7)

"Make room for us in your hearts. We have wronged no one, we have corrupted no one, we have exploited no one. I do not say this to condemn you; I have said before that you have such a place in our hearts that we would live or die with you."

"I have spoken to you with great frankness; I take great pride in you. I am greatly encouraged; in all our troubles my joy knows no bounds. For when we came into Macedonia, we had no rest, but we were harassed at every turn - conflicts on the outside, fears within.

But God, who comforts the downcast, comforted us by the coming of Titus, and not only by his coming but also by the comfort you had given him. He told us about your longing for me, your deep sorrow, your ardent concern for me, so that my joy was greater than ever." (2 Corinthians 7:2-7)

Paul transitions to a personal note, defending his actions and motives towards the Corinthians. He asks for openness, having wronged no one, corrupted no one, and exploited no one. It's a plea for mutual understanding and affection.

Then, Paul moves to express his joy over the Corinthians' response to his previous letter (likely referring to what we call 1 Corinthians). Despite the severe challenges and the "godly sorrow" it produced, it led to their repentance. Notice how Paul distinguishes between worldly sorrow, leading to death, and godly sorrow, leading to salvation.

This section asks us to reflect on our own responses to correction. Do we respond with defensiveness and denial, or with a soft heart that leads to genuine change? Paul's joy is not in the pain caused but in the transformation it led to. How do we view the discipline and correction of the Lord in our lives?

The Power of Godly Sorrow (7:8-11)

"Even if I caused you sorrow by my letter, I do not regret it. Though I did regret it - I see that my letter hurt you, but only for a little while - yet now I am happy, not because you were made sorry, but because your sorrow led you to repentance. For you became sorrowful as God intended and so were not harmed in any way by us. Godly sorrow brings repentance that leads to salvation and leaves no regret, but worldly sorrow brings death."

"See what this godly sorrow has produced in you: what earnestness, what eagerness to clear yourselves, what indignation, what alarm, what longing, what concern, what readiness to see justice done. At every point you have proved yourselves to be innocent in this matter." (2 Corinthians 7:8-11)

Here, Paul elaborates on the concept of godly sorrow. This isn't mere regret over consequences or a superficial apology. Godly sorrow involves a deep, heartfelt response to the realization that we have grieved God's heart. It's a sorrow that leads to decisive action, to earnestness, eagerness to clear oneself, indignation, alarm, longing, concern, and readiness to see justice done.

Look at the transformation in the Corinthians: from apathy and defiance to zeal and vindication. This is the fruit of true repentance, a complete turnaround not just in behaviour but in heart attitude. Let's ask ourselves: Does our sorrow over sin lead us to such transformation, or are we stuck in the cycle of worldly sorrow with no real change?

Reconciliation and Renewal (7:12-16)

"So even though I wrote to you, it was neither on account of the one who did the wrong nor on account of the injured party, but rather that before God you could see for yourselves how devoted to us you are. By all this we are encouraged. In addition to our own encouragement, we were especially delighted to see how happy Titus was, because his spirit has been refreshed by all of you. I had boasted to him about you, and you have not embarrassed me.

But just as everything we said to you was true, so our boasting about you to Titus has proved to be true as well. And his affection for you is all the greater when he remembers that you were all obedient, receiving him with fear and trembling. I am glad I can have complete confidence in you." (2 Corinthians 7:12-16)

In concluding the chapter, Paul reveals his deeper purpose: not just to defend himself or to cause pain, but to show his deep love for the Corinthians.

The outcome is joyful: Titus reports back about the Corinthians' longing, mourning, and zeal for Paul, reflecting a full circle of reconciliation and renewal.

This ending underscores the beauty of restored relationships within the body of Christ. It speaks to the power of sincere repentance and the depth of spiritual leadership that seeks restoration over punishment.

Conclusion

As we finish this chapter, let's take to heart the powerful lessons Paul has given us here. Let's not shy away from the cleansing pain of godly sorrow, for it has the power to lead us to true repentance and renewal.

May we respond to the Holy Spirit's conviction with openness and humility, allowing His godly sorrow to work deep within us, transforming us from the inside out. And as we experience this deep cleansing, may we also know the overwhelming joy of restored fellowship with God and with each other.

Let us pray now for the courage to embrace godly sorrow, for the grace to repent sincerely, and for the joy of deeper communion with our Father and with our brothers and sisters in Christ.

~ 2 CORINTHIANS 8 ~

Introduction

In this chapter, the Apostle Paul challenges us to consider the nature of giving, not merely as an obligation or a duty but as a privilege and a reflection of God's grace in our lives.

As we explore this profound chapter, let us open our hearts to what the Spirit might reveal about the way we view and practice giving.

The Example of the Macedonian Churches (8:1-5)

"And now, brothers and sisters, we want you to know about the grace that God has given the Macedonian churches. In the midst of a very severe trial, their overflowing joy and their extreme poverty welled up in rich generosity.

For I testify that they gave as much as they were able, and even beyond their ability. Entirely on their own, they urgently pleaded with us for the privilege of sharing in this service to the Lord's people. And they exceeded our expectations: They gave themselves first of all to the Lord, and then by the will of God also to us."
(2 Corinthians 8:1-5)

Paul begins with an inspiring account of the churches in Macedonia. Despite severe trial and extreme poverty, these believers overflowed with rich generosity, giving beyond their ability, entirely on their own initiative.

Notice, their giving was not primarily about the amount; it was about the attitude. They gave themselves first to the Lord and then by the will of God, also to Paul's mission.

This sets a profound precedent for us. True generosity starts with giving ourselves to God. It's about a heart fully surrendered and committed to God's purposes.

Reflect on your own giving: is it a reflection of a heart wholly given to God, or is it merely a religious obligation?

The Call to Excel in the Grace of Giving (8:6-8)

"So we urged Titus, just as he had earlier made a beginning, to bring also to completion this act of grace on your part.

But since you excel in everything - in faith, in speech, in knowledge, in complete earnestness and in the love we have kindled in you - see that you also excel in this grace of giving.

I am not commanding you, but I want to test the sincerity of your love by comparing it with the earnestness of others."
(2 Corinthians 8:6-8)

Paul encourages the Corinthian church to excel in the grace of giving, just as they excel in everything else - faith, speech, knowledge, and love. Here, giving is described as a grace, something that flows from God's own nature into ours. It's not about equalizing wealth but about expressing the equality of our shared commitment to one another in Christ.

Consider your own life: in what areas are you excelling? Is giving one of them? How does the understanding that giving is a grace, a gift from God, change the way you approach generosity?

The Example of Christ (8:9)

"For you know the grace of our Lord Jesus Christ, that though he was rich, yet for your sake he became poor, so that you through his poverty might become rich." (2 Corinthians 8:9)

In this single verse, Paul captures the essence of Christian giving by pointing to the example of Christ Himself: "Though he was rich, yet for your sake he became poor, so that you through his poverty might become rich." Jesus' act of giving was the ultimate act of grace - He gave Himself entirely for us.

This reality should profoundly impact our perspective on giving. Our giving is a response to the immense generosity we have received in Christ. How does the sacrificial giving of Jesus influence your own willingness to give?

Encouragement and Integrity in Giving (8:10-15)

"And here is my judgment about what is best for you in this matter. Last year you were the first not only to give but also to have the desire to do so. Now finish the work, so that your eager willingness to do it may be matched by your completion of it, according to your means. For if the willingness is there, the gift is acceptable according to what one has, not according to what one does not have.

Our desire is not that others might be relieved while you are hard pressed, but that there might be equality. At the present time your plenty will supply what they need, so that in turn their plenty will supply what you need.

The goal is equality, as it is written: "The one who gathered much did not have too much, and the one who gathered little did not have too little."(2 Corinthians 8:10-15)

Paul proceeds to offer practical advice about giving, urging the Corinthians to follow through on their earlier commitment. He speaks of the desire to give as being more important than the amount given. This teaches us that God values the disposition of our heart above the size of our gift.

Moreover, Paul emphasizes the importance of integrity and accountability in the handling of gifts. This reminds us that our stewardship of God's resources is a significant part of our Christian witness. How does this affect the way you view your commitments and the management of your resources?

The Role of Titus and the Other Brothers (8:16-24)

"Thanks be to God, who put into the heart of Titus the same concern I have for you. For Titus not only welcomed our appeal, but he is coming to you with much enthusiasm and on his own initiative. And we are sending along with him the brother who is praised by all the churches for his service to the gospel. What is more, he was chosen by the churches to accompany us as we carry the offering, which we administer in order to honour the Lord himself and to show our eagerness to help."

" We want to avoid any criticism of the way we administer this liberal gift. For we are taking pains to do what is right, not only in the eyes of the Lord but also in the eyes of man.

In addition, we are sending with them our brother who has often proved to us in many ways that he is zealous, and now even more so because of his great confidence in you. As for Titus, he is my partner and co-worker among you; as for our brothers, they are representatives of the churches and an honour to Christ. Therefore show these men the proof of your love and the reason for our pride in you, so that the churches can see it." (2 Corinthians 8:16-24)

Paul concludes the chapter by commending Titus and other brothers who have been entrusted with the task of administering this act of grace. Their dedication and integrity in service underscore the communal and collaborative nature of Christian giving. It's not just about individual acts of generosity but about the collective responsibility and mutual accountability within the body of Christ.

This passage invites us to consider our own roles within our community. Are we participating, supporting, and ensuring accountability in the acts of grace within our church and community?

Conclusion

As we reflect on chapter 8, let us be challenged and encouraged to view our resources and our capacity to give through the lens of God's grace. Let our giving not be grudging or forced but a joyful overflow of a heart in love with God, responding to the incomparable gift of Jesus Christ.

May we, like the Macedonian churches, give ourselves first to the Lord, allowing His grace to transform us into generous givers, reflecting the generosity of Christ Himself. Let this week be a time of examining our hearts and practices concerning giving, ensuring that they align with the principles of generosity, integrity, and love we find in God's Word.

~ 2 CORINTHIANS 9 ~

Introduction

In chapter 9 the Apostle Paul continues to unfold the principles of Christian giving, weaving together the themes of generosity, stewardship, and divine blessing. This chapter is not merely about the mechanics of giving but the heart behind it and the transformative power it holds for both the giver and the recipient. As we explore these verses, let's ask God to challenge and expand our understanding of generosity.

Preparation and the Heart of Giving (9:1-5)

"There is no need for me to write to you about this service to the Lord's people. For I know your eagerness to help, and I have been boasting about it to the Macedonians, telling them that since last year you in Achaia were ready to give; and your enthusiasm has stirred most of them to action. But I am sending the brothers in order that our boasting about you in this matter should not prove hollow, but that you may be ready, as I said you would be. For if any Macedonians come with me and find you unprepared, we - not to say anything about you - would be ashamed of having been so confident. So, I thought it necessary to urge the brothers to visit you in advance and finish the arrangements for the generous gift you had promised. Then it will be ready as a generous gift, not as one grudgingly given." (2 Corinthians 9:1-5)

Paul begins this chapter by addressing the readiness of the Corinthians to give, highlighting the importance of preparedness in our acts of generosity. He commends their eagerness, which has inspired others, yet he sends brothers ahead to ensure their promised gift is ready as a willing gift, not as an exaction.

This speaks to the heart of giving in the Christian life - it should be prepared, enthusiastic, and voluntary, not reluctant or under compulsion. Reflect on your approach to giving. Is it marked by readiness and eagerness? How can we prepare our hearts and resources to respond generously to the needs around us and to God's prompting?

The Principle of Sowing and Reaping (9:6-8)

"Remember this: Whoever sows sparingly will also reap sparingly, and whoever sows generously will also reap generously. Each of you should give what you have decided in your heart to give, not reluctantly or under compulsion, for God loves a cheerful giver.

And God is able to bless you abundantly, so that in all things at all times, having all that you need, you will abound in every good work." (2 Corinthians 9:6-8)

Paul introduces a powerful agricultural metaphor here: Whoever sows sparingly will also reap sparingly, and whoever sows generously will also reap generously. This is not a transactional formula but a spiritual principle reflecting the nature of God's kingdom. Our giving is likened to sowing seeds which, when planted generously, will result in a bountiful harvest.

This principle challenges us to examine our own giving. Are we sowing sparingly, giving the minimum, or are we sowing generously, trusting God for the harvest? Remember, the harvest is not just financial; it includes increased righteousness, enriched relationships, and the joy of seeing God's work unfold.

Cheerful Giving and God's Provision (9:9-11)

"As it is written: "They have freely scattered their gifts to the poor; their righteousness endures forever." Now he who supplies seed to the sower and bread for food will also supply and increase your store of seed and will enlarge the harvest of your righteousness. You will be enriched in every way so that you can be generous on every occasion, and through us your generosity will result in thanksgiving to God." (2 Corinthians 9:9-11)

Each person should give what they have decided in their heart to give, not reluctantly or under compulsion, for God loves a cheerful giver. This verse underscores the attitude with which we are to give. Our giving should not be grudging or out of guilt, but cheerful and from a heart of gratitude.

Moreover, Paul reassures us of God's abundant provision: God is able to bless you abundantly, so that in all things at all times, having all that you need, you will abound in every good work. This is the promise that accompanies our giving - God will not only meet our needs but will also enable us to continue being generous in His work.

How does the promise of God's provision impact your own willingness to give? Are you trusting in His supply, or are you holding back out of fear or uncertainty?

Paul continues, quoting Scripture to affirm that the one who supplies seed to the sower will also supply and increase your store of seed and will enlarge the harvest of your righteousness. Here, the harvest is explicitly connected to righteousness - a right standing and right living before God. Our generosity is not only an act of obedience but a pathway to greater righteousness.

This passage invites us to see giving as an integral part of our spiritual growth and expression of our faith. How does this view change your perception of generosity? Can you see your giving as a part of your journey towards righteousness?

Resulting in Thanksgiving to God (9:12-15)

"This service that you perform is not only supplying the needs of the Lord's people but is also overflowing in many expressions of thanks to God. Because of the service by which you have proved yourselves, others will praise God for the obedience that accompanies your confession of the gospel of Christ, and for your generosity in sharing with them and with everyone else. And in their prayers for you their hearts will go out to you, because of the surpassing grace God has given you. Thanks be to God for his indescribable gift!" (2 Corinthians 9:12-15)

Finally, Paul emphasizes that the service of giving does not only supply the needs of God's people but also overflows in many expressions of thanks to God. Our generosity then leads to thanksgiving, glorifying God as others recognize His provision and grace at work.

This completes the circle of generosity: from God to us, from us to others, and from others back to God in the form of praise. Consider the broader impact of your giving. How does it extend beyond the immediate context, contributing to a greater culture of gratitude and glorifying God in the community and beyond?

Conclusion

As we close, let's allow 2 Corinthians 9 to sink deeply into our hearts. God invites us into the joy and privilege of generosity, not as mere donors but as sowers in the field of His great kingdom, anticipating a wonderful harvest of righteousness, provision, and thanksgiving.

Let's commit to being cheerful givers, trusting in God's abundant provision, and looking forward to the harvest that our generosity will bring - not only in our lives but in the lives of those around us and in the very heart of God's kingdom.

~ 2 CORINTHIANS 10 ~

Introduction

Now the Apostle Paul confronts the challenges he faces with the Corinthian church, setting a firm foundation for understanding spiritual warfare, the nature of our ministry, and the true metrics of godly success.

As we explore this chapter, let us invite the Holy Spirit to reveal the deeper truths contained within these verses and how they apply to our lives today.

Spiritual Authority and Humility (10:1-2)

> *"By the humility and gentleness of Christ, I appeal to you - I, Paul, who am "timid" when face to face with you, but "bold" toward you when away! I beg you that when I come, I may not have to be as bold as I expect to be toward some people who think that we live by the standards of this world." (2 Corinthians 10:1-2)*

Paul begins this chapter with an appeal for understanding, basing his argument on the meekness and gentleness of Christ. Despite accusations of being bold from afar but timid when present, Paul asserts his readiness to exercise apostolic authority if necessary. This juxtaposition of meekness with assertiveness introduces us to the Christian paradox: true strength is found in humility and gentleness, grounded in the character of Christ.

Reflect on your own approach to conflict and authority. Do you rely on worldly standards of aggression and force, or do you operate from a place of Christlike gentleness, rooted in the confidence of your spiritual authority in Him?

The Nature of Our Warfare (10:3-6)

> *"For though we live in the world, we do not wage war as the world does. The weapons we fight with are not the weapons of the world. On the contrary, they have divine power to demolish strongholds."*

"We demolish arguments and every pretension that sets itself up against the knowledge of God, and we take captive every thought to make it obedient to Christ. And we will be ready to punish every act of disobedience, once your obedience is complete."
(2 Corinthians 10:3-6)

Paul shifts the focus from his personal defence to the broader spiritual conflict at hand, asserting, "For though we live in the world, we do not wage war as the world does." He emphasizes that the weapons we fight with are not the weapons of the world but have divine power to demolish strongholds. This passage challenges us to re-evaluate our strategies in facing life's battles. Are we engaging in spiritual warfare with the tools and tactics of the world, or are we utilizing the spiritual weapons provided to us by God - prayer, the Word of God, righteousness, faith, the gospel of peace, salvation, and the Spirit?

Paul also speaks of taking captive every thought to make it obedient to Christ. This is a powerful reminder of the battlefield within the mind and the importance of aligning our thoughts with the truth of God's Word. How are you guarding your mind and taking your thoughts captive in obedience to Christ?

Boasting in the Lord (10:7-12)

"You are judging by appearances. If anyone is confident that they belong to Christ, they should consider again that we belong to Christ just as much as they do. So even if I boast somewhat freely about the authority the Lord gave us for building you up rather than tearing you down, I will not be ashamed of it. I do not want to seem to be trying to frighten you with my letters. For some say, "His letters are weighty and forceful, but in person he is unimpressive and his speaking amounts to nothing." Such people should realize that what we are in our letters when we are absent, we will be in our actions when we are present. We do not dare to classify or compare ourselves with some who commend themselves. When they measure themselves by themselves and compare themselves with themselves, they are not wise."
(2 Corinthians 10:7-12)

Paul addresses the issue of boasting, urging the Corinthians to look beyond the surface and consider the truth of Christ within them. He defends his ministry, not on the basis of outward appearances or human commendation but on the authority and area of influence God has assigned to him.

This prompts us to consider the basis of our own boasting. Is it in our achievements, appearances, or human approval? Or is our boasting solely in the Lord, in what He has done in us and through us? Let's examine where our true confidence lies.

Staying Within Our God-Given Boundaries (10:13-18)

"We, however, will not boast beyond proper limits, but will confine our boasting to the sphere of service God himself has assigned to us, a sphere that also includes you.

We are not going too far in our boasting, as would be the case if we had not come to you, for we did get as far as you with the gospel of Christ.

Neither do we go beyond our limits by boasting of work done by others. Our hope is that, as your faith continues to grow, our sphere of activity among you will greatly expand, so that we can preach the gospel in the regions beyond you.

For we do not want to boast about work already done in someone else's territory. But, "Let the one who boasts boast in the Lord." For it is not the one who commends himself who is approved, but the one whom the Lord commends." (2 Corinthians 10:13-18)

Paul concludes by underscoring the importance of staying within the boundaries God has set for us, not overextending ourselves beyond our God-given sphere. Here Paul emphasizes that true commendation comes from the Lord, not from self-praise.

In our own lives, this calls us to a humble assessment of our ministries and responsibilities. Are we trying to operate beyond what God has called and equipped us to do, or are we faithfully stewarding the roles and opportunities He has entrusted to us?

Conclusion

As we close, let's reflect on the lessons from Chapter 10. We are called to wage spiritual warfare, not with worldly tactics but with divine power that can break down strongholds. We are urged to embrace humility, align our thoughts with Christ, and find our boasting only in the Lord.

May we leave here empowered to fight our spiritual battles with the weapons God has given us, standing firm in the truth of His Word, and walking in the humility and authority of Christ.

Let us pray for the grace to apply these truths in our daily lives, that we might be effective soldiers for the Kingdom, advancing not our agendas, but the glorious gospel of our Lord Jesus Christ.

~ 2 CORINTHIANS 11 ~

Introduction

In this chapter, the Apostle Paul wants to expose false apostles and defend his apostolic authority, not for his sake but for the integrity of the Gospel and the well-being of the Corinthian church. As we explore this chapter, let's open our hearts to the Holy Spirit's guidance, discerning the truths that safeguard our faith and the purity of our devotion to Christ.

The Jealousy of God and the Simplicity of Christ (11:1-4)

> *"I hope you will put up with me in a little foolishness. Yes, please put up with me! I am jealous for you with a godly jealousy. I promised you to one husband, to Christ, so that I might present you as a pure virgin to him.*
>
> *But I am afraid that just as Eve was deceived by the serpent's cunning, your minds may somehow be led astray from your sincere and pure devotion to Christ.*
>
> *For if someone comes to you and preaches a Jesus other than the Jesus we preached, or if you receive a different spirit from the Spirit you received, or a different gospel from the one you accepted, you put up with it easily enough."*
> (2 Corinthians 11:1-4)

Paul begins with a plea for patience as he enters into what he calls a "foolish" boast. His tone is ironic, yet behind it lies a deep concern: the spiritual well-being of the Corinthian believers. He expresses a godly jealousy, for he has betrothed them to one husband, Christ, but fears that just as Eve was deceived, their minds might be led astray from the simplicity and purity of devotion to Christ.

This introduction challenges us: Are we maintaining our pure devotion to Christ, or are we, like the early Corinthians, susceptible to being led astray by seemingly "new" or "more sophisticated" teachings that distort the simplicity of the Gospel?

The Danger of False Apostles (5:5-15)

"I do not think I am in the least inferior to those 'super-apostles.' I may indeed be untrained as a speaker, but I do have knowledge. We have made this perfectly clear to you in every way. Was it a sin for me to lower myself in order to elevate you by preaching the gospel of God to you free of charge? I robbed other churches by receiving support from them so as to serve you.

And when I was with you and needed something, I was not a burden to anyone, for the brothers who came from Macedonia supplied what I needed. I have kept myself from being a burden to you in any way and will continue to do so. As surely as the truth of Christ is in me, nobody in the regions of Achaia will stop this boasting of mine. Why? Because I do not love you? God knows I do!

And I will keep on doing what I am doing in order to cut the ground from under those who want an opportunity to be considered equal with us in the things they boast about. For such people are false apostles, deceitful workers, masquerading as apostles of Christ.

And no wonder, for Satan himself masquerades as an angel of light. It is not surprising, then, if his servants also masquerade as servants of righteousness. Their end will be what their actions deserve." (2 Corinthians 11:5-15)

Paul contrasts himself with the so-called "super-apostles," asserting that he is in no way inferior to them, despite his humble manner and speech. He warns the Corinthians about these false teachers who masquerade as apostles of Christ, just as Satan disguises himself as an angel of light. The deception is subtle, and the stakes are high: the very Gospel of Christ.

This segment of Scripture calls us to vigilance and discernment. False teachings often appear attractive, even enlightening, but they lead away from the truth of Christ. How can we, as modern believers, guard against such deception? Are we grounding ourselves in the Word of God, enabling us to discern between truth and falsehood?

In verses 7-12, Paul explains the reasoning behind his refusal to accept support from the Corinthians: to cut the ground from under those who seek to discredit his apostolic calling. He defends his choice to preach the Gospel free of charge as a mark of his genuine love for them and commitment to the Gospel, not as a sign of unworthiness. This passage challenges our basic understanding of ministry and sacrifice. Paul's example prompts us to consider: What are we willing to endure for the sake of the Gospel? Are our leaders and we ourselves motivated by love and sacrifice, or by personal gain and recognition?

Paul's Sufferings for Christ (11:16-33)

"I repeat: Let no one take me for a fool. But if you do, then tolerate me just as you would a fool, so that I may do a little boasting. In this self-confident boasting I am not talking as the Lord would, but as a fool.

Since many are boasting in the way the world does, I too will boast. You gladly put up with fools since you are so wise! In fact, you even put up with anyone who enslaves you or exploits you or takes advantage of you or puts on airs or slaps you in the face. To my shame I admit that we were too weak for that!

Whatever anyone else dares to boast about - I am speaking as a fool — I also dare to boast about. Are they Hebrews? So am I. Are they Israelites? So am I. Are they Abraham's descendants? So am I. Are they servants of Christ? (I am out of my mind to talk like this.) I am more.

I have worked much harder, been in prison more frequently, been flogged more severely, and been exposed to death again and again. Five times I received from the Jews the forty lashes minus one. Three times I was beaten with rods, once I was pelted with stones, three times I was shipwrecked, I spent a night and a day in the open sea, I have been constantly on the move. I have been in danger from rivers, in danger from bandits, in danger from my fellow Jews, in danger from Gentiles; in danger in the city, in danger in the country, in danger at sea; and in danger from false believers."

"I have laboured and toiled and have often gone without sleep; I have known hunger and thirst and have often gone without food; I have been cold and naked. Besides everything else, I face daily the pressure of my concern for all the churches. Who is weak, and I do not feel weak? Who is led into sin, and I do not inwardly burn?

If I must boast, I will boast of the things that show my weakness. The God and Father of the Lord Jesus, who is to be praised forever, knows that I am not lying. In Damascus the governor under King Aretas had the city of the Damascenes guarded in order to arrest me. But I was lowered in a basket from a window in the wall and slipped through his hands." (2 Corinthians 11:16-33)

Paul continues his 'foolish' boasting, listing the hardships he has endured for the sake of the Gospel. This is no ordinary boast; it is a litany of sufferings – beatings, imprisonments, shipwrecks, and constant dangers. These are the important credentials of his apostleship, not the worldly successes but the sufferings that align him with Christ.

This part of the chapter is a sobering reminder that the Christian life and ministry are not paths to glory and comfort but often to suffering and sacrifice. How does Paul's example of suffering for Christ challenge our expectations of the Christian life? Are we prepared to bear hardships for the sake of His name?

Conclusion

As we conclude, let's reflect on the central messages of 2 Corinthians Chapter 11. Paul's passionate defence of his ministry and the stark warnings against false apostles compel us to examine our own faith and the teachings we embrace. In a world filled with spiritual deception, we must cling to the true Gospel, the simple yet profound message of Christ crucified and risen. May we, like Paul, be willing to endure all things for the sake of the Gospel, holding fast to the truth in love, grace, and with an unwavering commitment to our Lord Jesus Christ.

Introduction

As we approach the final stage of this wonderful letter, Paul shares some profound insights into suffering, strength, and the sufficiency of God's grace. In this chapter, Apostle Paul shares personal experiences that unveil the paradoxical truth of the Christian life: power is perfected in weakness. As we explore this scripture, let's open our hearts to the lessons God has for us, especially in understanding how our weaknesses can become platforms for God's power.

The Vision of Paradise (12:1-6)

> "I must go on boasting. Although there is nothing to be gained, I will go on to visions and revelations from the Lord. I know a man in Christ who fourteen years ago was caught up to the third heaven. Whether it was in the body or out of the body I do not know - God knows. And I know that this man - whether in the body or apart from the body I do not know, but God knows - was caught up to paradise and heard inexpressible things, things that no one is permitted to tell.
>
> I will boast about a man like that, but I will not boast about myself, except about my weaknesses. Even if I should choose to boast, I would not be a fool, because I would be speaking the truth. But I refrain, so no one will think more of me than is warranted by what I do or say ..." (2 Corinthians 12:1-6)

Paul begins with a reluctant but necessary defence of his own apostolic authority, sharing an extraordinary experience of being caught up to the third heaven - Paradise. He speaks of 'a man in Christ' who had a vision fourteen years ago, referring to himself in the third person out of humility. This man heard inexpressible things, which no one is permitted to tell. This introduction sets a tone of humility and mystery. Even in recounting a sublime spiritual experience, Paul remains reticent, focusing not on his own spiritual achievements but on the revelations granted by God Himself.

This challenges us to reflect: How do we share our spiritual experiences? Are we seeking to glorify God or are we wanting to elevate ourselves?

The Thorn in the Flesh (12:7-10)

"... or because of these surpassingly great revelations. Therefore, in order to keep me from becoming conceited, I was given a thorn in my flesh, a messenger of Satan, to torment me.

Three times I pleaded with the Lord to take it away from me. But he said to me, "My grace is sufficient for you, for my power is made perfect in weakness."

Therefore, I will boast all the more gladly about my weaknesses, so that Christ's power may rest on me. That is why, for Christ's sake, I delight in weaknesses, in insults, in hardships, in persecutions, in difficulties.

For when I am weak, then I am strong." (2 Corinthians 12:7-10)

The heart of this chapter — and perhaps the most moving part — deals with Paul's "thorn in the flesh," a mysterious affliction that tormented him. Despite pleading with the Lord three times to take it away, God's response was, *"My grace is sufficient for you, for my power is made perfect in weakness."*

Here lies a profound kingdom principle: God's power is most clearly displayed not in our strengths, but in our weaknesses. Paul's response to this revelation is radical: he boasts gladly about his weaknesses, so that Christ's power may rest on him. He says that he takes pleasure in weaknesses, insults, hardships, persecutions, and difficulties for Christ's sake.

Let's ponder this in our context. We all have thorns - chronic pain, unresolved issues, persistent struggles. How do we respond to these? Do we continually seek removal, or can we find grace to embrace them as opportunities for God's power to shine through us?

Concern for the Corinthian Church (12:11-21)

"I have made a fool of myself, but you drove me to it. I ought to have been commended by you, for I am not in the least inferior to the "super-apostles," even though I am nothing. I persevered in demonstrating among you the marks of a true apostle, including signs, wonders and miracles. How were you inferior to the other churches, except that I was never a burden to you? Forgive me this wrong!

Now I am ready to visit you for the third time, and I will not be a burden to you, because what I want is not your possessions but you. After all, children should not have to save up for their parents, but parents for their children. So I will very gladly spend for you everything I have and expend myself as well. If I love you more, will you love me less? Be that as it may, I have not been a burden to you. Yet, crafty fellow that I am, I caught you by trickery! Did I exploit you through any of the men I sent to you? I urged Titus to go to you and I sent our brother with him. Titus did not exploit you, did he? Did we not walk in the same footsteps by the same Spirit?

Have you been thinking all along that we have been defending ourselves to you? We have been speaking in the sight of God as those in Christ; and everything we do, dear friends, is for your strengthening. For I am afraid that when I come, I may not find you as I want you to be, and you may not find me as you want me to be. I fear that there may be discord, jealousy, fits of rage, selfish ambition, slander, gossip, arrogance and disorder. I am afraid that when I come again my God will humble me before you, and I will be grieved over many who have sinned earlier and have not repented of the impurity, sexual sin and debauchery in which they have indulged." (2 Corinthians 12:11-21)

Paul shifts his focus back to the Corinthian church, expressing concern for their spiritual well-being. He fears that upon visiting, he might find them not as he wishes and that he himself may not be as they wish. His heart is laid completely bare, with worries about quarrels, jealousy, anger, factions, slander, arrogance, gossip, and disorder among them.

This section invites us to examine our community life. Do our church environments reflect the character of Christ, or are they marred by divisions and sins? Paul's willingness to confront these issues head-on challenges us to address conflicts and sins within our communities truthfully and lovingly.

Conclusion

As we close, let's draw near to the heart of this message. Paul's journey in this chapter—from heavenly visions to painful thorns, from apostolic authority to personal concern for the church - teaches us about the true nature of Christian strength.

May we learn to embrace our weaknesses, not as failures or curses, but as opportunities for the power of Christ to work through us. Let's shift our focus from self-reliance to dependence on God, from boasting in our strengths to boasting in our weaknesses, so that the power of Christ may dwell in us.

Let us move forward in humility and strength, not our own, but the strength that comes from God, whose grace is sufficient for every weakness, every trial, and every thorn. May our lives, individually and collectively, reflect the paradoxical beauty of Christ's power made perfect in weakness.

~ 2 CORINTHIANS 13 ~

Introduction

We now turn our hearts and minds to the closing chapter of Paul's second letter to the Corinthians. This chapter brings us face to face with the themes of self-examination, correction, restoration, and power found in weakness - a fitting conclusion to a letter that weaves deep personal vulnerability with apostolic authority.

Let us now explore this incredibly rich passage, as we seek to understand and apply its truths to our lives.

Examine Yourselves (13:1-6)

"This will be my third visit to you. "Every matter must be established by the testimony of two or three witnesses." I already gave you a warning when I was with you the second time. I now repeat it while absent: On my return I will not spare those who sinned earlier or any of the others, since you are demanding proof that Christ is speaking through me. He is not weak in dealing with you, but is powerful among you.

For to be sure, he was crucified in weakness, yet he lives by God's power. Likewise, we are weak in him, yet by God's power we will live with him in our dealing with you.

Examine yourselves to see whether you are in the faith; test yourselves. Do you not realize that Christ Jesus is in you — unless, of course, you fail the test? And I trust that you will discover that we have not failed the test." (2 Corinthians 13:1-6)

Paul begins this chapter with a stern warning: he is coming to Corinth for the third time and will not spare those who have sinned earlier. He invokes the principle of every matter being established by two or three witnesses - standard of justice from the law. But this is not just about external judgment; it's a call for self-examination. "*Examine yourselves to see whether you are in the faith; test yourselves.*"

This is a profound exhortation to each of us. It's not about proving our worthiness to others, but about affirming our own faith and commitment to Christ. Are we living out the truth of the gospel in our daily lives? Is Christ evident in our thoughts, words, and actions?

Paul addresses accusations about his weakness, turning the argument on its head. Yes, Christ was crucified in weakness, yet He lives by God's power. Similarly, Paul might be weak in their eyes, but he lives with Christ by God's power. This echoes the earlier themes in the letter of strength perfected in weakness. Here, Paul invites us to find strength not in ourselves but in Christ. In our weaknesses, failures, and vulnerabilities, Christ's power is made perfect. How does this truth change the way you view your struggles and weaknesses?

Aim for Restoration (13:7-11)

> *"Now we pray to God that you will not do anything wrong - not so that people will see that we have stood the test but so that you will do what is right even though we may seem to have failed. For we cannot do anything against the truth, but only for the truth. We are glad whenever we are weak but you are strong; and our prayer is that you may be fully restored. This is why I write these things when I am absent, that when I come, I may not have to be harsh in my use of authority - the authority the Lord gave me for building you up, not for tearing you down. Finally, brothers and sisters, rejoice! Strive for full restoration, encourage one another, be of one mind, live in peace. And the God of love and peace will be with you." (2 Corinthians 13:7-11)*

Paul's final exhortations are rich with wisdom and love. He does not wish to use his authority to tear down but to build up. He prays not for the Corinthians to fail, but for their restoration.

This reflects the heart of God: He disciplines us not to punish, but to restore and renew. *"Rejoice. Strive for full restoration, encourage one another, be of one mind, live in peace."* These are not mere platitudes but powerful principles for life in the Christian community.

They call us to a higher standard of unity, peace, and mutual support. How can we, as a church family, better embody these principles?

The Grace of the Lord Jesus Christ (13:12-14)

> *"Greet one another with a holy kiss. All God's people here send their greetings. May the grace of the Lord Jesus Christ, and the love of God, and the fellowship of the Holy Spirit be with you all."* (2 Corinthians 13:12-14)

Paul concludes with a beautiful benediction, invoking the grace of the Lord Jesus Christ, the love of God, and the fellowship of the Holy Spirit. This Trinitarian blessing encapsulates the essence of our faith and the source of our strength. It's a reminder that we are not alone; we live in the grace, love, and fellowship of God.

As we reflect on this, let's remember that our strength comes from this divine fellowship. In every trial, in every weakness, in every moment of self-examination, we are sustained and enriched by the grace of Christ, the love of God, and the fellowship of the Holy Spirit.

Conclusion

As we conclude our journey through 2 Corinthians, let us take to heart the lessons of this final chapter. Let's commit to regular self-examination, not as an exercise in self-judgment, but as a means to affirm and deepen our faith. Let us embrace our weaknesses, allowing them to become conduits of Christ's power. And let us aim for restoration, building each other up in love and peace.

May the grace of our Lord Jesus Christ, the love of God, and the fellowship of the Holy Spirit be with us all, always guiding us, strengthening us, and uniting us in our walk of faith.

~ GALATIANS ~

Introduction

We now begin our brief journey through the book of Galatians, a powerful letter from the Apostle Paul to the churches in Galatia. In this opening chapter, Paul addresses a disturbing issue: the distortion of the Gospel. As we explore this important letter, we will discover the true essence of the Gospel and the dangers of deviating from it.

Galatians 1:

Paul's authority and greeting (Galatians 1:1-5): Paul's greeting and his emphasis on the authority given to him not by man but by Jesus Christ and God the Father. Highlight the importance of divine calling over human endorsement.

No other Gospel (Galatians 1:6-10): Paul identifies a major problem with the Galatians turning to a different gospel, which is really no gospel at all. We need to always be aware of the danger of perverting the true Gospel and the importance of seeking God's approval over human approval.

Paul's defence of his Apostleship (Galatians 1:11-24): Paul now reflects on his personal testimony and journey from persecutor of the church to apostle of Christ. Here we are reminded of the transformative power of the Gospel and the authenticity of Paul's mission and message.

Galatians 2:

In the second chapter of Galatians, we witness a pivotal moment as Paul's confronts Peter. This passage reveals the importance of consistency between belief and behaviour and the truth of the Gospel for all people, Jew and Gentile alike.

Paul's acceptance by the Apostles (Galatians 2:1-10): Here we see the validation of Paul's ministry by the pillars of the church and the agreement that the Gospel should go to both the Jews and the Gentiles.

Paul confronts Peter (Galatians 2:11-14): Paul outlines the incident at Antioch where he confronted Peter for hypocrisy, stressing the impact of our actions on the truth of the Gospel.

Justification by faith (Galatians 2:15-21): This is where we find the doctrine of justification by faith, not by works of the Law. Highlight Paul's argument that we live by faith in Christ, the essence of the Gospel message.

We should all be challenged to live out our faith authentically, aligning actions with beliefs, as we embrace the doctrine of justification by faith as the cornerstone of our relationship with God, in Christ.

Galatians 3:

In this chapter Paul presents a powerful argument from on the supremacy of faith over the Law. As we explore these verses, we'll confront the question of what truly justifies us before God.

Faith or works of the Law (Galatians 3:1-14): Paul addresses the foolishness of relying on the Law after beginning by the Spirit, discussing the example of Abraham and the role of faith in our relationship with God.

The Law and the promise (Galatians 3:15-29): Examines the purpose of the Law and its relationship to the promises which were given to Abraham. Emphasizes that the Law as our guardian and tutor until Christ came, so that we might be justified by faith.

Paul reminds us that we are called to live by faith, not by trying to adhere to the Law to earn salvation. Paul reinforces our identity in Christ that comes from faith, making us all children of God.

Galatians 4:

In this heartfelt chapter, Paul uses the analogy of sons and heirs to illustrate our relationship with God through Christ. We'll look at how this status affects our freedom and our identity.

Slavery Versus Sonship (Galatians 4:1-11): Contrasts our former slavery under the basic principles of the world with our new status as God's adopted children.

Paul's Concern for the Galatians (Galatians 4:12-20): Reflects on Paul's personal appeal to the Galatians, his concern for their spiritual well-being, and the danger of turning back to slavery.

The Allegory of Hagar and Sarah (Galatians 4:21-31): Discusses the allegory of Hagar and Sarah to illustrate the difference between living under the law and living by the promise through faith.

Paul encourages us to embrace our identity as children of God, living in the freedom granted through Christ and warns against becoming ensnared again by legalistic practices that negate the grace of God. Highlights the importance of nurturing our spiritual freedom and not taking it for granted.

Galatians 5:

Paul calls us to live in the freedom that Christ has secured for us. He contrasts the works of the flesh with the fruit of the Spirit, guiding us on how to walk by the Spirit and not gratify the desires of the flesh.

Stand Firm in Freedom (Galatians 5:1-15): Paul's exhortation to stand firm in the freedom we have in Christ and not to be burdened again by the yoke of slavery. Discuss the implications of using our freedom as an opportunity for the flesh versus serving one another in love.

Walking by the Spirit (Galatians 5:16-26): Addresses the conflict between the flesh and the Spirit. List and explain the works of the flesh contrasted with the fruit of the Spirit, encouraging self-reflection.

Living in the Spirit (Galatians 5:25-26): Paul now stresses the importance of living in accordance with the Spirit, avoiding conceit, provoking, and envying.

In this chapter we are urged to examine our lives in light of Paul's contrast between flesh and Spirit. We are encouraged to make a commitment to walking in the Spirit, thus producing fruit that reflects our true freedom in Christ.

Chapter 6:

In the concluding chapter of Galatians, Paul focuses on practical applications of living out the Gospel, emphasizing the law of Christ, which is fulfilled in love and service to others.

Bearing One Another's Burdens (Galatians 6:1-5): Discusses the importance of supporting one another during times of weakness and temptation, highlighting the balance between bearing one another's burdens and taking responsibility for our own actions.

Sowing and Reaping (Galatians 6:6-10): Explores the principle of sowing and reaping, encouraging us not to grow weary in doing good, for at the proper time, we will reap a harvest if we do not give up. Stresses the importance of doing good to all, especially to those in the family of faith.

Final Warnings and Benediction (Galatians 6:11-18): Paul's final warnings against those who would compel the Galatians to be circumcised merely to boast in the flesh. Reiterates that the only thing worth boasting in is the cross of our Lord Jesus Christ.

The Apostle offers a strong motivation to practical Christian living - bearing burdens, sharing in all good things, and doing good to all people. We are reminded of the ultimate goal: new creation in Christ Jesus, as Paul encourages us to live lives that glorify God and serve others, thereby fulfilling the law of Christ.

Now I will unpack each of the six chapters of Galatians in more detail as we wrestle with profound truths in this letter.

~ GALATIANS 1 ~

Introduction

Paul's letter to the Church in Galatia is charged with urgency and divine clarity, as it addresses a crisis of faith, a turning away from the true Gospel. Let's explore the depths of this first chapter, as we seek to embrace its profound implications for our lives today.

Context and Greeting (1:1-5)

"Paul, an apostle - sent not from men nor by a man, but by Jesus Christ and God the Father, who raised him from the dead - and all the brothers and sisters with me, to the churches in Galatia: Grace and peace to you from God our Father and the Lord Jesus Christ, who gave himself for our sins to rescue us from the present evil age, according to the will of our God and Father, to whom be glory for ever and ever. Amen." (Galatians 1:1-5)

Paul opens with a greeting, but this is no ordinary salutation. He asserts his apostleship not from men or by man, but by Jesus Christ and God the Father. In a world that often seeks human endorsement, Paul reminds us of a higher calling and divine commission. As we reflect on these opening verses, let's ask ourselves: Whose approval are we seeking? Are we living by the standards of men or by the call of God?

Paul mentions Jesus who gave himself for our sins to rescue us from the present evil age. This is the gospel in a nutshell—Christ's sacrifice, our rescue. Every word pulses with the gravity of our salvation and the cost at which it was purchased. Let this resonate with you: Christ gave Himself for you. How does this truth shape your life today?

No Other Gospel (1:6-10)

"I am astonished that you are so quickly deserting the one who called you to live in the grace of Christ and are turning to a different gospel - which is really no gospel at all. Evidently some people are throwing you into confusion and are trying to pervert the gospel of Christ."

"But even if we or an angel from heaven should preach a gospel other than the one we preached to you, let them be under God's curse! As we have already said, so now I say again: If anybody is preaching to you a gospel other than what you accepted, let them be under God's curse! Am I now trying to win the approval of human beings, or of God? Or am I trying to please people? If I were still trying to please people, I would not be a servant of Christ." (Galatians 1:6-10)

The heart of the matter swiftly unfolds in these verses. Paul expresses astonishment at how quickly the Galatians are now deserting the one who called them to live in the grace of Christ. Here, Paul uses the term "astonished," which conveys not just surprise but also deep distress. Have you ever felt a profound disappointment when someone you mentored, loved, or taught strayed from the truth?

The Galatians were turning to a different gospel - an altered, perverted gospel, which is really no gospel at all. This is a stark reminder that not all that glitters is gold, not all that claims to be truth is truth. In our lives, we encounter various teachings, ideologies, and philosophies. Paul's words compel us to discern: Are we embracing the true Gospel, or are we being swayed by counterfeits?

Paul is unapologetic and quite stern here about the consequences of distorting the Gospel. He says if anyone preaches a gospel other than the one they received, let them be under God's curse. This is a very solemn reminder of the seriousness with which we should guard the purity of the Gospel. In a world full of grey compromise, are we standing firm in the truth of Christ?

Paul's Divine Commission (1:11-24)

"I want you to know, brothers and sisters, that the gospel I preached is not of human origin. I did not receive it from any man, nor was I taught it; rather, I received it by revelation from Jesus Christ. For you have heard of my previous way of life in Judaism, how intensely I persecuted the church of God and tried to destroy it."

"I was advancing in Judaism beyond many of my own age among my people and was extremely zealous for the traditions of my fathers. But when God, who set me apart from my mother's womb and called me by his grace, was pleased to reveal his Son in me so that I might preach him among the Gentiles, my immediate response was not to consult any human being. I did not go up to Jerusalem to see those who were apostles before I was, but I went into Arabia. Later I returned to Damascus.

Then after three years, I went up to Jerusalem to get acquainted with Cephas and stayed with him fifteen days. I saw none of the other apostles – only James, the Lord's brother. I assure you before God that what I am writing you is no lie.

Then I went to Syria and Cilicia. I was personally unknown to the churches of Judea that are in Christ. They only heard the report: 'The man who formerly persecuted us is now preaching the faith he once tried to destroy.' And they praised God because of me."
(Galatians 1:11-24)

Paul transitions from confrontation to testimony, emphasizing that the Gospel he preaches is not of human origin. This is vital: the Gospel is divine, not devised by human intellect or reasoning. It came through a revelation of Jesus Christ. When Paul recounts his past life in Judaism and how radically he was transformed, it serves as a powerful testimony to the transforming power of the Gospel. Paul, once a brutal persecutor of the church, became a proclaimer of faith.

This brings us to reflect on our own lives. What transformations have we experienced since encountering the true Gospel? How has our understanding of Christ's love changed our direction, purpose, and priorities?

Conclusion

As we conclude, let's consider the gravity of Paul's message in Galatians Chapter 1. The true Gospel is not just good news; it is the only news that brings life. It is not a message of human origin; it is the revelation of Jesus Christ Himself.

We are seriously challenged in this chapter to examine what we believe. Are we clinging to the true Gospel - the message of Jesus Christ crucified and resurrected for our sins, offering grace and freedom - or have we been seduced by a distorted gospel that seeks to add to or subtract from the finished work of Christ?

Let us be like Paul, unashamed of the Gospel, for it is the power of God for salvation to everyone who believes. May we stand firm in the true grace of Christ, not moved by other so-called 'gospels' that seek to enslave us once more.

Let's pray for discernment, for a deepening understanding of the true Gospel, and for the courage to live it out in every aspect of our lives.

~ GALATIANS 2 ~

Introduction

In chapter 2, the Apostle Paul presents us with pivotal moments in his ministry and the early church's life. He confronts not only the essence of the Gospel but also how it should manifest in our lives, especially in terms of unity and truth. Let's journey through this chapter to understand the courage of conviction and the call to live out the truth of the Gospel in every aspect of our lives.

Unity in Diversity (2:1-10)

> *"Then after fourteen years, I went up again to Jerusalem, this time with Barnabas. I took Titus along also. I went in response to a revelation and, meeting privately with those esteemed as leaders, I presented to them the gospel that I preach among the Gentiles. I wanted to be sure I was not running and had not been running my race in vain. Yet not even Titus, who was with me, was compelled to be circumcised, even though he was a Greek.*
>
> *This matter arose because some false believers had infiltrated our ranks to spy on the freedom we have in Christ Jesus and to make us slaves. We did not give in to them for a moment, so that the truth of the gospel might be preserved for you.*
>
> *As for those who were held in high esteem - whatever they were makes no difference to me; God does not show favouritism - they added nothing to my message. On the contrary, they recognized that I had been entrusted with the task of preaching the gospel to the uncircumcised, just as Peter had been to the circumcised.*
>
> *For God, who was at work in Peter as an apostle to the circumcised, was also at work in me as an apostle to the Gentiles. James, Cephas and John, those esteemed as pillars, gave me and Barnabas the right hand of fellowship when they recognized the grace given to me. They agreed that we should go to the Gentiles, and they to the circumcised. All they asked was that we should continue to remember the poor, the very thing I had been eager to do all along." (Galatians 2:1-10)*

Paul begins this section by recounting his journey to Jerusalem, bringing along Titus, a Gentile Christian. This visit was not just a formality but a significant moment of truth - a testament to the universal reach of the Gospel. Despite pressures, Titus was not compelled to be circumcised, highlighting the conviction that salvation is for everybody, irrespective of cultural or religious backgrounds.

Here, Paul demonstrates the importance of unity in diversity within the church. The Jerusalem leaders recognized the grace given to Paul and agreed that he should continue his ministry among the Gentiles while they ministered to the Jews. This moment underscores that while our missions may differ, our message - the Gospel of Jesus Christ - remains the same.

We should reflect on our church's diversity. Are we embracing and celebrating our differences while maintaining the unity of our faith? Let us strive to support each other's ministries, understanding that the same grace works within us all.

Confrontation in Antioch (2:11-14)

> *"When Cephas came to Antioch, I opposed him to his face, because he stood condemned. For before certain men came from James, he used to eat with the Gentiles. But when they arrived, he began to draw back and separate himself from the Gentiles because he was afraid of those who belonged to the circumcision group. The other Jews joined him in his hypocrisy, so that by their hypocrisy even Barnabas was led astray.*
>
> *When I saw that they were not acting in line with the truth of the gospel, I said to Cephas in front of them all, "You are a Jew, yet you live like a Gentile and not like a Jew. How is it, then, that you force Gentiles to follow Jewish customs?" (Galatians 2:11-14)*

The scene shifts to Antioch, where Paul confronts Peter, a pillar of the church, for withdrawing from eating with Gentile believers out of fear of criticism from certain Jewish Christians. This wasn't a mere social faux pas; it was a fundamental contradiction of the Gospel message.

By his actions, Peter was implying that Gentile Christians were second-class believers and that adherence to Jewish customs was necessary for salvation.

Paul's confrontation with Peter is a powerful lesson in integrity and truth. It shows us that the truth of the Gospel must prevail over cultural preferences and peer pressure. When practices or traditions, even those deeply ingrained, stand in contradiction to the Gospel's truth, they must be re-evaluated.

Let us consider our own lives and church community. Are there practices or traditions we hold that may contradict the message of grace and unity in Christ? Let us have the courage to confront and align our actions with the truth of the Gospel.

Justification by Grace through Faith (2:15-21)

> *"We who are Jews by birth and not sinful Gentiles know that a person is not justified by the works of the law, but by faith in Jesus Christ. So we, too, have put our faith in Christ Jesus that we may be justified by faith in Christ and not by the works of the law, because by the works of the law no one will be justified.*

> *But if, in seeking to be justified in Christ, we Jews find ourselves also among the sinners, doesn't that mean that Christ promotes sin? Absolutely not! If I rebuild what I destroyed, then I really would be a lawbreaker.*

> *For through the law, I died to the law so that I might live for God. I have been crucified with Christ and I no longer live, but Christ lives in me. The life I now live in the body, I live by faith in the Son of God, who loved me and gave himself for me. I do not set aside the grace of God, for if righteousness could be gained through the law, Christ died for nothing!" (Galatians 2:15-21)*

Paul uses this incident to delve into the heart of the Gospel - justification by grace through faith, not by works of the law. He argues that if righteousness could be gained through the law, Christ died for nothing. This is a truly profound statement which underscores the sufficiency of life, death and resurrection of Christ for our salvation.

This section calls us to reflect on the foundation of our faith. Are we trying to earn God's favour through our actions, or are we resting in the finished work of Christ? Paul's message is clear: We live by faith in the Son of God, who loved us and gave Himself for us.

This text should encourage you to examine your heart. Are there areas in your life where you are relying on your own righteousness rather than Christ's? Let us recommit ourselves to living by faith, recognizing that it is only through Christ's grace that we are saved.

Conclusion

Galatians Chapter 2 challenges us to live out the truth of the Gospel authentically and courageously. It calls for unity in diversity, integrity in our actions, and faith in the sufficiency of Christ's sacrifice. As we go forth, let us hold fast to these truths, allowing them to shape our lives and our community.

May we be a church that not only believes the Gospel but lives it out in every aspect of our lives. Amen.

~ GALATIANS 3 ~

Introduction

Now we come to the heart of the Apostle Paul's impassioned plea to the Galatians. This chapter confronts us with fundamental questions about the nature of our faith, the role of the law, and the true path to righteousness. Paul challenges us to consider what lies at the core of our relationship with God. Let us now examine these rich verses to uncover the transformative power of the gospel and the purpose of the law in our lives.

The Foolishness of Abandoning Faith (3:1-5)

"You foolish Galatians! Who has bewitched you? Before your very eyes Jesus Christ was clearly portrayed as crucified. I would like to learn just one thing from you: Did you receive the Spirit by the works of the law, or by believing what you heard? Are you so foolish? After beginning by means of the Spirit, are you now trying to finish by means of the flesh? Have you experienced so much in vain - if it really was in vain? So again, I ask, does God give you his Spirit and work miracles among you by the works of the law, or by your believing what you heard?" (Galatians 3:1-5)

Paul begins with a heart-breaking question, calling the Galatians 'foolish' for abandoning the spirit of faith that initially brought them salvation. He reminds them, and us, of the simplicity and power of faith - a faith that brought about miracles and the indwelling of the Holy Spirit.

This opening rebuke is not merely a chastisement but a call to return to the essential, to the profound yet simple truth that our relationship with God begins and ends with faith, not human efforts or adherence to the law.

Reflect on your own spiritual journey. Have you drifted into legalism or reliance on personal achievements for your standing with God? Let us remember that it is through faith that we received the Spirit; let us continue to walk in that same faith.

Abraham's Example (3:6-9)

"So also Abraham 'believed God, and it was credited to him as righteousness.' Understand, then, that those who have faith are children of Abraham. Scripture foresaw that God would justify the Gentiles by faith, and announced the gospel in advance to Abraham: "All nations will be blessed through you." So those who rely on faith are blessed along with Abraham, the man of faith." (Galatians 3:6-9)

Paul directs us to the example of Abraham, the patriarch of faith, to illustrate that righteousness has always been a matter of faith. Abraham believed God, and that belief was credited to him as righteousness.

This pivotal moment in history underscores that God's blessings come through faith, a principle that transcends law, culture, and time. It's a powerful reminder that we, as believers, are children of Abraham not through ethnic lineage or adherence to a set of rules, but through faith in Christ Jesus.

Consider what it means to be a child of Abraham. Are you living in the assurance and freedom of faith, or are you ensnared by the need to prove your worth? Let Abraham's example lead you back to a faith that trusts wholly in God's promises.

The Purpose of the Law (3:10-25)

"For all who rely on the works of the law are under a curse, as it is written: "Cursed is everyone who does not continue to do everything written in the Book of the Law." Clearly no one who relies on the law is justified before God, because "the righteous will live by faith."

The law is not based on faith; on the contrary, it says, "The person who does these things will live by them." Christ redeemed us from the curse of the law by becoming a curse for us, for it is written: "Cursed is everyone who is hung on a pole." He redeemed us in order that the blessing given to Abraham might come to the Gentiles through Christ Jesus, so that by faith we might receive the promise of the Spirit."

"Brothers and sisters, let me take an example from everyday life. Just as no one can set aside or add to a human covenant that has been duly established, so it is in this case. The promises were spoken to Abraham and to his seed. Scripture does not say "and to seeds," meaning many people, but "and to your seed," meaning one person, who is Christ. What I mean is this: The law, introduced 430 years later, does not set aside the covenant previously established by God and thus do away with the promise. For if the inheritance depends on the law, then it no longer depends on the promise; but God in his grace gave it to Abraham through a promise.

Why, then, was the law given at all? It was added because of transgressions until the Seed to whom the promise referred had come. The law was given through angels and entrusted to a mediator. A mediator, however, implies more than one party; but God is one.

Is the law, therefore, opposed to the promises of God? Absolutely not! For if a law had been given that could impart life, then righteousness would certainly have come by the law. But Scripture has locked up everything under the control of sin, so that what was promised, being given through faith in Jesus Christ, might be given to those who believe.

Before the coming of this faith, we were held in custody under the law, locked up until the faith that was to come would be revealed. So, the law was our guardian until Christ came that we might be justified by faith. Now that this faith has come, we are no longer under a guardian." (Galatians 3:10-25)

Here, Paul addresses a challenging but crucial concept: the purpose of the law. He clarifies that the law was never meant to impart life or righteousness; rather, it was given to reveal sin and our need for a saviour. The law serves as a "guardian" - leading us to Christ so that we might be justified by faith.

This passage invites us to re-evaluate our understanding of the law, not as a means to earn God's favour, but as a tool to guide us to the profound need for Christ's redeeming love.

How than do you view God's commandments? As burdensome obligations or as a mirror reflecting your need for Christ. Let this understanding reshape your relationship with God, seeing His laws as a pathway that leads to the grace found in faith.

Children of God Through Faith (3:26-29)

> *"So in Christ Jesus you are all children of God through faith, for all of you who were baptized into Christ have clothed yourselves with Christ. There is neither Jew nor Gentile, neither slave nor free, nor is there male and female, for you are all one in Christ Jesus. If you belong to Christ, then you are Abraham's seed, and heirs according to the promise." (Galatians 3:26-29)*

Paul concludes this chapter with an exhilarating declaration: In Christ, we are all children of God through faith. This profound truth demolishes barriers of ethnicity, social status, and gender within the community of believers. We are all one in Christ Jesus, heirs according to the promise. This is the culmination of faith's journey - unity and identity not grounded in worldly distinctions but in Christ alone.

So, look around your own community. Do you see the unity and equality that Paul speaks of? Let this vision of oneness in Christ inspire us to live out our faith in a way that transcends societal divisions, embracing our identity as God's children, united in His promise.

Conclusion

Galatians Chapter 3 beckons us back to the heart of the Gospel and the call to live by faith. It challenges us to consider where we've placed our trust: in our own efforts, in the adherence to the law, or in the all-sufficient sacrifice of Jesus Christ.

As we move forward, let us hold fast to faith as the foundation of our lives, the source of our righteousness, and the bond that unites us as the family of God. Let us walk in the freedom and unity that faith in Christ brings.

~ GALATIANS 4 ~

Introduction

My heart is full of expectation as we now explore the profound depths of Galatians Chapter 4, where Paul delves into the themes of inheritance, freedom, and identity. In this chapter, he uses the powerful analogy of slavery versus sonship to illustrate our incredible transformation through Christ. As we navigate these sacred verses, let us open our hearts to the lessons God wants to imprint upon us, revealing our true identity as His beloved children.

From Slaves to Heirs (4:1-7)

> *"What I am saying is that as long as an heir is underage, he is no different from a slave, although he owns the whole estate. The heir is subject to guardians and trustees until the time set by his father. So also, when we were underage, we were in slavery under the elemental spiritual forces of the world.*
>
> *But when the set time had fully come, God sent his Son, born of a woman, born under the law, to redeem those under the law, that we might receive adoption to sonship. Because you are his sons and daughters, God sent the Spirit of his Son into our hearts, the Spirit who calls out, "Abba, Father." So you are no longer a slave, but God's child; and since you are his child, God has made you also an heir." (Galatians 4:1-7)*

Paul begins this chapter with an analogy: as long as the heir is a child, he is no different from a slave. This image sets the stage for one of the most liberating truths of the Gospel. We were once slaves under the basic principles of the world, but when the time was fully come, God sent His Son to redeem us. Through Christ, we are no longer slaves but sons and daughters, and if we are children, then we are heirs of God's glorious inheritance.

Reflect on your own spiritual journey. Do you still live as if you are a slave to old laws, fears, and sins? Or do you embrace the freedom and rights of God's children?

Remember, in Christ, you are an heir to the kingdom, entitled to the promises and blessings of God.

Paul's Personal Appeal (4:8-20)

> "Formerly, when you did not know God, you were slaves to those who by nature are not gods. But now that you know God - or rather are known by God - how is it that you are turning back to those weak and miserable forces? Do you wish to be enslaved by them all over again? You are observing special days and months and seasons and years! I fear for you, that somehow I have wasted my efforts on you.
>
> I plead with you, brothers and sisters, become like me, for I became like you. You did me no wrong. As you know, it was because of an illness that I first preached the gospel to you, and even though my illness was a trial to you, you did not treat me with contempt or scorn. Instead, you welcomed me as if I were an angel of God, as if I were Christ Jesus himself. Where, then, is your blessing of me now? I can testify that, if you could have done so, you would have torn out your eyes and given them to me. Have I now become your enemy by telling you the truth?
>
> Those people are zealous to win you over, but for no good. What they want is to alienate you from us, so that you may have zeal for them. It is fine to be zealous, provided the purpose is good, and to be so always, not just when I am with you. My dear children, for whom I am again in the pains of childbirth until Christ is formed in you, how I wish I could be with you now and change my tone, because I am perplexed about you!" (Galatians 4:8-20)

In this section, Paul becomes quite personal, reminiscing about his previous visit and the warm reception he received from the Galatians. He expresses his perplexity and deep pain over their willingness to return to bondage, urging them to remain in the freedom Christ granted.

This passage isn't just a historical account; it's a timeless appeal to every believer who has ever been tempted to turn back to their old ways.

So, consider the areas in your life where you might be slipping back into 'spiritual slavery.' What old habits, traditions, or beliefs are you clinging to that prevent you from fully embracing the freedom Christ offers? Let Paul's earnest appeal resonate with you, prompting a return to the liberating truth of the Gospel.

The Allegory of Sarah and Hagar (4:21-31)

"Tell me, you who want to be under the law, are you not aware of what the law says? For it is written that Abraham had two sons, one by the slave woman and the other by the free woman. His son by the slave woman was born according to the flesh, but his son by the free woman was born as the result of a divine promise.

These things are being taken figuratively: The women represent two covenants. One covenant is from Mount Sinai and bears children who are to be slaves: This is Hagar. Now Hagar stands for Mount Sinai in Arabia and corresponds to the present city of Jerusalem, because she is in slavery with her children. But the Jerusalem that is above is free, and she is our mother. For it is written: "Be glad, barren woman, you who never bore a child; shout for joy and cry aloud, you who were never in labour; because more are the children of the desolate woman than of her who has a husband."

Now you, brothers and sisters, like Isaac, are children of promise. At that time the son born according to the flesh persecuted the son born by the power of the Spirit. It is the same now.

But what does Scripture say? "Get rid of the slave woman and her son, for the slave woman's son will never share in the inheritance with the free woman's son." Therefore, brothers and sisters, we are not children of the slave woman, but of the free woman." (Galatians 4:21-31)

Paul uses the allegory of Sarah and Hagar to distinguish between two covenants: one born of flesh, leading to slavery, and the other born of promise, leading to freedom. This allegory is not just an ancient story but a vivid representation of two ways of life.

Hagar represents the old covenant of the Law, which always leads to bondage, while Sarah symbolizes the new covenant of grace, bringing freedom and life.

So, which covenant are you really living under? Are you labouring under the weight of legalism, trying to earn God's favour, or are you resting in the promise of grace, living as a child of freedom? This allegory invites us to step out of the shadows of slavery and into the light of promise.

Conclusion

Galatians chapter 4 is a profound reminder of our transformation through Christ. We are no longer slaves but beloved children of God. This new identity carries with it the promise of freedom, inheritance, and a new way of life. As we leave today, let us shed the remnants of our spiritual bondage and embrace the fullness of our adoption as God's heirs.

Let us live not as those who are burdened by the yoke of slavery but as those who are free, rejoicing in the promise given to Abraham, fulfilled in Christ Jesus.

As children of promise, let us walk in the freedom and faith that define our heritage in Christ. Amen.

~ GALATIANS 5 ~

Introduction

In this chapter, Paul issues a clarion call to stand firm in the freedom Christ has secured for us. In this text he challenges us to examine our walk with Christ, urging us to live by the Spirit and not be ensnared again by the yoke of bondage. As we explore these potent verses, let's allow the Holy Spirit to guide us into a deeper understanding of true Christian freedom and how it transforms our lives.

The Call to Freedom (5:1-6)

"It is for freedom that Christ has set us free. Stand firm, then, and do not let yourselves be burdened again by a yoke of slavery. Mark my words! I, Paul, tell you that if you let yourselves be circumcised, Christ will be of no value to you at all. Again, I declare to every man who lets himself be circumcised that he is obligated to obey the whole law.

You who are trying to be justified by the law have been alienated from Christ; you have fallen away from grace. For through the Spirit, we eagerly await by faith the righteousness for which we hope. For in Christ Jesus neither circumcision nor uncircumcision has any value. The only thing that counts is faith expressing itself through love." (Galatians 5:1-6)

Paul begins with a powerful exhortation: *"It is for freedom that Christ has set us free."* He warns against returning to the yoke of slavery, which is, in this context, the legalistic observance of the Law, particularly circumcision, as a means to righteousness. Paul makes it abundantly clear that in Christ, neither circumcision nor uncircumcision has any value. What matters is faith expressing itself through love.

Reflect therefore on your own life. Are there areas where you've allowed yourself to be burdened again by a yoke of slavery, perhaps through legalism, guilt, or trying to earn God's love? Remember, true freedom is found in Christ alone.

Strong Words (5:7-12)

"You were running a good race. Who cut in on you to keep you from obeying the truth? That kind of persuasion does not come from the one who calls you. "A little yeast works through the whole batch of dough." I am confident in the Lord that you will take no other view. The one who is throwing you into confusion, whoever that may be, will have to pay the penalty. Brothers and sisters, if I am still preaching circumcision, why am I still being persecuted? In that case the offense of the cross has been abolished. As for those agitators, I wish they would go the whole way and emasculate themselves!" (Galatians 5:7-12)

Paul uses a racing metaphor to question the Galatians about who misled them from the truth of the Gospel. He emphasizes that their diversion isn't inspired by God, who called them to faith. The "little yeast" metaphor illustrates how minor false teachings can corrupt the whole community, highlighting the danger of deviation from the Gospel.

Paul expresses confidence that the Galatians will reject the false teachings and return to the true Gospel. He also warns that those misleading them will face consequences, showing his trust in divine justice. Responding to accusations of preaching circumcision, Paul points to his persecution as evidence against such claims. He emphasizes the scandalous nature of salvation through Christ alone, which negates the necessity of circumcision. Paul's frustration with the false teachers culminates in a hyperbolic wish that they would emasculate themselves. This statement underscores the severity of the spiritual threat their teachings pose to the community.

In these verses Paul passionately defends the true Gospel against false teachings that threaten the spiritual health of the Galatian church. His metaphors and strong language reveal his deep concern for the Galatians' adherence to the faith and his unwavering commitment to the Gospel's integrity.

Life by the Spirit (5:13-18)

"You, my brothers and sisters, were called to be free. But do not use your freedom to indulge the flesh; rather, serve one another humbly in love.

For the entire law is fulfilled in keeping this one command: "Love your neighbour as yourself." If you bite and devour each other, watch out or you will be destroyed by each other.

So, I say, walk by the Spirit, and you will not gratify the desires of the flesh. For the flesh desires what is contrary to the Spirit, and the Spirit what is contrary to the flesh. They are in conflict with each other, so that you are not to do whatever you want. But if you are led by the Spirit, you are not under the law."
(Galatians 5:13-18)

Paul transitions from the theme of freedom to its proper use. He cautions against using liberty as an opportunity for the flesh but encourages us to serve one another humbly in love.

Here, Paul introduces the concept of walking by the Spirit, which stands in opposition to gratifying the desires of the flesh. Paul provides a stark contrast between the acts of the flesh and the fruit of the Spirit, underscoring that living by the Spirit leads to true freedom.

Examine your daily walk. Are you living according to the flesh or by the Spirit? Are the fruits of the Spirit evident in your life?

Let this reflection guide you to live by the Spirit more fully, embracing the freedom that produces love, joy, peace, and other fruits that glorify God.

The Battle Between Flesh and Spirit (5:19-26)

"The acts of the flesh are obvious: sexual immorality, impurity and debauchery; idolatry and witchcraft; hatred, discord, jealousy, fits of rage, selfish ambition, dissensions, factions and envy; drunkenness, orgies, and the like. I warn you, as I did before, that those who live like this will not inherit the kingdom of God."

"But the fruit of the Spirit is love, joy, peace, forbearance, kindness, goodness, faithfulness, gentleness and self-control. Against such things there is no law. Those who belong to Christ Jesus have crucified the flesh with its passions and desires. Since we live by the Spirit, let us keep in step with the Spirit. Let us not become conceited, provoking and envying each other."
(Galatians 5:19-26)

In this segment, Paul lists the acts of the flesh and contrasts them with the fruit of the Spirit. This passage serves as a mirror, allowing us to see whether our lives align more with the flesh or with the Spirit. Paul reminds us that those who belong to Christ have crucified the flesh with its passions and desires. Therefore, as we live by the Spirit, let us also keep in step with the Spirit.

Consider the list of the acts of the flesh and the fruit of the Spirit. Where do you see yourself in these lists? This is a call to self-examination and repentance, urging us to align our lives more closely with the Spirit's leading.

Conclusion

Galatians Chapter 5 presents us with a profound dichotomy between the freedom we have in Christ and the bondage of the law and the flesh. Paul's message is clear: We have been called to freedom, but we must stand firm in this freedom and not use it as an excuse for self-indulgence. Instead, we are to serve one another in love, walk by the Spirit, and thereby fulfill the law of Christ.

As we conclude this chapter, let us commit to living by the Spirit, allowing Him to guide our thoughts, actions, and desires. Let us embrace the freedom we have in Christ - not as a license for the flesh, but as an empowerment to live a life that is pleasing to God, fruitful, and filled with love.

May our lives reflect the beauty of the Spirit's work within us, demonstrating the true freedom that comes from walking with Christ. Amen.

Introduction

As we approach the concluding chapter of the Apostle Paul's letter to the church in Galatia, we find ourselves beckoned into a community of care, restoration, and mutual support. In this chapter Paul invites us to consider the practical implications of living by the Spirit in our interactions with one another. This passage challenges us to embody the law of Christ through acts of kindness, humility, and perseverance.

Bearing One Another's Burdens (6:1-5)

"Brothers and sisters, if someone is caught in a sin, you who live by the Spirit should restore that person gently. But watch yourselves, or you also may be tempted. Carry each other's burdens, and in this way you will fulfill the law of Christ. If anyone thinks they are something when they are not, they deceive themselves. Each one should test their own actions. Then they can take pride in themselves alone, without comparing themselves to someone else, for each one should carry their own load."
(Galatians 6:1-5)

Paul opens this chapter with a call to gently restore those caught in sin, emphasizing the need for self-examination and humility. He speaks about us bearing one another's burdens, thereby fulfilling the law of Christ. This instruction is not merely about physical assistance, it includes emotional and spiritual support.

Look around you; see the community God has placed you in. Are there burdens you can help to bear? Are you open to letting others help you with your burdens? This is a call to active participation in the life of the church, a call to empathy, support, and genuine love.

Sowing and Reaping (6:6-10)

"Nevertheless, the one who receives instruction in the word should share all good things with their instructor. Do not be deceived: God cannot be mocked. A man reaps what he sows."

> *"Whoever sows to please their flesh, from the flesh will reap destruction; whoever sows to please the Spirit, from the Spirit will reap eternal life. Let us not become weary in doing good, for at the proper time we will reap a harvest if we do not give up. Therefore, as we have opportunity, let us do good to all people, especially to those who belong to the family of believers."* (Galatians 6:6-10)

Paul continues with the metaphor of sowing and reaping, teaching us that what we invest in spiritually will determine what we harvest. He encourages us not to grow weary in doing good, for at the proper time, we will reap a harvest if we do not give up. This principle applies to our personal lives and our interactions with others, reminding us of the eternal impact of our earthly actions.

Reflect on your own life: What are you sowing? Are your actions driven by the Spirit, leading to a harvest of righteousness? Are you contributing positively to the lives of those around you? Remember, the investment you make in goodness and faithfulness will not return void.

Final Instructions and Blessings (6:11-18)

> *"See what large letters I use as I write to you with my own hand! Those who want to impress people by means of the flesh are trying to compel you to be circumcised. The only reason they do this is to avoid being persecuted for the cross of Christ. Not even those who are circumcised keep the law, yet they want you to be circumcised that they may boast about your circumcision in the flesh.*
>
> *May I never boast except in the cross of our Lord Jesus Christ, through which the world has been crucified to me, and I to the world. Neither circumcision nor uncircumcision means anything; what counts is the new creation. Peace and mercy to all who follow this rule - to the Israel of God.*
>
> *From now on, let no one cause me trouble, for I bear on my body the marks of Jesus. The grace of our Lord Jesus Christ be with your spirit, brothers and sisters. Amen."* (Galatians 6:11-18)

In his concluding remarks, Paul reiterates the insignificance of circumcision or uncircumcision, highlighting instead the importance of being a new creation in Christ. He bears witness to the scars he has for the sake of Christ, marks that signify his own bearing of burdens and suffering for the Gospel. Paul's closing blessing is a prayer for peace and mercy upon those who follow this rule - to live as new creations in Christ.

As we conclude our journey through Galatians, let's take a moment to reflect on our identity in Christ. Are we walking as new creations? Are our lives marked by the grace of our Lord Jesus Christ? Let's commit to living out the truth of the Gospel, bearing the marks of Jesus in our daily lives.

Conclusion

Galatians is a call to communal living that reflects the heart of the Gospel. It's about more than individual morality; it's about how we engage with one another, carrying each other's burdens, and working for the good of all. As we move forward, let us take these words to heart, seeking to apply them in our lives and our community.

Therefore, let us not become weary in doing good. Let us look for opportunities to support one another, to restore with gentleness, to share each other's burdens, and thus fulfill the law of Christ. As we do, we will truly live as the family of God, sowing seeds of righteousness that will yield a harvest of eternal life.

~ EPHESIANS ~

Introduction

The Epistle to the Ephesians is one of the thirteen New Testament letters attributed to the Apostle Paul, though its authorship has been debated. It's typically dated to around 60-62 A.D., written during Paul's imprisonment in Rome. The letter is directed to the Christian community in Ephesus, a major city of Asia Minor (modern Turkey). Unlike other Pauline letters, Ephesians lacks personal greetings and specific issues within the community, leading some scholars to propose it was a circular letter meant for a much broader audience.

The book is composed of six chapters and can be divided into two sections: doctrinal (chapters 1-3) and practical (chapters 4-6).

Chapters 1-3: Doctrinal Insights

Chapter 1 introduces the spiritual blessings Christians possess in Christ, emphasizing themes like predestination, redemption, and the indwelling of the Holy Spirit. This chapter sets the tone for the entire letter, underscoring the grace and peace from God and the spiritual wealth believers enjoy in Christ.

Chapter 2 further expands on the themes of grace, salvation, and unity. Paul contrasts the former state of Gentile believers (separated from Christ, without hope and without God) with their new status as fellow citizens with the saints and members of God's household.

A key passage is Ephesians 2:8-10, which underscores that salvation is a gift of God's grace, not a result of works. This chapter also emphasizes the breaking down of the wall of hostility between Jews and Gentiles, illustrating the new man in Christ and the reconciliation of all-in-one body through the cross.

Chapter 3 reveals the mystery of Christ, which Paul explains is the union of Jews and Gentiles in one body.

Paul reflects on his role as a minister of this gospel and prays for the spiritual strength of the believers in Ephesus, understanding, and comprehension of the vast love of Christ, which surpasses knowledge.

Chapter 4 transitions from doctrine to duty, urging believers to live a life worthy of their calling. Unity and diversity within the body of Christ are highlighted, alongside the importance of spiritual growth and renewal. Paul emphasizes the need for humility, patience, and love in maintaining the unity of the Spirit. He also discusses the roles of various gifts and offices within the church, intended for building up the body of Christ.

Chapter 5 continues with practical exhortations, instructing believers to imitate God and live in love, avoiding all forms of immorality, impurity, and greed. This chapter contains specific advice on Christian living, including relationships between husbands and wives, which is famously encapsulated in the concept of mutual submission and love, mirroring the relationship between Christ and the Church.

Chapter 6 then covers a range of relational duties, including instructions for children, parents, servants, and masters, highlighting a spirit of obedience and service as unto the Lord. The letter concludes with a vivid description of the armour of God, an allegory representing the spiritual resources available to believers in their battle against evil forces. This includes the belt of truth, the breastplate of righteousness, and the sword of the Spirit, which is the word of God.

Paul's Epistle to the followers of Christ in Ephesus very cleverly intertwines profound theological concepts with practical advice for living a life faithful to Christ. Its emphasis on unity, love, and the transformative power of the gospel has made it a cornerstone for understanding Christian identity and conduct.

Ephesians challenges believers to consider their position in Christ and how that informs their relationship with others, encouraging a life that reflects God's love and grace to the world.

This letter's broad themes and lack of specific controversies make it universally applicable, offering insights into the nature of the Church, the plan and purpose of God, and the practical outworking of Christian doctrine in everyday life. Its messages about reconciliation, community, and spiritual warfare continue to resonate with Christians worldwide, providing guidance, encouragement, and a deeper understanding of their faith.

Theological Themes

Unity and Diversity in the Body of Christ: Ephesians emphasizes the Church as one body composed of diverse members. This has practical implications for church life and relationships among believers, advocating for unity, mutual respect, and the valuing of different gifts and roles.

The Cosmic Scope of Christ's Work: Paul presents a vision of Christ's work that extends beyond individual salvation to the unification of all things in heaven and on earth. This elevates the narrative from personal faith to a cosmic plan, encouraging believers to view their faith in light of God's total redemptive purpose.

The Church as a New Humanity: The letter presents the Church not just as a collection of individuals but as a new humanity created in Christ. This challenges us to live out our new identity in every aspect of life, breaking down racial, social, and cultural barriers.

Spiritual Warfare: The final chapter's depiction of the armour of God frames the Christian life as a battle not against flesh and blood but against spiritual forces. This perspective impacts how believers view adversity, temptation, and conflict.

Personal and Community Application

Personal Identity in Christ: Ephesians calls individuals to consider their identity as chosen, adopted, redeemed, and sealed in Christ. This has profound implications for self-worth, purpose, and daily living.

Community Relationships: Paul's exhortations to unity, mutual submission, and love have direct applications to how believers interact within families, churches, and society. Ephesians challenges Christians to embody the reconciliation and peace that Christ achieved.

Ethical Living: The contrasts between the old and new life in Ephesians provide a framework for ethics and morality that is rooted in the believer's new identity in Christ, guiding decision-making and behaviour.

Engagement with the World:
The letter's teaching on spiritual warfare and the armour of God equips believers for engagement with the world that is spiritual and strategic, grounded in truth, righteousness, and prayer.

Summary

Ephesians is a rich and multi-faceted letter that interweaves lofty theological concepts with practical advice for living out the Christian faith. Its themes of unity, identity, and spiritual engagement are as relevant today as they were in the first century. In studying Ephesians, believers are called to reflect on the magnitude of God's grace, the depth of Christ's love, and the high calling of the Christian life, motivated to live out these truths in community with others and in the face of spiritual opposition.

By engaging with each verse and allowing its truths to penetrate deeply, individuals and churches can experience transformation and growth into the maturity of faith that Paul envisioned for the Ephesian believers.

Now I will unpack each of the six chapters in more detail as we explore this amazing document in more detail.

~ EPHESIANS 1 ~

Introduction

Paul opens his epistle to the church in Ephesus with a celebration of the spiritual blessings we have received through Christ. These blessings are not of this world; they are heavenly, spiritual, and eternal. They remind us of our identity and purpose in Christ.

Our Blessings in Christ (1:1-14)

"Paul, an apostle of Christ Jesus by the will of God, to God's holy people in Ephesus, the faithful in Christ Jesus: Grace and peace to you from God our Father and the Lord Jesus Christ.

Praise be to the God and Father of our Lord Jesus Christ, who has blessed us in the heavenly realms with every spiritual blessing in Christ. For he chose us in him before the creation of the world to be holy and blameless in his sight. In love he predestined us for adoption to sonship through Jesus Christ, in accordance with his pleasure and will - to the praise of his glorious grace, which he has freely given us in the One he loves.

In him we have redemption through his blood, the forgiveness of sins, in accordance with the riches of God's grace that he lavished on us. With all wisdom and understanding, he made known to us the mystery of his will according to his good pleasure, which he purposed in Christ, to be put into effect when the times reach their fulfillment - to bring unity to all things in heaven and on earth under Christ.

In him we were also chosen, having been predestined according to the plan of him who works out everything in conformity with the purpose of his will, in order that we, who were the first to put our hope in Christ, might be for the praise of his glory.

And you also were included in Christ when you heard the message of truth, the gospel of your salvation. When you believed, you were marked in him with a seal, the promised Holy Spirit, who is a deposit guaranteeing our inheritance until the redemption of those who are God's possession - to the praise of his glory." (Ephesians 1:1-14)

After Paul' opening greeting, he begins by praising God for the spiritual blessings that we, as believers, have in Christ. Notice, Paul says we are blessed with *"every spiritual blessing in the heavenly places."* This is profound. We are not just given one or two blessings; we have been given every blessing possible through our union with Christ. These blessings include our election (v.4), our adoption as sons and daughters (v.5), our redemption and forgiveness (v.7), and the revelation of His will to us (v.9). These are not mere earthly blessings that can fade or be taken away. These are eternal, secured in Christ.

What does this mean for us today? It means that our value and identity are not determined by worldly standards but by God's immense love and grace towards us. It's a call to live in response to these blessings - not in pursuit of them, since we already possess them in Christ.

Paul speaks of the mystery of God's will, revealed to us in Christ. This mystery is that in the fullness of time, all things in heaven and on earth will be united under Christ. This is the divine plan of redemption that encompasses not just us, but all of creation. This perspective changes how we view our lives and the world around us.

We are part of a larger, divine narrative. Our lives, our choices, and our actions should align with God's ultimate plan of bringing unity and reconciliation through Christ. How are we contributing to this divine purpose?

Paul continues to expand on our spiritual blessings by talking about our inheritance in Christ. We, who were the first to hope in Christ, are destined according to the purpose of Him who works all things according to the counsel of His will.

This inheritance is not like earthly inheritances that can deplete; it is imperishable, undefiled, and unfading. And how do we know we have this inheritance? We have been sealed with the Holy Spirit, the guarantee of our inheritance until we acquire possession of it.

This should give us immense security and hope. No matter what we face in this life, our future is secure in Christ. The presence of the Holy Spirit in our lives is our constant reminder that we belong to God and that He will fulfill all His promises to us.

Paul's Prayer for Enlightenment (1:15-23)

"For this reason, ever since I heard about your faith in the Lord Jesus and your love for all God's people, I have not stopped giving thanks for you, remembering you in my prayers. I keep asking that the God of our Lord Jesus Christ, the glorious Father, may give you the Spirit of wisdom and revelation, so that you may know him better.

I pray that the eyes of your heart may be enlightened in order that you may know the hope to which he has called you, the riches of his glorious inheritance in his holy people, and his incomparably great power for us who believe. That power is the same as the mighty strength he exerted when he raised Christ from the dead and seated him at his right hand in the heavenly realms, far above all rule and authority, power and dominion, and every name that is invoked, not only in the present age but also in the one to come.

And God placed all things under his feet and appointed him to be head over everything for the church, which is his body, the fullness of him who fills everything in every way."
(Ephesians 1:15-23)

Paul concludes this chapter with a wonderful prayer for the Ephesian believers, that God may give them the Spirit of wisdom and revelation, so they may know Him better. He prays for their hearts to be enlightened to know the hope to which they are called, the riches of His glorious inheritance in the saints, and the incomparable power for us who believe.

This should be our prayer for ourselves today, that we would not just know about these spiritual blessings but that we would know them deeply and personally. That we would live in the reality of what God has done for us in Christ, and that this reality would transform our lives.

Conclusion

As we close, let us reflect on the spiritual blessings we have in Christ. We are chosen, adopted, redeemed, forgiven, and sealed with the Holy Spirit. Let us live in the light of these truths, walking in a manner worthy of the calling we have received. Let us pray for a deeper understanding of these blessings and for the power to live them out in our daily lives.

Ephesians Chapter 1 bursts with the joy of being chosen by God, revealing the incredible spiritual blessings we have in Christ. From being predestined for adoption to receiving redemption through His blood, this chapter reminds us of our identity and inheritance in Him. It speaks of the power of the Holy Spirit as a seal of our salvation, ensuring us of our glorious hope.

As we understand these truths, we're called to live in the fullness of God's grace, empowered by His might, and enveloped in His love, recognizing that we are part of His grand plan to unite all things in Christ.

Introduction

As we explore Paul's teaching in Ephesians chapter 2, we will be taken from the depths of despair to the heights of divine grace. Paul illustrates the dramatic transformation that occurs in the life of every believer: from spiritual death to eternal life, solely through the grace and mercy of our Lord Jesus Christ.

From Death to Life (2:1-10)

> *"As for you, you were dead in your transgressions and sins, in which you used to live when you followed the ways of this world and of the ruler of the kingdom of the air, the spirit who is now at work in those who are disobedient.*
>
> *All of us also lived among them at one time, gratifying the cravings of our flesh and following its desires and thoughts. Like the rest, we were by nature deserving of wrath.*
>
> *But because of his great love for us, God, who is rich in mercy, made us alive with Christ even when we were dead in transgressions — it is by grace you have been saved. And God raised us up with Christ and seated us with him in the heavenly realms in Christ Jesus, in order that in the coming ages he might show the incomparable riches of his grace, expressed in his kindness to us in Christ Jesus.*
>
> *For it is by grace you have been saved, through faith - and this is not from yourselves, it is the gift of God - not by works, so that no one can boast. For we are God's handiwork, created in Christ Jesus to do good works, which God prepared in advance for us to do." (Ephesians 2:1-10)*

In the opening verses, Paul delivers a stark reminder: "*As for you, you were dead in your transgressions and sins.*" Here, the Apostle does not mince his words. He describes a state of spiritual death, a life ensnared by the ways of the world, influenced by the ruler of the kingdom of the air – a reference to Satan's pervasive power.

Yet, the tone shifts dramatically with two of the most hope-filled words in all of Scripture: "*But God...*" These words mark a divine intervention, as Paul recounts how God, rich in mercy and love, made us alive with Christ even when we were dead in sins. It's a gift of grace, not a result of our works, so that none of us may boast. This grace is our foundation, the bedrock of our faith. As we ponder these truths, let us ask ourselves: Do we truly appreciate the gravity of our past state and the magnificence of God's intervention?

Unity in Christ (2:11-18)

"Therefore, remember that formerly you who are Gentiles by birth and called "uncircumcised" by those who call themselves "the circumcision" (which is done in the body by human hands) - remember that at that time you were separate from Christ, excluded from citizenship in Israel and foreigners to the covenants of the promise, without hope and without God in the world. But now in Christ Jesus you who once were far away have been brought near by the blood of Christ.

For he himself is our peace, who has made the two groups one and has destroyed the barrier, the dividing wall of hostility, by setting aside in his flesh the law with its commands and regulations. His purpose was to create in himself one new humanity out of the two, thus making peace, and in one body to reconcile both of them to God through the cross, by which he put to death their hostility. He came and preached peace to you who were far away and peace to those who were near. For through him we both have access to the Father by one Spirit." (Ephesians 2:11-18)

Paul then transitions to address the unity between Jewish and Gentile believers, symbolizing the broader unity all believers share in Christ. He reminds the Gentiles that previously, they were outsiders to the covenants and promises of Israel. But now, in Christ, the dividing wall of hostility has been demolished. Through His flesh and His sacrifice, Christ has created one new humanity, thus making peace. This unity is not superficial; it is rooted in the spiritual reconciliation we have with God through the cross.

How then, can we apply this to our church today? Are there "dividing walls" within our own community that Christ has called us to tear down?

A Holy Temple (2:19-22)

> *"Consequently, you are no longer foreigners and strangers, but fellow citizens with God's people and also members of his household, built on the foundation of the apostles and prophets, with Christ Jesus himself as the chief cornerstone.*
>
> *In him the whole building is joined together and rises to become a holy temple in the Lord. And in him you too are being built together to become a dwelling in which God lives by his Spirit."* (Ephesians 2:19-22)

In the closing verses, Paul uses the metaphor of a building to describe the growing church. We are no longer strangers or aliens, but fellow citizens with God's people and members of God's household. This building, with Christ as the cornerstone, grows into a holy temple in the Lord. Each of us, as part of this structure, is being built together to become a dwelling in which God lives by His Spirit. This imagery challenges us to consider our role in the church. Are we contributing to the growth and sanctification of God's temple, or are we hindering it?

Conclusion

As we reflect on this chapter, let us consider our own spiritual journey. Have we moved from death to life, embracing the grace that has been so freely given to us? Are we working towards unity within the body of Christ, tearing down walls of division and embracing our brothers and sisters with open arms? And finally, are we actively contributing to the building of God's holy temple, supporting the growth and sanctification of His church? Let us face the days ahead with a renewed commitment to carrying the message of grace, unity, and growth into our daily lives. For we are God's workmanship, created in Christ Jesus to do good works, which God prepared in advance for us to do.

~ EPHESIANS 3 ~

Introduction

In this chapter, we explore the revelation of a mystery hidden for ages, the role of Paul in God's grand design, and the deep, heartfelt prayer he offers for the believers. This chapter invites us to embrace the boundless dimensions of Christ's love and to recognize our place in the mosaic of God's family.

The Mystery Revealed (3:1-6)

> *"For this reason, I, Paul, the prisoner of Christ Jesus for the sake of you Gentiles. Surely you have heard about the administration of God's grace that was given to me for you, that is, the mystery made known to me by revelation, as I have already written briefly.*
>
> *In reading this, then, you will be able to understand my insight into the mystery of Christ, which was not made known to people in other generations as it has now been revealed by the Spirit to God's holy apostles and prophets.*
>
> *This mystery is that through the gospel the Gentiles are heirs together with Israel, members together of one body, and sharers together in the promise in Christ Jesus." (Ephesians 3:1-6)*

Paul begins this chapter referring to himself as a *"prisoner of Christ Jesus for the sake of you Gentiles."* It's a striking introduction, reminding us that Paul's physical bonds in no way limit the power or reach of the gospel. Despite his imprisonment, Paul is entrusted with a divine mystery, one that would change the course of history.

This mystery, as revealed to Paul, is that through the gospel, Gentiles are heirs together with Israel, members together of one body, and sharers together in the promise in Christ Jesus. Reflect on that for a moment.

The wall that divided Jews from Gentiles has been demolished. This was radical news! In God's family, there are no second-class citizens.

Let us consider our own lives. Are there walls we have erected? Are there people we consider 'outside' the love of God? Paul's revelation challenges us to dismantle these barriers and to embrace the inclusive nature of the gospel.

Paul's Role as Minister (3:7-13)

> "I became a servant of this gospel by the gift of God's grace given me through the working of his power. Although I am less than the least of all the Lord's people, this grace was given me: to preach to the Gentiles the boundless riches of Christ, and to make plain to everyone the administration of this mystery, which for ages past was kept hidden in God, who created all things.
>
> His intent was that now, through the church, the manifold wisdom of God should be made known to the rulers and authorities in the heavenly realms, according to his eternal purpose that he accomplished in Christ Jesus our Lord. In him and through faith in him we may approach God with freedom and confidence. I ask you, therefore, not to be discouraged because of my sufferings for you, which are your glory." (Ephesians 3:7-13)

Paul views his commission as a gift of God's grace. He, a former persecutor of Christians, is now tasked with bringing to light the plan of the mystery hidden for ages in God. It's a beautiful testament to how God can transform and use anyone for His purposes. Paul's mission isn't just to spread the gospel but to illuminate the multifaceted wisdom of God. The church is to be a display of God's wisdom, a testament to His plan for unity and reconciliation. This should encourage us. Regardless of our past, we have a role in God's redemptive plan. Like Paul, let us embrace our calling with humility and boldness.

Prayer for Spiritual Empowerment (3:14-21)

> "For this reason, I kneel before the Father, from whom every family in heaven and on earth derives its name. I pray that out of his glorious riches he may strengthen you with power through his Spirit in your inner being, so that Christ may dwell in your hearts through faith."

"And I pray that you, being rooted and established in love, may have power, together with all the Lord's holy people, to grasp how wide and long and high and deep is the love of Christ, and to know this love that surpasses knowledge - that you may be filled to the measure of all the fullness of God.

Now to him who is able to do immeasurably more than all we ask or imagine, according to his power that is at work within us, to him be glory in the church and in Christ Jesus throughout all generations, for ever and ever! Amen." (Ephesians 3:14-21)

Paul, with a pastor's heart, kneels in prayer for the Ephesians, and it's here we find one of the most moving prayers in the Bible. He prays not for material blessings but for spiritual strength and understanding. He desires for them to grasp the width, length, height, and depth of Christ's love a love that truly surpasses all knowledge.

Paul's prayer is for us too. It's a prayer to be filled to the measure of all the fullness of God. Imagine that—being filled with the fullness of God! This is the life to which we are called, a life empowered by the Spirit, rooted in love, and overflowing with the fullness of God.

Conclusion

As we reflect on this amazing chapter, let us truly embrace the revelation of this mystery - our unity in Christ. Let us walk in our calling with humility and courage, no matter our past. Let us also pray for each other, that we may be strengthened in our inner beings; comprehend the vastness of Christ's love; and be filled with the fullness of God.

Remember, in Christ, we are no longer strangers or aliens; we are fellow citizens with the saints and members of the household of God. Let us live in a manner worthy of this calling, breaking down walls, building bridges, and filling our hearts and our communities with the love of Christ.

Introduction

This chapter stands as a beacon of light guiding us toward unity, maturity, and a life transformed by the grace of God. As we explore these verses, we're invited to reflect deeply on how we, as individuals and as a community, can live lives that are worthy of the calling we have received in Christ Jesus.

Living in Humility, Gentleness, and Patience (4:1-3)

"As a prisoner for the Lord, then, I urge you to live a life worthy of the calling you have received. Be completely humble and gentle; be patient, bearing with one another in love. Make every effort to keep the unity of the Spirit through the bond of peace."
(Ephesians 4:1-3)

Paul's call for us to live a life worthy of our calling is not just an aspirational goal; it's a practical, daily commitment to embody the virtues of Christ. Humility, gentleness, and patience are not signs of weakness but of strength. They are the marks of a community deeply rooted in Christ's love, where every member values and upholds the dignity and worth of the others. This mutual respect and love are essential for maintaining the unity of the Spirit. We are reminded that peace is not merely the absence of conflict but the presence of justice and love.

Diversity in Unity (4:4-16)

"There is one body and one Spirit, just as you were called to one hope when you were called; one Lord, one faith, one baptism; one God and Father of all, who is over all and through all and in all. But to each one of us grace has been given as Christ apportioned it. This is why it says: "When he ascended on high, he took many captives and gave gifts to his people."

(What does "he ascended" mean except that he also descended to the lower, earthly regions? He who descended is the very one who ascended higher than all the heavens, in order to fill the whole universe.)"

"So Christ himself gave the apostles, the prophets, the evangelists, the pastors and teachers, to equip his people for works of service, so that the body of Christ may be built up until we all reach unity in the faith and in the knowledge of the Son of God and become mature, attaining to the whole measure of the fullness of Christ.

Then we will no longer be infants, tossed back and forth by the waves, and blown here and there by every wind of teaching and by the cunning and craftiness of people in their deceitful scheming. Instead, speaking the truth in love, we will grow to become in every respect the mature body of him who is the head, that is, Christ. From him the whole body, joined and held together by every supporting ligament, grows and builds itself up in love, as each part does its work." (Ephesians 4:4-16)

In these verses, Paul celebrates the diversity within the body of Christ. He uses the metaphor of a body to illustrate how our different gifts, perspectives, and roles are essential for the health and growth of the church.

The diversity of gifts - from apostles and prophets to pastors and teachers - is not for personal glory but for the common good, to equip and build up the church.

This process of building up the church is ongoing, leading us toward maturity in faith and deeper knowledge of Christ. In this maturity, we are not easily swayed by false doctrines but are anchored in the truth of the gospel, growing in every way more like Christ, who is the head of the church.

The Old Way of Life (4:17-19)

"So I tell you this, and insist on it in the Lord, that you must no longer live as the Gentiles do, in the futility of their thinking. They are darkened in their understanding and separated from the life of God because of the ignorance that is in them due to the hardening of their hearts. Having lost all sensitivity, they have given themselves over to sensuality so as to indulge in every kind of impurity, and they are full of greed." (Ephesians 4:17-19)

Paul paints a stark picture of the Gentile (non-Christian) way of life, not to shame, but to remind us of the radical transformation that has occurred in us through Christ. This transformation requires a conscious decision to reject our former way of life - the deceitful desires and practices that lead us away from God. The Gentile way of life is characterized by a pursuit of vanity and a hardening of the heart against God's truth and love.

Renewal and Transformation (4:20-24)

> *"That, however, is not the way of life you learned when you heard about Christ and were taught in him in accordance with the truth that is in Jesus. You were taught, with regard to your former way of life, to put off your old self, which is being corrupted by its deceitful desires; to be made new in the attitude of your minds; and to put on the new self, created to be like God in true righteousness and holiness." (Ephesians 4:20-24)*

The Christian life is marked by continual renewal. This renewal of our minds is not a one-time event but a daily process of transformation that shapes our thoughts, attitudes, and actions. As we put on the new self, created to be like God in true righteousness and holiness, we are invited into a life that reflects God's character.

This new life is not just about avoiding sin; it's about actively pursuing righteousness, participating in God's work of renewal in the world.

Truth, Anger, and Forgiveness (4:25-27)

> *"Therefore, each of you must put off falsehood and speak truthfully to your neighbour, for we are all members of one body. "In your anger do not sin:" Do not let the sun go down while you are still angry, and do not give the devil a foothold." (Ephesians 4:25-27)*

Speaking the truth in love is foundational to building trust and fostering genuine relationships within the church. Paul acknowledges that anger is a natural emotion but cautions us against allowing it to lead us into sin.

Instead, we are to deal with our anger constructively, seeking reconciliation and understanding. Forgiveness is not optional but a mandate, reflecting the forgiveness we have received in Christ.

Positive Speech and Generosity (4:28-32)

> *"Anyone who has been stealing must steal no longer, but must work, doing something useful with their own hands, that they may have something to share with those in need. Do not let any unwholesome talk come out of your mouths, but only what is helpful for building others up according to their needs, that it may benefit those who listen.*
>
> *And do not grieve the Holy Spirit of God, with whom you were sealed for the day of redemption. Get rid of all bitterness, rage and anger, brawling and slander, along with every form of malice. Be kind and compassionate to one another, forgiving each other, just as in Christ God forgave you." (Ephesians 4:28-32)*

Paul emphasizes the importance of our words and actions in reflecting our new identity in Christ. Our speech should not tear down but build up, bringing grace to those who hear. Similarly, our actions, especially our generosity, are a testimony of God's love and grace at work in our lives. The call to put away all bitterness, rage, anger, brawling, and slander is a call to live in a manner that promotes peace, harmony, and edification.

Conclusion

Ephesians 4 presents a vision of the Christian life that is both challenging and inspiring. It calls us to unity, maturity, and a lifestyle that reflects our new identity in Christ. As we reflect on this chapter, let us commit to embodying these values in our lives, to be agents of God's love and grace in a world that so desperately needs it. Let us remember that living a life worthy of our calling is not about attaining perfection but about striving every day to reflect the love, grace, and truth of Jesus Christ in all that we do. May God give us the strength, wisdom, and courage to live out this calling.

~ EPHESIANS 5 ~

Introduction

Ephesians Chapter 5, a passage rich with instruction and insight for living a life that honours God. Paul, in this chapter, calls us to imitate God's character, walking in love, light, and wisdom. This is not merely a call to individual holiness but a summons to embody these virtues in a way that transforms our relationships and communities. Let us dive into these sacred words to uncover the depth of Paul's message for our lives today.

Walking in Love (5:1-2)

> *"Follow God's example, therefore, as dearly loved children and walk in the way of love, just as Christ loved us and gave himself up for us as a fragrant offering and sacrifice to God."*
> *(Ephesians 5:1-2)*

This call to follow God's example is rooted in our identity as God's beloved children, an identity that shapes our actions and interactions. To imitate God is to walk in love, just as Christ loved us and gave Himself up for us. This sacrificial love is our model, guiding us in our relationships with others. It challenges us to consider, how does love manifest in our actions, especially towards those who are difficult to love?

The sacrificial love of Christ, a fragrant offering and sacrifice to God, stands in contrast to the selfish desires that often motivate our actions. This love is not based on what we can gain but on what we can give. It calls us to look beyond our own needs and desires to the needs of others, just as Christ did for us.

Walking as Children of Light (5:3-14)

> *"But among you there must not be even a hint of sexual immorality, or of any kind of impurity, or of greed, because these are improper for God's holy people. Nor should there be obscenity, foolish talk or coarse joking, which are out of place, but rather thanksgiving."*

"For of this you can be sure: No immoral, impure or greedy person - such a person is an idolater - has any inheritance in the kingdom of Christ and of God. Let no one deceive you with empty words, for because of such things God's wrath comes on those who are disobedient. Therefore, do not be partners with them.

For you were once darkness, but now you are light in the Lord. Live as children of light (for the fruit of the light consists in all goodness, righteousness and truth) and find out what pleases the Lord. Have nothing to do with the fruitless deeds of darkness, but rather expose them. It is shameful even to mention what the disobedient do in secret.

But everything exposed by the light becomes visible - and everything that is illuminated becomes a light. This is why it is said: "Wake up, sleeper, rise from the dead, and Christ will shine on you." (Ephesians 5:3-14)

Paul exhorts us to put away all forms of immorality, impurity, and greed. These deeds of darkness have no place among God's people. Instead, we are called to live as children of light, for light produces goodness, righteousness, and truth.

This complete transformation from darkness to light is not only a personal moral endeavour but a communal witness to the transformative power of the gospel.

As children of light, our lives not only reflect God's character but also expose the unfruitful works of darkness. This is not a call to judgment but to a life so radically transformed by God's grace that it challenges and convicts the world around us. Our lives should raise questions about the hope that is within us, leading others out of darkness and into the marvellous light of Christ.

Walking in Wisdom (5:15-20)

"Be very careful, then, how you live — not as unwise but as wise, making the most of every opportunity, because the days are evil. Therefore, do not be foolish, but understand what the Lord's will is. Do not get drunk on wine, which leads to debauchery."

"Instead, be filled with the Spirit, speaking to one another with psalms, hymns, and songs from the Spirit. Sing and make music from your heart to the Lord, always giving thanks to God the Father for everything, in the name of our Lord Jesus Christ." (Ephesians 5:15-20)

In a world marked by foolishness and folly, Paul calls us to walk wisely, making the most of every opportunity. This wisdom is not merely intellectual but practical, guiding us in how to live in a manner which is worthy of our calling. It involves discernment, understanding God's will, and aligning our lives accordingly.

In a culture that often values busyness and productivity over spiritual health, how are we making time for what truly matters?

Paul contrasts the drunkenness of wine, which leads to reckless living, with being filled with the Spirit, which leads to lives marked by gratitude, singing, and mutual submission.

This filling of the Spirit is not a one-time event but a continual process of surrendering to God's leading and transforming power. It completely changes how we interact with one another, fostering relationships marked by love, respect, and humility.

Relationships as Reflections of Christ's Love (5:21-32)

"Submit to one another out of reverence for Christ. Wives, submit yourselves to your own husbands as you do to the Lord. For the husband is the head of the wife as Christ is the head of the church, his body, of which he is the Saviour. Now as the church submits to Christ, so also wives should submit to their husbands in everything.

Husbands, love your wives, just as Christ loved the church and gave himself up for her to make her holy, cleansing her by the washing with water through the word, and to present her to himself as a radiant church, without stain or wrinkle or any other blemish, but holy and blameless. In this same way, husbands ought to love their wives as their own bodies. He who loves his wife loves himself."

"After all, no one ever hated their own body, but they feed and care for their body, just as Christ does the church - for we are members of his body." For this reason, a man will leave his father and mother and be united to his wife, and the two will become one flesh."

This is a profound mystery - but I am talking about Christ and the church. However, each one of you also must love his wife as he loves himself, and the wife must respect her husband."(Ephesians 5:21-32)

Before diving into specific relational roles, Paul establishes a foundational principle: mutual submission out of reverence for Christ. This verse sets the tone for the following directives, emphasizing that Christian relationships are to be grounded in mutual respect and selflessness, mirroring our submission to Christ Himself.

Paul calls wives to submit to their husbands as to the Lord. This submission is not about inferiority or suppression but reflects the Church's submission to Christ. It's a voluntary act of love, respect, and support that mirrors the Church's unique relationship with Jesus.

Husbands are called to love their wives as Christ loved the Church and gave Himself up for her. This sacrificial love goes beyond mere affection; it's a selfless commitment to the well-being and sanctification of their wives. Husbands are to cherish and nourish their wives, recognizing them as integral parts of their own bodies, just as Christ does for the Church.

Paul quotes Genesis 2:24, highlighting the profound mystery of marriage - the union of two individuals into one flesh. This mystery is a profound illustration of Christ's intimate and unbreakable union with the Church.

In Christian marriage, the joining of lives is not just a social contract but a spiritual bond that reflects Christ's covenant relationship with His people.

Conclusion

In Ephesians 5, Paul gives us a transformative way of living that challenges us to walk in love, light, and wisdom. The chapter culminates in a profound exploration of Christian marriage as a reflection of Christ's sacrificial love for the Church. But whether married or single, the principles of love, sacrifice, and mutual submission are applicable to all Christians in their various relationships.

As we reflect on this chapter, let us be challenged to examine our lives and relationships through the lens of the Gospel. Are we walking in love, reflecting Christ's love in our actions and interactions? Are we living as children of light, illuminating the darkness around us with the truth of the Gospel? Are we walking in wisdom, making the most of every opportunity to glorify God in all we do?

The challenge to each of us today is to make a fresh commitment to embodying these principles, allowing the Holy Spirit to work in us and through us, transforming us more into the likeness of Christ. May our lives be a testament to the power of the Gospel, not just in what we say but in how we live, love, and relate to one another.

~ EPHESIANS 6 ~

Introduction

We now conclude our journey through this amazing Epistle to the Ephesians, arriving at a powerful finale in Chapter 6. Here, the Apostle Paul equips us for a reality that every believer faces: spiritual warfare.

This passage isn't just about a battle; it's about preparation, strength, and understanding the profound resources available to us in Christ. Let's explore these verses to discover how we can stand firm against the schemes of the devil, fully armoured and fully reliant on the Lord.

The Christian Household (6:1-4)

> *"Children, obey your parents in the Lord, for this is right.*
> *"Honour your father and mother"- which is the first*
> *commandment with a promise - "so that it may go well with you*
> *and that you may enjoy long life on the earth." Fathers, do not*
> *exasperate your children; instead, bring them up in the training*
> *and instruction of the Lord." (Ephesians 6:1-4)*

In the opening verses Paul addresses two critical aspects of the Christian life: our conduct within the household and our stance against spiritual forces. These instructions are not disjointed; rather, they reveal the comprehensive nature of our walk with Christ, touching on both our everyday relationships and our spiritual warfare.

Paul begins with a direct message to children, urging them to obey their parents *"in the Lord, for this is right."* This obedience is not blind but is anchored in a desire to live according to God's will, recognizing the God-given authority of all parents.

The promise attached to this commandment - that it may go well with you and that you may live long on the earth - highlights the blessings tied to honouring God's design for family structures.

However, Paul's instructions quickly turn to parents, specifically fathers, cautioning them not to provoke their children to anger. Instead, they are to bring them up in the discipline and instruction of the Lord.

This directive shifts the focus from mere obedience to nurturing - a difficult process involving patience, teaching, and modelling godly virtues. It's a reminder that authority is not for domineering but for stewarding the spiritual growth of the next generation.

Bondservants and Masters (6:5-9)

> *"Slaves, obey your earthly masters with respect and fear, and with sincerity of heart, just as you would obey Christ. Obey them not only to win their favour when their eye is on you, but as slaves of Christ, doing the will of God from your heart.*
>
> *Serve wholeheartedly, as if you were serving the Lord, not people, because you know that the Lord will reward each one for whatever good they do, whether they are slave or free.*
>
> *And masters, treat your slaves in the same way. Do not threaten them, since you know that he who is both their Master and yours is in heaven, and there is no favouritism with him."*
> *(Ephesians 6:5-9)*

The discourse on bondservants and masters might seem distant from our contemporary context, but at its core, Paul addresses the Christian ethic in all forms of work and leadership.

The call for bondservants to obey their earthly masters with sincerity and respect underscores the principle of working as unto the Lord. It's a transformative perspective that elevates every task, no matter how mundane, into an act of worship.

Masters, too, are reminded of their accountability to their Master in heaven, challenging any notion of absolute power over others. This mutual accountability before God lays the groundwork for just and compassionate relationships, transcending social and economic statuses.

The Call to Stand Firm (6:10-13)

"Finally, be strong in the Lord and in his mighty power. Put on the full armour of God, so that you can take your stand against the devil's schemes. For our struggle is not against flesh and blood, but against the rulers, against the authorities, against the powers of this dark world and against the spiritual forces of evil in the heavenly realms.

Therefore, put on the full armour of God, so that when the day of evil comes, you may be able to stand your ground, and after you have done everything, to stand." (Ephesians 6:10-13)

Paul's starting point is not our strength but God's. He urges us to find our strength in the Lord's vast reservoir of power. This is crucial because our adversary, the devil, is cunning and relentless.

The 'full armour of God' is a metaphorical representation of all the resources God provides for our defence. The purpose? So we may stand firm. This standing firm isn't just about holding our ground; it's about maintaining our faith and integrity despite the onslaughts of temptation, doubt, and fear.

Ask yourself: Am I relying on my own strength, or am I drawing power from God? Am I equipped with His full armour to face daily spiritual battles?

The Armor Detailed (6:14-17)

"Stand firm then, with the belt of truth buckled around your waist, with the breastplate of righteousness in place, and with your feet fitted with the readiness that comes from the gospel of peace. In addition to all this, take up the shield of faith, with which you can extinguish all the flaming arrows of the evil one. Take the helmet of salvation and the sword of the Spirit, which is the word of God." (Ephesians 6:14-17)

Paul details each piece of this metaphorical armour, emphasizing its importance and symbolic meaning:

Belt of Truth:
This represents honesty, integrity, and the truth of God's Word, which holds everything together.

Breastplate of Righteousness:
This signifies the righteousness we receive through faith in Christ, protecting our hearts and moral centre.

Shoes of the Gospel of Peace:
Ready feet symbolize our preparedness to spread the Good News and to stand firm in peace, even amidst chaos.

Shield of Faith:
Our faith can extinguish all the flaming arrows of the evil one. It's our trust in God, our fundamental defence against doubt and fear.

Helmet of Salvation:
Our assurance of salvation protects our minds from despair and hopelessness.

Sword of the Spirit:
The only offensive weapon in the armour, representing the Word of God, which is powerful and effective in spiritual combat.

Are we equipping ourselves daily with these spiritual resources? How am we using the Word of God in our lives?

Prayer and Alertness (6:18-20)

"And pray in the Spirit on all occasions with all kinds of prayers and requests. With this in mind, be alert and always keep on praying for all the Lord's people. Pray also for me, that whenever I speak, words may be given me so that I will fearlessly make known the mystery of the gospel, for which I am an ambassador in chains. Pray that I may declare it fearlessly, as I should."
(Ephesians 6:18-20)

The armour is complete, but the strategy includes constant communication with our Commander in Chief through prayer. Paul underscores the necessity of prayer: It is the way we activate the armour and remain vigilant.

Being 'alert' means being aware of spiritual dangers and being ready to counter them with prayer. We're not only to pray for ourselves but for all believers, understanding that we're part of a larger battle affecting the entire body of Christ.

So, consider this: Is prayer my first response in times of trouble? Am I mindful of the needs of others in my prayers?

Conclusion

As we close this study in Ephesians, let us always remember that spiritual warfare is a reality for every believer. But Ephesians doesn't leave us in fear; it equips us with hope, strength, and strategy.

We are called to stand firm, fully armoured, deeply rooted in prayer, and connected to our fellow soldiers in Christ. May the Lord strengthen and protect each one of us as we stand firm in His mighty power.

~ PHILIPPIANS ~

Introduction

The New Testament book of Philippians, one of Paul's prison epistles, is a profound piece of scripture primarily focused on joy, humility, and the imitation of Christ.

Despite being written from prison, the tone of this whole letter is overwhelmingly positive, emphasizing the joy of Christian faith even in adversity. Allow me to give you an overview of this whole letter before we explore the text in more detail

Chapter 1: Christ Is My Life

Paul starts by expressing his gratitude and affection for the Philippians, thanking God for their partnership in the gospel from the very beginning (1:3-5). This sets a tone of mutual respect and love, highlighting the strong bond between Paul and the church.

The central theme of Chapter 1 is that Christ is to be magnified in all circumstances. Paul talks about his own situation, being in chains, and how it has served to advance the gospel rather than hinder it (1:12-14).

He asserts that whether through life or death, his ultimate goal is to honour Christ. His famous declaration, *"For to me, to live is Christ and to die is gain"* (1:21), encapsulates his deep commitment to Jesus and the gospel.

Paul also addresses the issue of suffering and persecution, emphasizing that it is a privilege granted on behalf of Christ (1:29-30).

This sets a precedent for the rest of the letter, advocating for a perspective that sees suffering as a component of Christian discipleship and a means to further deepen one's connection with Christ.

Chapter 2: Humility and Unity in Christ

This chapter is home to one of the most poignant passages in the New Testament, the Christ Hymn (2:6-11). Paul uses the example of Jesus Christ to instruct the Philippians on humility, service, and obedience. He encourages them to have the same mindset as Christ - who, despite being in the form of God, humbled Himself by becoming obedient to death, even death on a cross.

Paul calls the community to unity and selflessness, urging them to *"do nothing out of selfish ambition or vain conceit, but in humility consider others better than yourselves"* (2:3). This appeal is grounded in the example of Christ's own humility and is a call to live a life that reflects His character.

The latter part of Chapter 2 shifts to more personal matters, discussing Timothy and Epaphroditus, two men who embody the teachings Paul has been expounding. Their examples further reinforce the letter's themes of service, sacrifice, and Christian fellowship.

Chapter 3: Righteousness Through Faith and Pressing On

Chapter 3 marks a shift as Paul warns against false teachers and stresses the importance of righteousness through faith in Christ rather than through legalistic adherence to the law. He shares his own background as a Pharisee and considers all his previous achievements as "garbage" compared to the surpassing worth of knowing Christ (3:8).

The concept of pressing on toward the goal for the prize of the upward call of God in Christ Jesus (3:14) is central to this chapter. Paul speaks about the Christian life as a race, emphasizing the importance of focus, perseverance, and the ultimate goal of heavenly citizenship.

Chapter 4: Rejoice Always and Final Exhortations

The final chapter of Philippians is packed with exhortations and practical advice. Paul's call to *"rejoice in the Lord always"* (4:4) reiterates the letter's overarching theme of joy.

He speaks about the peace of God, which transcends all understanding, and how it will guard the hearts and minds of those in Christ Jesus (4:7).

Paul also addresses the importance of contentment, stating that he has learned now to be content whatever the circumstances (4:11-13). He speaks to the secret of facing both plenty and hunger, abundance, and need through Christ who strengthens him.

The letter concludes with thanks for the financial support he has received from the Philippians, affirming their generosity as a *"fragrant offering, an acceptable sacrifice, pleasing to God"* (4:18). Yet, beyond the material support, Paul emphasizes their shared bond in Christ and the eternal value of their spiritual partnership.

Summary

Paul's letter to the believers in Philippi offers profound insights into Christian life and spirituality, emphasizing joy, humility, unity, and perseverance. Through personal reflections, strong theological exhortations, and practical advice, Paul encourages the Philippian church - and by extension, all Christians - to live lives that reflect the values and attitude of Christ.

It's a reminder that the source of true joy and peace lies not in external circumstances but in a deep, abiding relationship with Jesus Christ.

Now I will unpack each of the four chapters in more detail as we explore this encouraging epistle in more detail.

~ PHILIPPIANS 1 ~

Introduction

Paul's letter to the Philippians is full of encouragement and joy. It is written not from a place of comfort, but from the confines of a prison cell.

In this first chapter, we find a profound message of hope, purpose, and joy that transcends circumstances, a message that is just as relevant to us today as it was to the early church in Philippi.

The Joy of Fellowship (1:1-11)

"Paul and Timothy, servants of Christ Jesus, to all God's holy people in Christ Jesus at Philippi, together with the overseers and deacons: Grace and peace to you from God our Father and the Lord Jesus Christ.

I thank my God every time I remember you. In all my prayers for all of you, I always pray with joy because of your partnership in the gospel from the first day until now, being confident of this, that he who began a good work in you will carry it on to completion until the day of Christ Jesus.

It is right for me to feel this way about all of you, since I have you in my heart and, whether I am in chains or defending and confirming the gospel, all of you share in God's grace with me. God can testify how I long for all of you with the affection of Christ Jesus.

And this is my prayer: that your love may abound more and more in knowledge and depth of insight, so that you may be able to discern what is best and may be pure and blameless for the day of Christ, filled with the fruit of righteousness that comes through Jesus Christ - to the glory and praise of God." (Philippians 1:1-11)

Paul begins his letter with expressions of gratitude and joy for the fellowship and partnership he shares with the Philippians in the gospel.

Notice how Paul's joy is not rooted in his physical well-being or material comfort, but in the spiritual bond he shares with his fellow believers. Despite his chains, Paul is overflowing with gratitude, praying with joy for the believers in Philippi (1:4).

Let us ask ourselves: Where does our joy come from? In a world that often equates happiness with material success and personal comfort, Paul reminds us that our true joy lies in our relationship with Christ and our fellowship with one another. As we navigate through our own trials and tribulations, may we find strength and joy in the community of faith, just as Paul did.

The Advancement of the Gospel (1:12-18)

> *"Now I want you to know, brothers and sisters, that what has happened to me has actually served to advance the gospel. As a result, it has become clear throughout the whole palace guard and to everyone else that I am in chains for Christ. And because of my chains, most of the brothers and sisters have become confident in the Lord and dare all the more to proclaim the gospel without fear.*
>
> *It is true that some preach Christ out of envy and rivalry, but others out of goodwill. The latter do so out of love, knowing that I am put here for the defence of the gospel. The former preach Christ out of selfish ambition, not sincerely, supposing that they can stir up trouble for me while I am in chains. But what does it matter? The important thing is that in every way, whether from false motives or true, Christ is preached. And because of this I rejoice. Yes, and I will continue to rejoice ..."* (Philippians 1:12-18)

One of the most striking aspects of this first chapter is Paul's perspective on his own imprisonment. Instead of seeing it as a setback, Paul views his chains as a means to further the gospel. His imprisonment has emboldened other believers to speak the word of God more courageously and fearlessly (1:14).

Paul's situation teaches us a valuable lesson: our circumstances, no matter how dire, can be used by God for His purposes. Instead of asking *"Why me?"* we are encouraged to ask, *"How can God use this for His glory?"*

Whether we face personal challenges, health issues, or professional setbacks, let us remember that God can use our situations to advance His kingdom, just as He did with Paul's imprisonment.

To Live Is Christ (1:19-26)

> " ... for I know that through your prayers and God's provision of the Spirit of Jesus Christ what has happened to me will turn out for my deliverance. I eagerly expect and hope that I will in no way be ashamed but will have sufficient courage so that now as always Christ will be exalted in my body, whether by life or by death.
>
> For to me, to live is Christ and to die is gain. If I am to go on living in the body, this will mean fruitful labour for me. Yet what shall I choose? I do not know! I am torn between the two: I desire to depart and be with Christ, which is better by far; but it is more necessary for you that I remain in the body.
>
> Convinced of this, I know that I will remain, and I will continue with all of you for your progress and joy in the faith, so that through my being with you again your boasting in Christ Jesus will abound on account of me." (Philippians 1:19-26)

In one of the most powerful passages of the New Testament, Paul declares boldly the words I have placed on the title page of this book, "*For to me, to live is Christ and to die is gain*" (v.21).

These words are a testament to Paul's unwavering commitment to Jesus Christ. For Paul, life is an opportunity to serve Christ and advance the gospel, while death is the gateway to eternal union with the Lord.

What does it mean for us to say, "*To live is Christ*"? It means that our lives are not our own; they are dedicated to reflecting Christ's love, serving others, and spreading the good news of the gospel.

Every breath we take, every decision we make, should be guided by our desire to glorify Christ. Let this be our guiding principle, our purpose, and our joy.

Standing Firm in One Spirit (1:27-30)

"Whatever happens, conduct yourselves in a manner worthy of the gospel of Christ. Then, whether I come and see you or only hear about you in my absence, I will know that you stand firm in the one Spirit, striving together as one for the faith of the gospel without being frightened in any way by those who oppose you. This is a sign to them that they will be destroyed, but that you will be saved - and that by God. For it has been granted to you on behalf of Christ not only to believe in him, but also to suffer for him, since you are going through the same struggle you saw I had, and now hear that I still have." (Philippians 1:27-30)

Paul concludes the chapter by urging the Philippians to conduct themselves in a manner worthy of the gospel of Christ. He calls them to stand firm in one spirit, striving together as one for the faith of the gospel 1:27). This is a call to unity, perseverance, and courage in the face of opposition.

As followers of Christ, we are called to stand together, united by our common faith and purpose. The world around us may be filled with conflict and division, but in Christ, we find common ground and a shared mission. Let us strive to live out our faith with courage and unity, supporting one another in love and standing firm against the challenges of this world.

Conclusion

Philippians Chapter 1 offers us a treasure trove of spiritual wisdom and encouragement. It reminds us that our joy and purpose are not dictated by our circumstances, but by our relationship with Christ and our commitment to the gospel.

As we embrace the days ahead, let us carry with us the lessons of Paul's letter: to find joy in fellowship, to see opportunities for the gospel in our challenges, to live for Christ in all things, and to stand firm in our faith, united in spirit and purpose.

~ PHILIPPIANS 2 ~

Introduction

We now venture into the profound depths of chapter 2, a passage that challenges us, encourages us, and calls us to live in a manner radically different from the world around us. In this chapter, the Apostle Paul presents the ultimate example of humility and selflessness: Jesus Christ Himself. As we explore these sacred verses, let us open our hearts to the transformative message of love and humility.

Unity through Humility (2:1-4)

> *"Therefore, if you have any encouragement from being united with Christ, if any comfort from his love, if any common sharing in the Spirit, if any tenderness and compassion, then make my joy complete by being like-minded, having the same love, being one in spirit and of one mind. Do nothing out of selfish ambition or vain conceit. Rather, in humility value others above yourselves, not looking to your own interests but each of you to the interests of the others." (Philippians 2:1-4)*

Paul begins this chapter with an appeal that resonates with the heart's deep longing for true community and unity. He speaks of being like-minded, having the same love, being one in spirit and purpose. But how do we achieve such unity? Paul offers a radical solution: humility. He calls us to value others above ourselves, not looking to our own interests but to the interests of the others.

This call to humility is counter cultural. It goes against the grain of a western society that often promotes individualism and self-promotion. Yet, it is the secret to genuine community and unity in Christ.

As followers of Jesus, we are called to embody this humility in our relationships, our families, our workplaces, and our church. Imagine the impact we could make if we truly lived out this principle, putting the needs and interests of others before our own!

The Example of Christ (2:5-11)

"In your relationships with one another, have the same mindset as Christ Jesus: Who, being in very nature God, did not consider equality with God something to be used to his own advantage; rather, he made himself nothing by taking the very nature of a servant, being made in human likeness.

And being found in appearance as a man, he humbled himself by becoming obedient to death - even death on a cross! Therefore, God exalted him to the highest place and gave him the name that is above every name, that at the name of Jesus every knee should bow, in heaven and on earth and under the earth, and every tongue acknowledge that Jesus Christ is Lord, to the glory of God the Father." (Philippians 2:5-11)

In the heart of Philippians Chapter 2 lies one of the most beautiful and profound passages of the New Testament, often referred to as the Kenosis Hymn (from the Greek word for "emptying"). Paul points us to the example of Jesus Christ, who, though being in very nature God, did not consider equality with God something to be grasped. Instead, He emptied Himself, taking the form of a servant, being made in human likeness, He humbled Himself by becoming obedient to death - even death on a cross!

This passage challenges us to the core. Christ's humility led Him from the highest heights of glory to the deepest depths of suffering - out of love for us. As we reflect on Christ's self-emptying, let's ask ourselves: How does His example impact the way we live? Are we willing to humble ourselves, to serve, to put others first, to love selflessly? The mind of Christ is a mindset of radical humility and sacrificial love. Let us strive to adopt this mindset in all aspects of our lives.

Working Out Our Salvation (2:12-13)

"Therefore, my dear friends, as you have always obeyed - not only in my presence, but now much more in my absence - continue to work out your salvation with fear and trembling, for it is God who works in you to will and to act in order to fulfill his good purpose." (Philippians 2:12-13)

Paul transitions from the example of Christ to the practical application, urging us to "*work out your salvation with fear and trembling.*" This is not a call to earn our salvation through works but to live out the implications of our salvation with seriousness and commitment. It is God who works in us to will and to act according to His good purpose.

This is a reminder that the Christian life is both a gift and a responsibility. It is a life of cooperation with the Holy Spirit, allowing Him to transform us from the inside out. As we reflect Christ's humility and love, we become lights in a dark world, shining the beauty of the gospel for all to see.

Shining as Stars (2:14-18)

"Do everything without grumbling or arguing, so that you may become blameless and pure, "children of God without fault in a warped and crooked generation." Then you will shine among them like stars in the sky as you hold firmly to the word of life.

And then I will be able to boast on the day of Christ that I did not run or labour in vain. But even if I am being poured out like a drink offering on the sacrifice and service coming from your faith, I am glad and rejoice with all of you. So you too should be glad and rejoice with me." (Philippians 2:14-18)

Paul calls us to shine like stars in the universe as we hold out the word of life. In a world marked by complaining and arguing, we are to be different. Our lives should be marked by gratitude, unity, and joy. Even in the midst of a crooked and depraved generation, our lives can display the transforming power of the gospel.

This is no small task, but it is what we are called to as followers of Christ. Let us examine our hearts and lives: Are we shining as lights in our community? Are our workplaces, our homes, and our social circles better because we are there? Let us commit to living out our faith boldly and joyfully, making the gospel attractive through our words and actions.

Models of Service and Sacrifice (2:19-30)

> *"I hope in the Lord Jesus to send Timothy to you soon, that I also may be cheered when I receive news about you. I have no one else like him, who will show genuine concern for your welfare. For everyone looks out for their own interests, not those of Jesus Christ.*
>
> *But you know that Timothy has proved himself, because as a son with his father he has served with me in the work of the gospel. I hope, therefore, to send him as soon as I see how things go with me. And I am confident in the Lord that I myself will come soon.*
>
> *But I think it is necessary to send back to you Epaphroditus, my brother, co-worker and fellow soldier, who is also your messenger, whom you sent to take care of my needs. For he longs for all of you and is distressed because you heard he was ill. Indeed he was ill, and almost died. But God had mercy on him, and not on him only but also on me, to spare me sorrow upon sorrow.*
>
> *Therefore, I am all the more eager to send him, so that when you see him again you may be glad and I may have less anxiety. So then, welcome him in the Lord with great joy, and honour people like him, because he almost died for the work of Christ. He risked his life to make up for the help you yourselves could not give me."*
> *(Philippians 2:19-30)*

Paul shifts from theological exposition to personal reflections and outlines his plans regarding two key individuals in his ministry: Timothy and Epaphroditus. This passage provides us with profound insights into Christian service, leadership, and the nature of the Christian community as characterized by genuine concern, selflessness, and sacrifice.

Paul expresses his intention to send Timothy to the Philippian church soon, highlighting Timothy's unique quality of genuine concern for the welfare of the Philippians.

Unlike others who seek their own interests, Timothy's care for the Philippians mirrors that of Paul. This mutual concern is not based on personal gain but on the interests of Jesus Christ.

Timothy embodies the selfless mindset Paul has been advocating for in Philippians 2, serving as a living example of looking out for the interests of others. Timothy is not just a helper but a son to Paul in the service of the gospel. His proven worth comes from his faithful service alongside Paul, akin to a son with a father.

This metaphor underscores the depth of their relationship, bound not by blood but by shared commitment to the gospel. Timothy's service and loyalty set a standard for Christian ministry, emphasizing faithfulness and dedication.

Paul's mention of his hope to send Timothy "soon" and his own anticipation of visiting the Philippians reflect a deep trust in God's providence. Despite his imprisonment, Paul remains hopeful and plans for the future, showing a steadfast faith in the Lord's guidance. This attitude encourages believers to trust in God's timing and provision, even in uncertain circumstances.

Epaphroditus is introduced with titles that reflect his character and service: brother, fellow worker, and fellow soldier. These descriptors not only highlight his close relationship with Paul but also his active participation in the work of the gospel and his endurance in spiritual battles. Epaphroditus represents the ideal of Christian brotherhood, labouring and fighting for the faith alongside his fellow believers.

Paul recounts how Epaphroditus nearly died for the work of Christ, risking his life to make up for the help the Philippians could not give Paul. This act of sacrifice reveals the extent of Epaphroditus's dedication to serving God and supporting Paul.

His willingness to lay down his life for the sake of the gospel exemplifies the call to take up one's cross and follow Jesus. The Philippians are urged to receive him back with joy and to honour such individuals who display such commitment and sacrifice.

In highlighting the examples of Timothy and Epaphroditus, Paul provides the Philippian church (and us) with concrete illustrations of the Christlike humility and selflessness he has been teaching.

These men embody the principles of looking beyond one's interests to serve others and being willing to sacrifice for the sake of Christ and His church. Their stories encourage believers to adopt a similar mindset in their communities, serving faithfully and risking for the gospel.

As we reflect on the lives of Timothy and Epaphroditus, let us be inspired to cultivate genuine concern for our fellow believers, to serve the Lord with proven worth, and to embrace the risks associated with living out our faith boldly. May their examples spur us on to greater love, service, and sacrifice.

Conclusion

Philippians Chapter 2 presents us with a stunning vision of Christian life and community. It calls us to unity through humility, to live out the sacrificial love of Christ, to work out our salvation with fear and trembling, and to shine as lights in a dark world.

As we go forth from here, let the mind of Christ be in us. Let us embrace humility, serve one another in love, and shine as beacons of hope and grace. May our lives reflect the beauty and humility of Jesus, drawing others to Him and transforming the world around us.

Let us pray that God would empower us to live out these truths, for the glory of His name and the advancement of His kingdom.

~ PHILIPPIANS 3 ~

Introduction

In this chapter, the Apostle Paul probes deep into the heart of the Christian experience, challenging us to reconsider what we value most in life. In this chapter, Paul contrasts the worthlessness of worldly achievements with the incomparable value of knowing Christ. As we explore these timeless truths, let's open our hearts to the transformative power of the Gospel.

The Loss of All Things for Christ (3:1-11)

"Further, my brothers and sisters, rejoice in the Lord! It is no trouble for me to write the same things to you again, and it is a safeguard for you. Watch out for those dogs, those evildoers, those mutilators of the flesh. For it is we who are the circumcision, we who serve God by his Spirit, who boast in Christ Jesus, and who put no confidence in the flesh - though I myself have reasons for such confidence.

If someone else thinks they have reasons to put confidence in the flesh, I have more: circumcised on the eighth day, of the people of Israel, of the tribe of Benjamin, a Hebrew of Hebrews; in regard to the law, a Pharisee; as for zeal, persecuting the church; as for righteousness based on the law, faultless.

But whatever were gains to me I now consider loss for the sake of Christ. What is more, I consider everything a loss because of the surpassing worth of knowing Christ Jesus my Lord, for whose sake I have lost all things. I consider them garbage, that I may gain Christ and be found in him, not having a righteousness of my own that comes from the law, but that which is through faith in[a] Christ - the righteousness that comes from God on the basis of faith.

I want to know Christ — yes, to know the power of his resurrection and participation in his sufferings, becoming like him in his death, 11 and so, somehow, attaining to the resurrection from the dead."
(Philippians 3:1-11)

Paul begins this chapter with a stark warning against placing confidence in the flesh – that is, confidence in our own abilities, achievements, or religious credentials. Paul then lists his own impressive qualifications: circumcised on the eighth day, of the people of Israel, a Hebrew of Hebrews, a Pharisee, zealous, and blameless under the law. Yet, Paul considers all these things as loss compared to the surpassing worth of knowing Christ Jesus his Lord.

This passage invites us to examine our own hearts: What are we relying on for our identity and worth? Are we clinging to our accomplishments, our social status, our religious activities? Paul's testimony challenges us to count all these things as loss for the sake of Christ. Knowing Jesus is not just another item on the list of life's achievements; it is the only thing that truly matters.

Paul emphasizes that his righteousness does not come from obeying the law but from faith in Christ. This righteousness is not our own doing; it is given through faith in Christ, the righteousness that comes from God on the basis of faith. This is the heart of the gospel: we are saved not by our works but by faith in the finished work of Christ on the cross.

Here lies the radical freedom of the Christian life. We are liberated from the endless cycle of trying to earn God's favour through our own efforts. Instead, we are invited to rest in the perfect righteousness that is ours through faith in Christ. Let us then live lives marked by this faith, fully relying on the grace of God rather than our own merits.

Pressing On Toward the Goal (3:12-14)

> *"Not that I have already obtained all this, or have already arrived at my goal, but I press on to take hold of that for which Christ Jesus took hold of me. Brothers and sisters, I do not consider myself yet to have taken hold of it. But one thing I do: Forgetting what is behind and straining toward what is ahead, I press on toward the goal to win the prize for which God has called me heavenward in Christ Jesus." (Philippians 3:12-14)*

In one of the most stirring calls to spiritual perseverance in the Scriptures, Paul declares that he has not yet obtained all this, nor has he already been made perfect. But he presses on to take hold of that for which Christ Jesus took hold of him. He forgets what is behind and strains toward what is ahead, pressing on toward the goal to win the prize for which God has called him heavenward in Christ Jesus.

This is a powerful metaphor for the Christian life. Like athletes in a race, we are called to keep moving forward, focusing on the finish line, not getting entangled in past failures or resting on past laurels.

This pressing on is not just some solitary endeavour but one we undertake as part of the community of faith, encouraging and supporting each other in our journey toward Christlikeness.

Citizenship in Heaven (3:15-16)

"All of us, then, who are mature should take such a view of things. And if on some point you think differently, that too God will make clear to you. Only let us live up to what we have already attained." (Philippians 3:15-16)

Paul addresses believers with a call to maturity and consistency in the Christian life. This brief yet profound passage provides crucial insights into Paul's understanding of spiritual growth and the communal pursuit of faithfulness. He begins by speaking to the "mature," implying a level of spiritual development and understanding. He encourages these mature believers to adopt the same mindset he has been expounding upon - specifically, the attitude of pressing on toward the goal for the prize of the upward call of God in Christ Jesus (3:14).

This call to maturity is not about achieving perfection based on human standards but about continually striving for spiritual growth and deeper relationship with Christ. Paul acknowledges that not everyone may share this perspective but expresses confidence that God will reveal the truth to those who are open to it.

Paul then urges the Philippians to live up to what they have already attained. This exhortation to "hold true" to the progress they've made in their spiritual journey emphasizes the importance of consistency and perseverance. It's a reminder that the Christian life is not characterized by momentary flashes of insight or sporadic growth spurts but by a steady, ongoing walk in obedience to the truth already revealed.

This verse underscores the communal aspect of spiritual growth. By urging believers to walk by the same rule and mind the same thing, Paul highlights the importance of unity and mutual encouragement within the body of Christ. The Christian faith, while personal, is not solitary; it's lived out within a community of believers striving together toward maturity in Christ.

These two short verses encapsulate Paul's strong call to spiritual maturity and communal faithfulness. It reminds us that while we are each at different stages in our spiritual journey, we are called to press on toward the goal of knowing Christ more deeply. Moreover, it challenges us to maintain the ground we've gained in our spiritual lives, not regressing or becoming complacent but continually moving forward in unity with our fellow believers. In essence, these verses encourage us to embody the truths we've embraced, walking together in a manner worthy of the gospel.

Citizenship in Heaven (3:17-21)

"Join together in following my example, brothers and sisters, and just as you have us as a model, keep your eyes on those who live as we do. For, as I have often told you before and now tell you again even with tears, many live as enemies of the cross of Christ. Their destiny is destruction, their god is their stomach, and their glory is in their shame. Their mind is set on earthly things.

But our citizenship is in heaven. And we eagerly await a Saviour from there, the Lord Jesus Christ, who, by the power that enables him to bring everything under his control, will transform our lowly bodies so that they will be like his glorious body." (Philippians 3:17-21)

Paul concludes the chapter by reminding us that our citizenship is in heaven, from which we eagerly await a Saviour, the Lord Jesus Christ. This perspective is crucial in a world where we are constantly bombarded with messages urging us to find our identity and satisfaction in temporary, earthly things.

As citizens of heaven, our values, our priorities, and our hopes are shaped not by the shifting sands of cultural trends but by the eternal realities of the kingdom of God. This heavenly perspective empowers us to live in this world as ambassadors of Christ, shining as lights in the darkness, and holding firmly to the word of life.

Conclusion

Philippians Chapter 3 calls us to a radical re-evaluation of our values and priorities. It challenges us to find our worth not in our achievements or social status but in the surpassing worth of knowing Christ. It invites us to embrace the righteousness that comes through faith, to press on toward the goal, and to live as citizens of heaven.

As we leave this place, let us take these truths to heart. May we count everything as loss for the sake of Christ. May we press on toward the goal, supported by our fellow believers. And may we live each day as citizens of heaven, eagerly awaiting our Saviour, the Lord Jesus Christ.

Let us pray that the Holy Spirit would work these truths deep into our hearts, transforming us more into the likeness of Christ, for His glory and for the extension of His kingdom.

Introduction

We stand on the sacred ground as we approach chapter 4 of Philippians, a passage that offers profound insights into the Christian way of life marked by peace, contentment, and reliance on God.

This chapter, penned by the Apostle Paul from his prison cell, serves as a beacon of hope and instruction for all who seek to live in the fullness of Christ's joy and peace.

Stand Firm in the Lord (4:1-3)

"Therefore, my brothers and sisters, you whom I love and long for, my joy and crown, stand firm in the Lord in this way, dear friends! I plead with Euodia and I plead with Syntyche to be of the same mind in the Lord.

Yes, and I ask you, my true companion, help these women since they have contended at my side in the cause of the gospel, along with Clement and the rest of my co-workers, whose names are in the book of life." (Philippians 4:1-3)

Paul begins this final chapter with an affectionate appeal to the Philippian believers, urging them to stand firm in the Lord. This call to steadfastness is not just a call to doctrinal purity but to a lived-out faith that withstands the challenges of life. It's a reminder that our strength doesn't come from ourselves but from our union with Christ.

Moreover, Paul highlights the importance of unity within the church, making a personal appeal to Euodia and Syntyche to be of the same mind in the Lord. This tells us that our individual relationships within the church impact our collective witness.

As a community of believers, let us strive for reconciliation, unity, and mutual support, standing firm together in the Lord.

Rejoice Always (4:4-7)

"Rejoice in the Lord always. I will say it again: Rejoice! Let your gentleness be evident to all. The Lord is near. Do not be anxious about anything, but in every situation, by prayer and petition, with thanksgiving, present your requests to God. And the peace of God, which transcends all understanding, will guard your hearts and your minds in Christ Jesus." (Philippians 4:4-7)

Paul's command to rejoice is not based on our circumstances but on our relationship with the Lord. This joy is not fleeting or superficial but a deep, abiding sense of God's presence and goodness, even in the midst of trials.

Paul then connects this joy with the peace of God, which transcends all understanding. He instructs us to present our requests to God with thanksgiving, turning our anxieties into prayers. This peace guards our hearts and minds in Christ Jesus. As we face the worries and stresses of life, let us be people of prayer, trusting that the peace of God will guard our hearts in Christ Jesus.

Think on These Things (4:8-9)

"Finally, brothers and sisters, whatever is true, whatever is noble, whatever is right, whatever is pure, whatever is lovely, whatever is admirable - if anything is excellent or praiseworthy - think about such things. Whatever you have learned or received or heard from me or seen in me - put it into practice. And the God of peace will be with you." (Philippians 4:8-9)

Paul provides a guide for our thoughts: whatever is true, noble, right, pure, lovely, admirable, excellent, or praiseworthy, think about such things. In an age of negativity and cynicism, this call to focus on the positive aspects of life and faith is revolutionary.

Our thoughts shape our attitudes, our emotions, and ultimately our actions. Let us fill our minds with things that elevate rather than degrade, that heal rather than wound, that build up rather than tear down.

Learning Contentment (4:10-13)

"I rejoiced greatly in the Lord that at last you renewed your concern for me. Indeed, you were concerned, but you had no opportunity to show it. I am not saying this because I am in need, for I have learned to be content whatever the circumstances. I know what it is to be in need, and I know what it is to have plenty. I have learned the secret of being content in any and every situation, whether well fed or hungry, whether living in plenty or in want. I can do all this through him who gives me strength." (Philippians 4:10-13)

One of the most personal and powerful sections of this chapter is Paul's reflection on contentment. He speaks of learning to be content in any and every situation, whether well fed or hungry, whether living in plenty or in want. This contentment is not complacency but a deep trust in God who provides strength in all circumstances.

This is a challenging word for a world constantly seeking more. Paul's secret to contentment lies in his relationship with Christ: "I can do all this through him who gives me strength." May we, too, learn this secret of contentment, relying on Christ's strength rather than our own.

The Gift of Giving (4:14-20)

"Yet it was good of you to share in my troubles. Moreover, as you Philippians know, in the early days of your acquaintance with the gospel, when I set out from Macedonia, not one church shared with me in the matter of giving and receiving, except you only; for even when I was in Thessalonica, you sent me aid more than once when I was in need. Not that I desire your gifts; what I desire is that more be credited to your account. I have received full payment and have more than enough. I am amply supplied, now that I have received from Epaphroditus the gifts you sent. They are a fragrant offering, an acceptable sacrifice, pleasing to God. And my God will meet all your needs according to the riches of his glory in Christ Jesus. To our God and Father be glory for ever and ever. Amen." (Philippians 4:14-20)

Paul draws his letter to a close with words of gratitude for the financial support he received from the Philippian church. Their giving was an act of worship, a *"fragrant offering, an acceptable sacrifice, pleasing to God."* This reminds us that our giving is not merely a financial transaction but an act of worship and partnership in the gospel. Moreover, Paul assures them that God will meet all their needs according to the riches of his glory in Christ Jesus. This is the beautiful cycle of God's economy: as we give out of our resources, God supplies our needs, creating a community of mutual support and provision.

Final Greetings (4:21-23)

> *"Greet all God's people in Christ Jesus. The brothers and sisters who are with me send greetings. All God's people here send you greetings, especially those who belong to Caesar's household. The grace of the Lord Jesus Christ be with your spirit. Amen."*
> *(Philippians 4:21-23)*

Paul concludes his epistle by extending his final greetings and blessings to the Philippian believers, encapsulating themes of unity, grace, and the inclusiveness of the Christian community. Paul's request for the Philippians to greet every saint in Christ Jesus underlines the interconnectedness and individual importance of each member within the Christian community. This inclusivity and personal attention to each and every believer emphasize the value of every person in the body of Christ, regardless of their status or role.

The mention of the brothers who are with Paul sends a message of unity and solidarity. Despite physical distances, the bond among believers, strengthened through shared faith and mutual support, transcends geographical barriers, highlighting the universal nature of the Christian church.

Paul finishes with a benediction of grace, praying that the grace of the Lord Jesus Christ would be with their spirit. This final blessing is a powerful reminder of the source of their strength, fellowship, and salvation.

Grace is the foundation and sustenance of the believers' lives, encompassing Paul's desire for the Philippians to experience God's empowering presence and assistance in all aspects of their lives.

These concluding verses beautifully wrap up the epistle, leaving the readers with a sense of belonging, encouragement, and the assurance of God's grace. Paul's heartfelt closing reiterates the central Christian themes of love, unity, and the sustaining power of grace.

Conclusion

As we conclude our journey through Philippians, let us take to heart the lessons Paul has imparted: Stand firm in the Lord, rejoice always, let your gentleness be evident to all, bring your anxieties to God in prayer, focus your thoughts on what is good and pure, learn contentment in Christ, and give generously as an act of worship.

May the grace of the Lord Jesus Christ be with your spirit as you seek to live out these truths. Let Philippians be a guide for your life, leading you into deeper peace, joy, and contentment in the Lord.

Let us pray for God's grace to empower us to live out these commands, that our lives may reflect the peace and joy of Christ to a world in desperate need. Amen.

~ COLOSSIANS ~

Introduction

The Book of Colossians is an epistle (letter) from the Apostle Paul, directed to the Christian community in Colossae, a city in Asia Minor (modern-day Turkey).

This letter, composed of four chapters, deals with theological teachings, practical Christian living, and specific admonitions to the Colossian church. It's a blend of doctrinal instruction and practical advice, reflecting early Christian thought and challenges.

Chapter 1:

This chapter sets the tone for the entire letter. Paul begins with a greeting and a prayer of thanks for the Colossian believers, acknowledging their faith, love, and hope.

The central part of the chapter is a rich theological section that presents Jesus Christ as the preeminent creator and redeemer. Paul asserts Christ's supremacy over all creation and emphasizes that through Him, God has reconciled all things to Himself.

This reconciliation is available to the Colossians, who were once alienated from God but are now presented as holy and blameless. Paul ends the chapter by discussing his own ministry, highlighting his struggles and the energy Christ powerfully inspires within him for the sake of the church.

Chapter 2:

Paul warns the believers against deceptive philosophy, legalism, mysticism, and asceticism. He is concerned that external traditions and philosophies might lead the Colossians away from the gospel's simplicity and the supremacy of Christ.

Paul reminds them that in Christ, all the fullness of Deity lives in bodily form, and they have been filled in Him.

Therefore, they should continue to live their lives rooted and built up in Him, established in faith, and overflowing with thankfulness, not being captivated by human traditions or elemental spiritual forces.

Chapter 3:

This chapter shifts from doctrinal teaching to practical application, illustrating what the Christian life should look like in response to the truths presented. Paul urges the Colossians to set their hearts and minds on things above, where Christ is, rather than on earthly things.

This 'heavenly' mindset should be reflected in their earthly relationships and conduct. Paul outlines a series of 'put off' and 'put on' instructions, advocating for the total removal of old behaviours like anger, malice, and lying, and the adoption of new behaviours like compassion, kindness, and patience.

The chapter closes with specific instructions for wives, husbands, children, and servants, emphasizing Christlike submission and service in household relationships.

Chapter 4:

Paul concludes his letter with final instructions and greetings. He encourages the Colossians to devote themselves to prayer, be watchful, and be thankful. Paul also instructs them to conduct themselves wisely towards outsiders, making the most of every opportunity. He asks for prayers for himself and his companions, that God may open a door for their message.

The epistle ends with personal greetings to and from various individuals, highlighting the communal and interconnected nature of the early Christian communities.

In summary, the Book of Colossians presents a comprehensive view of Christian doctrine and practical living. It emphasizes the supremacy and sufficiency of Christ in all things, challenging believers to continue to live in Him, rooted and built up in faith.

The letter addresses the dangers of deviating towards either legalistic traditions or mystical experiences that detract from the centrality of Christ.

It calls for a transformation that impacts not only individual behaviour but also communal relationships and interactions with the outside world.

Colossians remains relevant for contemporary Christianity, reminding believers of the core truths of their faith and the lifestyle that should naturally flow from those beliefs.

Now I will unpack each of the four chapters in more detail as we explore this letter in more detail.

~ COLOSSIANS 1 ~

Introduction

What a blessing it is to be able to explore the incredible richness of Colossians Chapter 1, a passage that not only introduces us to the heart of Apostle Paul but also to the magnificent supremacy of our Lord Jesus Christ.

This chapter serves as a profound reminder of the grace and peace we've been granted through faith, and it beckons us to a much deeper understanding and appreciation of the divine mystery that is Christ in us, the hope of glory.

Thanksgiving and Prayer (1:1-14)

"Paul, an apostle of Christ Jesus by the will of God, and Timothy our brother, to God's holy people in Colossae, the faithful brothers and sisters in Christ: Grace and peace to you from God our Father.

We always thank God, the Father of our Lord Jesus Christ, when we pray for you, because we have heard of your faith in Christ Jesus and of the love you have for all God's people - the faith and love that spring from the hope stored up for you in heaven and about which you have already heard in the true message of the gospel that has come to you.

In the same way, the gospel is bearing fruit and growing throughout the whole world - just as it has been doing among you since the day you heard it and truly understood God's grace. You learned it from Epaphras, our dear fellow servant, who is a faithful minister of Christ on our behalf, and who also told us of your love in the Spirit.

For this reason, since the day we heard about you, we have not stopped praying for you. We continually ask God to fill you with the knowledge of his will through all the wisdom and understanding that the Spirit gives, so that you may live a life worthy of the Lord and please him in every way.."

" ... bearing fruit in every good work, growing in the knowledge of God, being strengthened with all power according to his glorious might so that you may have great endurance and patience, and giving joyful thanks to the Father, who has qualified you to share in the inheritance of his holy people in the kingdom of light. For he has rescued us from the dominion of darkness and brought us into the kingdom of the Son he loves, in whom we have redemption, the forgiveness of sins." (Colossians 1:1-14)

These opening verses of Colossians serve as an introduction and a profound prayer, offering deep theological insights and practical advice for the Christian life. This passage is structured around Paul's greeting to the church, his thanksgiving for their faith, and his prayer for their spiritual growth.

Paul, with Timothy, starts by identifying himself as an apostle of Jesus Christ by the will of God, emphasizing his divine calling and authority. The letter is addressed to the holy and faithful brothers and sisters in Christ at Colossae. This greeting acknowledges the recipients' identity in Christ and sets the tone for the letter, underlining the themes of holiness, faithfulness, and unity in Christ.

Paul expresses his gratitude for the faith, love, and hope evident in the Colossian church. These virtues are foundational to Christian life, showing a response to the gospel's work among them. The reference to the gospel's fruitfulness highlights its transformative power and universal reach, reinforcing the idea that the message of Christ has global implications.

Paul also mentions Epaphras, commending his role in spreading the gospel in Colossae and serving as a faithful minister of Christ on Paul's behalf.

Paul's prayer for the Colossians is rich in theological depth, focusing on spiritual wisdom, understanding, and living a life worthy of the Lord. He prays for their knowledge of God's will, which encompasses both intellectual comprehension and practical application.

This knowledge is aimed at producing a life that is fully pleasing to God, characterized by good works, growth in the knowledge of God, endurance, patience, and joy.

Paul emphasizes the power of God to enable believers to live according to His will, pointing to the divine strength for enduring trials and challenges. The theme of redemption and forgiveness in verses 13-14 highlights the centrality of Christ's work on the cross, transferring believers from the domain of darkness to the kingdom of light, where Christ reigns supreme. This redemption is not just a future hope but has present-day implications for how believers live and relate to the world around them.

These 14 verses beautifully encapsulate key Christian doctrines, including the supremacy of Christ, the transformative power of the gospel, and the importance of living a life that reflects the lordship of Jesus.

Paul's prayerful introduction sets the stage for the rest of the letter, which will delve deeper into these themes, always pointing back to Christ as the source of the believer's life and hope.

The Supremacy of Christ (1:15-20)

> *"The Son is the image of the invisible God, the firstborn over all creation. For in him all things were created: things in heaven and on earth, visible and invisible, whether thrones or powers or rulers or authorities; all things have been created through him and for him.*
>
> *He is before all things, and in him all things hold together. And he is the head of the body, the church; he is the beginning and the firstborn from among the dead, so that in everything he might have the supremacy.*
>
> *For God was pleased to have all his fullness dwell in him, and through him to reconcile to himself all things, whether things on earth or things in heaven, by making peace through his blood, shed on the cross." (Colossians 1:15-20)*

This passage is the centrepiece of chapter 1. Paul presents Jesus not merely as a figure in history but as the image of the invisible God, the firstborn over all creation. In Him, all things were created: things in heaven and on earth, visible and invisible. This elevates Christ beyond our traditional view, placing Him at the centre of the universe, not just as a saviour but as the Creator.

This supremacy of Christ is not just a theological concept; it's a call to reorient our lives. If Christ is supreme, then our lives, our decisions, and our relationships should reflect His centrality. In our families, workplaces, and communities, Christ should remain at the core. This acknowledgment of Christ's supremacy challenges us to evaluate areas of our lives where He might not reign supreme.

Reconciliation Through Christ (1:21-23)

"Once you were alienated from God and were enemies in your minds because of your evil behaviour. But now he has reconciled you by Christ's physical body through death to present you holy in his sight, without blemish and free from accusation - if you continue in your faith, established and firm, and do not move from the hope held out in the gospel. This is the gospel that you heard and that has been proclaimed to every creature under heaven, and of which I, Paul, have become a servant."
(Colossians 1:21-23)

Moving forward, Paul discusses our reconciliation through Christ. Once alienated from God, we were enemies in our minds because of our evil behaviour. Yet, through Christ's physical body and death on the cross, we are presented holy and blameless in God's sight. This is not because of our merit – it's only because of His grace.

This message of reconciliation is particularly poignant in today's divided world. It calls us to be ambassadors of peace and reconciliation, just as Christ reconciled us to Himself. In our interactions, let us remember the depth of grace we've received and extend that grace to others, embodying the reconciliation we've experienced through Christ.

Rejoice in Suffering (1:24-25)

"Now I rejoice in what I am suffering for you, and I fill up in my flesh what is still lacking in regard to Christ's afflictions, for the sake of his body, which is the church. I have become its servant by the commission God gave me to present to you the word of God in its fullness ..." (Colossians 1:24-25)

This is a profound reflection on the nature of Christian ministry and suffering, articulated by Paul in the context of his mission to the church. This passage is part of a larger discourse that emphasizes the mystery of Christ and the church's role in God's redemptive plan.

Paul begins these two verses with a striking statement about rejoicing in his sufferings for the sake of the Colossians, which is a startling concept both then and now. He views his hardships as a continuation or filling up of what is lacking in Christ's afflictions, not suggesting that Christ's work on the cross was insufficient for salvation, but rather, that Paul participates in the ongoing suffering that the body of Christ, the church, endures.

This participation is not for the redemption that comes from Christ's sacrifice alone but for the sake of his body, the church, indicating a deep solidarity and commitment to the well-being and growth of the Christian community.

Paul identifies himself as a servant of the church, a role given to him by God. This service is described as a stewardship, implying responsibility, care, and trustworthiness in administering something valuable that belongs to another - in this case, the gospel itself.

The mystery mentioned here, which has been disclosed to the saints, refers to the previously hidden plan of God to unite all things in Christ, including Gentiles alongside Jews in God's redemptive plan. Paul's mission is to make this mystery fully known, which underscores the universal scope of the gospel and the inclusivity of the church as the body of Christ.

These two verses encapsulate key aspects of Paul's theological and ministerial perspective. His willingness to endure suffering for the benefit of the church demonstrates a profound understanding of Christian ministry as participation in the sufferings of Christ. This participation is not merely passive but is an active and joyful sharing in the afflictions of Christ for the sake of others. Furthermore, Paul's role as a steward of the divine mystery highlights the importance of faithful proclamation and teaching in the Christian community. These verses emphasize that the gospel is not just a message of individual salvation but a call to participate in the unfolding mystery of God's purpose to unite all things in Christ, a mission that entails both suffering and the stewardship of divine truth.

The Mystery Revealed (1:26-27)

"… the mystery that has been kept hidden for ages and generations, but is now disclosed to the Lord's people. To them God has chosen to make known among the Gentiles the glorious riches of this mystery, which is Christ in you, the hope of glory." (Colossians 1:26-27)

Paul speaks of a mystery hidden for ages but now disclosed to the saints: Christ in you, the hope of glory. This mystery, which is Christ within us, is not just a comfort but a revolutionary truth that changes how we view ourselves and our purpose. Our hope for glory is not in our achievements, status, or wealth but in Christ living within us.

This indwelling of Christ transforms us from the inside out, affecting how we live, how we view challenges, and how we interact with others. It's a call to live not just with Christ beside us but with Christ within us, guiding, comforting, and empowering us.

Paul's Labour for the Church (1:28-29)

"He is the one we proclaim, admonishing and teaching everyone with all wisdom, so that we may present everyone fully mature in Christ. To this end I strenuously contend with all the energy Christ so powerfully works in me." (Colossians 1:28-29)

Finally, we see Paul's labour for the church, striving with all the energy Christ so powerfully works in him. Paul's example challenges us to consider our service to the church and the world. Are we labouring for the gospel with the energy that Christ provides, or are we relying on our strength?

Paul's ministry was fuelled by the power of Christ within him. This same power is available to us as we serve and minister to others. Our calling is not to serve in our capacity but to tap into the divine strength that God provides, allowing us to minister effectively and endure challenges.

I often quote these verses when someone asks me about my ministry in the Church. In these two verses we have the message, method, manner, motive and means of ministry:

Message: *"He (Christ) is the one we proclaim."*

Method: *"Admonishing and teaching everyone."*

Manner: *"With all wisdom"*

Motive: *"So that we may present everyone mature in Christ"*

Means: *"I strenuously contend with all the energy Christ so powerfully works in me."*

Conclusion

Colossians Chapter 1 presents us with profound truths about Christ's supremacy, our reconciliation through His sacrifice, the mystery of Christ in us, and the model of Christian labour.

As we reflect on these truths, let us recommit ourselves to recognize Christ's supremacy in all areas of our lives, embrace the reconciliation offered through His sacrifice, live out the mystery of Christ within us, and serve with the energy that He provides. Let us pray that these truths would not just be words we hear but realities we live out every day. May Christ be all and in all to us.

~ COLOSSIANS 2 ~

Introduction

This passage is a treasure trove of spiritual wisdom, addressing the fullness of life in Christ, the dangers of deceptive teachings, and the principles of Christian freedom. As we navigate through these verses, let us open our hearts to the transformative power of God's Word.

The Fullness in Christ (1-5)

"I want you to know how hard I am contending for you and for those at Laodicea, and for all who have not met me personally. My goal is that they may be encouraged in heart and united in love, so that they may have the full riches of complete understanding, in order that they may know the mystery of God, namely, Christ, in whom are hidden all the treasures of wisdom and knowledge.

I tell you this so that no one may deceive you by fine-sounding arguments. For though I am absent from you in body, I am present with you in spirit and delight to see how disciplined you are and how firm your faith in Christ is." (Colossians 2:1-5)

Paul begins by expressing his deep concern and care for the believers in Colosse and Laodicea, and indeed for all who have not met him personally. His desire is for their hearts to be encouraged and united in love so that they may have the full riches of complete understanding, enabling them to know the mystery of God, namely, Christ. In Christ, Paul asserts, are hidden all the treasures of wisdom and knowledge.

Paul's mention of this "mystery" emphasizes the revelation of divine truths in Christ that were previously hidden but now are disclosed to the saints.

This knowledge and wisdom in Christ surpass earthly wisdom, offering a spiritual depth that Paul wishes for all believers to comprehend fully.

This comprehension is not just intellectual but is deeply relational and transformative, meant to bring the believers into a closer, more intimate relationship with God through Christ.

Paul also warns the believers about being deceived by fine-sounding arguments. This is a caution against the persuasive yet misleading teachings that were prevalent at that time, which could lead believers away from the simplicity and purity of their devotion to Christ. The false teachings in Colosse likely included elements of Jewish legalism, pagan philosophy, and early forms of Gnosticism, which claimed to offer a superior, esoteric knowledge of the divine.

Despite his physical absence, Paul speaks of his presence with them in spirit, rejoicing to see their good order and the firmness of their faith in Christ. This reflects Paul's pastoral heart, as he seeks to affirm and encourage the believers in their faith journey, highlighting the importance of community, steadfastness, and resilience in the face of challenges.

Colossians 2:1-5 is a rich passage that underscores the centrality of Christ in the believer's life, the value of spiritual wisdom and understanding found in Him, and the importance of vigilance against teachings that deviate from the gospel. It also beautifully showcases Paul's pastoral concern for the spiritual welfare of the early Christian communities.

The Fullness in Christ (2:6-7)

"So then, just as you received Christ Jesus as Lord, continue to live your lives in him, rooted and built up in him, strengthened in the faith as you were taught, and overflowing with thankfulness." (Colossians 2:6-7)

Paul begins with this heartfelt exhortation: The apostle reminds us that the Christian journey doesn't end with accepting Christ; it begins there. Our faith is meant to grow, deepening like roots into the soil of God's love, building up into a structure that stands firm against the winds of hardship and doubt.

This imagery of being rooted and built up in Christ compels us to ask ourselves: Are we growing in our faith? Are our lives reflecting the stability and strength that come from a deep relationship with Jesus? Let us strive to be believers whose faith is not shallow but deeply anchored in the truth of the Gospel, leading us to live with gratitude and strength.

Beware of Deception (2:8-15)

> *"See to it that no one takes you captive through hollow and deceptive philosophy, which depends on human tradition and the elemental spiritual forces of this world rather than on Christ.*
>
> *For in Christ all the fullness of the Deity lives in bodily form, and in Christ you have been brought to fullness. He is the head over every power and authority. In him you were also circumcised with a circumcision not performed by human hands. Your whole self, ruled by the flesh was put off when you were circumcised by Christ, having been buried with him in baptism, in which you were also raised with him through your faith in the working of God, who raised him from the dead.*
>
> *When you were dead in your sins and in the uncircumcision of your flesh, God made you[d] alive with Christ. He forgave us all our sins, having cancelled the charge of our legal indebtedness, which stood against us and condemned us; he has taken it away, nailing it to the cross. And having disarmed the powers and authorities, he made a public spectacle of them, triumphing over them by the cross." (Colossians 2:8-15)*

Paul warns the Colossians against being taken captive by hollow and deceptive philosophies, which depend on human tradition and the elemental spiritual forces of this world rather than on Christ. In our own lives, this warning is ever relevant.

The world around us is filled with ideologies and beliefs that can easily lead us astray if we are not anchored in the truth of Christ. Whether it's materialism, relativism, or legalism, these philosophies can enslave us and divert us from the freedom found in Jesus.

Paul reminds us that in Christ, "the whole fullness of deity dwells bodily," and we are filled in Him. He is the head over every power and authority. In Him, we find a completeness that the world cannot offer. Therefore, let us be discerning, testing every teaching against the truth of Scripture, and clinging to the solid foundation that is Christ.

Freedom from Legalism (2:16-23)

> *"Therefore, do not let anyone judge you by what you eat or drink, or with regard to a religious festival, a New Moon celebration or a Sabbath day. These are a shadow of the things that were to come; the reality, however, is found in Christ. Do not let anyone who delights in false humility and the worship of angels disqualify you. Such a person also goes into great detail about what they have seen; they are puffed up with idle notions by their unspiritual mind. They have lost connection with the head, from whom the whole body, supported and held together by its ligaments and sinews, grows as God causes it to grow.*
>
> *Since you died with Christ to the elemental spiritual forces of this world, why, as though you still belonged to the world, do you submit to its rules: "Do not handle! Do not taste! Do not touch!"? These rules, which have to do with things that are all destined to perish with use, are based on merely human commands and teachings. Such regulations indeed have an appearance of wisdom, with their self-imposed worship, their false humility and their harsh treatment of the body, but they lack any value in restraining sensual indulgence." (Colossians 2:16-23)*

The apostle goes on to address the issue of legalism within the church. He instructs the Colossians not to let anyone judge them by what they eat or drink, or with regard to a religious festival, a New Moon celebration, or a Sabbath day. These regulations, which were a shadow of the things that were to come, are no longer binding because the reality, Christ, has come.

This passage challenges us to examine our own practices, beliefs and attitudes: Are we imposing unnecessary religious rules on ourselves or others?

Are we focusing more on external rituals than on our relationship with Jesus? Paul's message is clear — our faith should not be a burden of rules but a liberating walk with Christ, who has freed us from the requirements of the law.

Conclusion

Colossians Chapter 2 offers us profound insights into the fullness of life in Christ, the dangers of worldly philosophies, and the trap of legalism. As we reflect on this chapter, let us commit to deepening our roots in Jesus, remaining vigilant against deceptive teachings, and embracing the freedom we have in Christ.

May we continue to live in Him, rooted and built up, strengthened in the faith, and overflowing with thankfulness. May our lives be a testament to the fullness and freedom that are found only in Christ Jesus. Amen.

Introduction

This chapter is a beacon of light guiding us toward a life hidden with Christ in God. It is a call from the Apostle Paul to cast off our old selves and embrace the new creation we are in Christ. Let us dive into this transformative message, understanding how it applies to our lives today.

Setting Our Hearts on Things Above (3:1-4)

"Since, then, you have been raised with Christ, set your hearts on things above, where Christ is, seated at the right hand of God. Set your minds on things above, not on earthly things. For you died, and your life is now hidden with Christ in God. When Christ, who is your[a] life, appears, then you also will appear with him in glory." (Colossians 3:1-4)

Paul starts this chapter with a powerful command to set our hearts on things above. This isn't mere advice; it's a directive for living a life that truly honours God. In our world filled with distractions and earthly desires, this message is particularly relevant. Our focus should not be on the transient but on the eternal, not on earthly gain but on heavenly glory.

But what does it mean to set our hearts on things above? It means prioritizing our spiritual well-being, spending time in prayer and the Word, and seeking to live out God's will in our everyday lives. It means measuring our decisions, not by how they will advance our status or wealth but by how they align with God's kingdom values.

Putting to Death the Old Self (3:5-11)

"Put to death, therefore, whatever belongs to your earthly nature: sexual immorality, impurity, lust, evil desires and greed, which is idolatry. Because of these, the wrath of God is coming. You used to walk in these ways, in the life you once lived. But now you must also rid yourselves of all such things as these: anger, rage, malice, slander, and filthy language from your lips."

"Do not lie to each other, since you have taken off your old self with its practices and have put on the new self, which is being renewed in knowledge in the image of its Creator. Here there is no Gentile or Jew, circumcised or uncircumcised, barbarian, Scythian, slave or free, but Christ is all, and is in all." (Colossians 3:5-11)

Paul then calls us to a drastic action: putting to death whatever belongs to our earthly nature. This is not a gentle nudging away from sin; it's a clear command to eliminate it entirely from our lives. Paul lists sexual immorality, impurity, lust, evil desires, and greed as examples, but this is not an exhaustive list. Anything that separates us from God needs to be eradicated.

This call challenges us to self-reflection and repentance. It's uncomfortable but necessary. We must ask ourselves tough questions about what we need to *"put to death"* in our lives. It's a continuous process, not a one-time act, and it's not something we can do in our strength alone. We need the Holy Spirit's power to overcome these earthly temptations.

Clothing Ourselves with the New Self (3:12-17)

"Therefore, as God's chosen people, holy and dearly loved, clothe yourselves with compassion, kindness, humility, gentleness and patience. Bear with each other and forgive one another if any of you has a grievance against someone. Forgive as the Lord forgave you. And over all these virtues put on love, which binds them all together in perfect unity.

Let the peace of Christ rule in your hearts, since as members of one body you were called to peace. And be thankful. Let the message of Christ dwell among you richly as you teach and admonish one another with all wisdom through psalms, hymns, and songs from the Spirit, singing to God with gratitude in your hearts.

And whatever you do, whether in word or deed, do it all in the name of the Lord Jesus, giving thanks to God the Father through him." (Colossians 3:12-17)

After instructing us to put off the old self, Paul guides us to "*clothe ourselves*" with virtues like compassion, kindness, humility, gentleness, and patience. This imagery of putting on new clothes signifies a transformation from the inside out. It's not about outward appearance but about allowing these virtues to become integral parts of our being.

Paul emphasizes forgiveness, mirroring the forgiveness we've received from Christ. He also speaks of love, the bond that unites all other virtues. This is a call to live in harmony, letting the peace of Christ rule in our hearts and the word of Christ dwell in us richly. It's a beautiful picture of the Christian community at its best – loving, teaching, and admonishing one another in wisdom.

Living Out Our New Identity in Christ (3:18-25)

> *"Wives, submit yourselves to your husbands, as is fitting in the Lord. Husbands, love your wives and do not be harsh with them. Children, obey your parents in everything, for this pleases the Lord. Fathers, do not embitter your children, or they will become discouraged.*
>
> *Slaves, obey your earthly masters in everything; and do it, not only when their eye is on you and to curry their favour, but with sincerity of heart and reverence for the Lord. Whatever you do, work at it with all your heart, as working for the Lord, not for human masters, since you know that you will receive an inheritance from the Lord as a reward. It is the Lord Christ you are serving. Anyone who does wrong will be repaid for their wrongs, and there is no favouritism." (Colossians 3:18-25)*

In the latter part of the chapter, Paul applies these principles to various relationships: wives and husbands, children and parents, slaves and masters.

While cultural contexts have changed, the underlying message remains relevant: our new identity in Christ should transform all our relationships. It's about submitting to one another out of reverence for Christ, obeying from the heart, and doing everything in the name of the Lord Jesus.

This section challenges us to reflect on how our new identity in Christ affects our daily interactions and responsibilities. Are we living out the virtues of the new self in our homes, workplaces, and community? Are we doing everything as if we were doing it for the Lord?

Conclusion

Colossians chapter 3 is a powerful call to spiritual renewal and transformation. It challenges us to shift our focus from earthly things to heavenly realities, to rid ourselves of sin, and to embrace a life characterized by godly virtues and loving relationships.

Let this chapter not just be a passage we read but a roadmap for our lives. Let us seek to live out these truths, allowing them to transform us from the inside out.

Let us pray for the strength to set our hearts on things above, to put to death our old selves, and to put on the new self, created to be like God in true righteousness and holiness. May God empower us to live lives worthy of the calling we have received, fully clothed in the love and holiness of Christ.

~ COLOSSIANS 4 ~

Introduction

Now Paul provides some practical advice on prayer, evangelism, and relationships within the Christian community and beyond. As we explore these instructions, let us consider how they apply to our lives and challenge us to live out our faith in a visible and tangible way.

Master and Slaves (4:1)

"Masters, provide your slaves with what is right and fair, because you know that you also have a Master in heaven." (Colossians 4:1)

Paul instructs masters to treat their slaves with fairness and justice, reminding them that they too have a Master in heaven. This verse emphasizes equality and accountability before God, challenging societal norms by advocating for the dignified treatment of all individuals, regardless of status. It's a call to reflect Christ's love and justice in every relationship.

Devotion to Prayer and Wisdom in Action (4:2-6)

"Devote yourselves to prayer, being watchful and thankful. And pray for us, too, that God may open a door for our message, so that we may proclaim the mystery of Christ, for which I am in chains. Pray that I may proclaim it clearly, as I should. Be wise in the way you act toward outsiders; make the most of every opportunity. Let your conversation be always full of grace, seasoned with salt, so that you may know how to answer everyone." (Colossians 4:2-6)

Paul is urging believers to not treat prayer as an afterthought or a last resort; it should be our first line of action, a vital part of our daily lives. Being watchful in prayer means being aware of the needs around us and staying alert to spiritual realities. Being thankful in prayer reminds us of God's past faithfulness and grounds us in His grace.

Moreover, Paul encourages us to pray for opportunities to witness and for clarity in presenting the gospel. This challenges us to view our interactions through the lens of eternity. Are we looking for opportunities to share the gospel? Are we ready to make the mystery of Christ clear to those who don't know Him?

Paul also instructs us to "*be wise in the way you act toward outsiders; making the most of every opportunity.*" This wisdom is not worldly cunning but a discernment grounded in love and respect. Our speech should be "always full of grace, seasoned with salt." This metaphor suggests our words should preserve and enhance, not corrupt or degrade. How do our words and actions reflect Christ to those outside the faith?

Interpersonal Relationships and Final Greetings (4:7-18)

"Tychicus will tell you all the news about me. He is a dear brother, a faithful minister and fellow servant[a] in the Lord. I am sending him to you for the express purpose that you may know about our circumstances and that he may encourage your hearts. He is coming with Onesimus, our faithful and dear brother, who is one of you. They will tell you everything that is happening here.

My fellow prisoner Aristarchus sends you his greetings, as does Mark, the cousin of Barnabas. (You have received instructions about him; if he comes to you, welcome him.) Jesus, who is called Justus, also sends greetings. These are the only Jews among my co-workers for the kingdom of God, and they have proved a comfort to me.

Epaphras, who is one of you and a servant of Christ Jesus, sends greetings. He is always wrestling in prayer for you, that you may stand firm in all the will of God, mature and fully assured. I vouch for him that he is working hard for you and for those at Laodicea and Hierapolis.

Our dear friend Luke, the doctor, and Demas send greetings. Give my greetings to the brothers and sisters at Laodicea, and to Nympha and the church in her house."

"After this letter has been read to you, see that it is also read in the church of the Laodiceans and that you in turn read the letter from Laodicea. Tell Archippus: "See to it that you complete the ministry you have received in the Lord."

I, Paul, write this greeting in my own hand. Remember my chains. Grace be with you." (Colossians 4:7-18)

In the latter part of the chapter, Paul turns to personal greetings and instructions, reflecting the interconnectedness and mutual care within the body of Christ. He mentions Tychicus, Onesimus, Aristarchus, Mark, and others, showing the diversity and unity of the early Christian community. This reminds us that Christianity is not a solitary faith; it is lived out in community.

Paul's specific instructions to Archippus, *"See to it that you complete the ministry you have received in the Lord,"* speak to each of us. We all have a calling and a service to complete. What has God entrusted to us, and how are we fulfilling that commission? The mention of Mark, who once had a falling out with Paul but is now recommended to the Colossians, illustrates the power of reconciliation within the church. It's a powerful reminder that no one is beyond redemption and that broken relationships can be restored through Christ.

Lastly, Paul's request for remembrance in their prayers and his final grace underline the importance of mutual support and the unifying love of Christ that should pervade all our relationships.

Conclusion

Colossians Chapter 4 serves as a powerful reminder of the practical aspects of our faith. As we reflect on this chapter, let us ask ourselves these questions:

How devoted are we to prayer, and how actively do we seek to share the gospel?

Are we wise and gracious in our interactions, especially with those outside the faith?

Do we recognize the value of our Christian community, nurturing and cherishing it?

Are we completing the work God has entrusted to us, living out our calling with diligence and passion?

As we conclude our journey through Colossians, let the message of this letter resonate in our hearts and manifest in our actions. Let us be devoted to prayer, wise in conduct, gracious in speech, and committed to the work God has given us.

May the Lord grant us the strength and courage to live out these truths, that we might be a beacon of His love and grace in a world in desperate need of the gospel. Amen.

~ 1 THESSALONIANS ~

Introduction

The first Epistle to the Thessalonians is considered one of Paul's earliest letters, possibly his first, written around AD 50-52 from Corinth.

This epistle is significant for its insights into the early Christian community's beliefs, particularly concerning the Second Coming of Christ. Below is a brief chapter-by-chapter commentary and analysis of 1 Thessalonians.

Chapter 1:

Thanksgiving and Encouragement: Paul opens with gratitude for the Thessalonians' faith, love, and hope, acknowledging their work produced by faith, labour prompted by love, and endurance inspired by hope in Jesus Christ.

This chapter sets a positive tone, praising the Thessalonians for turning to God from idols to serve the living and true God and to wait for His Son from heaven. The conversion of the Thessalonians and their exemplary faith have become well-known, serving as a model to believers in Macedonia and Achaia.

Chapter 2:

Paul's Ministry in Thessalonica: Paul defends his conduct among the Thessalonians against accusations of deceit or impure motives. He emphasizes his gentle and caring approach, likening himself to a nursing mother and an encouraging father. The chapter highlights the sincerity and hardship of Paul's mission, his efforts to not be a burden to the Thessalonian believers, and his deep longing to see them again.

This personal reflection underscores the genuine love and concern Paul had for the Thessalonian Christians, along with his commitment to spreading the gospel despite opposition.

Chapter 3:

Timothy's Encouraging Report: After being unable to visit Thessalonica himself due to obstacles (possibly from Jewish opponents), Paul sent Timothy to strengthen and encourage the church in their faith. Timothy's report brings good news of the Thessalonians' faith and love, alleviating Paul's fears of the tempter undermining his work. This chapter reveals Paul's anxiety over the spiritual well-being of the fledgling church and his relief and joy upon hearing of their steadfastness. It ends with prayers for the Thessalonians, that they may increase in love and be blameless in holiness before God.

Chapter 4:

Living to Please God: Paul instructs the Thessalonians on how to live in a way that pleases God, emphasizing the need for sexual purity, love among brethren, and a quiet life. He specifically addresses the issue of sexual immorality, urging them to control their own bodies in holiness and honour. Paul also encourages the believers to aspire to live quietly, mind their own affairs, and work with their hands to win the respect of outsiders and not be dependent on anyone.

The Coming of the Lord: The latter part of the chapter addresses concerns about the fate of those who have died before Christ's return. Paul assures them that the dead in Christ will rise first, followed by the living, who will be caught up together with them in the clouds to meet the Lord in the air. This passage, often referred to as the "rapture," offers comfort and hope regarding the resurrection and the eternal union with the Lord.

Chapter 5:

The Day of the Lord: Paul discusses the suddenness of the Lord's coming, comparing it to a thief in the night. He contrasts the destinies of those in darkness with those in light, urging vigilance, sobriety, and the wearing of faith, love, and hope as a breastplate and helmet. This imagery reinforces the need for preparedness and living in the light of Christ's teachings.

Final Instructions and Greetings: The epistle concludes with various exhortations: to respect and hold in love those who labour among them, to live in peace, to admonish the idle, encourage the fainthearted, help the weak, and be patient with everyone.

Paul calls for continual joy, prayer, and thanksgiving, the avoidance of quenching the Spirit and despising prophecies, and admonishes the community to test everything and hold fast to what is good. The letter closes with a benediction, praying for their sanctification and preservation at the coming of Jesus Christ.

1 Thessalonians is notable for its emphasis on the Parousia (the Second Coming of Christ), ethical living, and pastoral care. Paul's message combines eschatological hope with practical guidance on Christian living, encouraging the Thessalonians to remain steadfast in their faith amidst persecution and to live in a manner worthy of their calling.

The letter reflects the early Christian expectation of Christ's imminent return and serves as a source of comfort and exhortation for believers to lead a life pleasing to God, characterized by holiness, love, and work ethic.

Now I will unpack each of the five chapters in more detail as we explore this letter in more detail.

~ 1 THESSALONIANS 1 ~

Introduction

This letter opens with Paul, Silas, and Timothy expressing their gratitude and admiration for the Thessalonian believers. This church, despite facing severe persecution, became an exemplary model of faith and love. Let's explore what made them stand out and how we can emulate their faithfulness in our own walk.

The Power of Faithful Witness (1:1-3)

"Paul, Silas and Timothy, to the church of the Thessalonians in God the Father and the Lord Jesus Christ: Grace and peace to you. We always thank God for all of you and continually mention you in our prayers. We remember before our God and Father your work produced by faith, your labour prompted by love, and your endurance inspired by hope in our Lord Jesus Christ. "
(1 Thessalonians 1:1-3)

Paul begins by acknowledging, with thanks, the Thessalonians' work produced by faith, labour prompted by love, and endurance inspired by hope in our Lord Jesus Christ. This triad - faith, love, and hope - forms the bedrock of Christian life. The Thessalonians' faith was active; their love was laborious, and their hope was enduring. You may want to reflect on your personal and our communal faith. Does it actively manifest in works, labour in love, and endure in the hope of Christ's return? Let these virtues guide our daily lives shape our witness.

Imitating Christ and Inspiring Others (1:4-7)

"For we know, brothers and sisters loved by God, that he has chosen you, because our gospel came to you not simply with words but also with power, with the Holy Spirit and deep conviction. You know how we lived among you for your sake. You became imitators of us and of the Lord, for you welcomed the message in the midst of severe suffering with the joy given by the Holy Spirit. And so you became a model to all the believers in Macedonia and Achaia." (1 Thessalonians 1:4-7)

Paul commends the Thessalonians for becoming imitators of them and of the Lord, despite severe suffering. Their steadfastness in the face of persecution became a beacon of faith to all believers in Macedonia and Achaia.

Consider how adversity shapes us. Are we allowing our struggles to draw us closer to Christ, thereby becoming examples to those around us? Our response to trials can inspire faith in others and spread the gospel further than we can imagine.

The Echo of Faith (1:8-10)

> "The Lord's message rang out from you not only in Macedonia and Achaia - your faith in God has become known everywhere. Therefore, we do not need to say anything about it, for they themselves report what kind of reception you gave us. They tell how you turned to God from idols to serve the living and true God, 1and to wait for his Son from heaven, whom he raised from the dead - Jesus, who rescues us from the coming wrath."
> (1 Thessalonians 1:8-10)

The faith of the Thessalonian church echoed far and wide, so much so that Paul and his companions hardly needed to speak of it. Their turn from idols to serve the living and true God, and to await His Son from heaven, speaks volumes of the transformative power of the Gospel.

Does our faith echo in our community and beyond? Let us live in such a way that our actions proclaim the Gospel loudly, turning from idols to serve God fully and await Christ's return.

~ 1 THESSALONIANS 2 ~

Introduction

This second chapter invites us into a reflection on the nature of genuine Christian ministry. Paul defends his apostolic ministry, not out of pride, but to affirm the purity, sincerity, and parental care that characterized his relationship with the Thessalonian believers. Through this, we glean timeless principles for how we, too, are called to serve one another in love and truth.

Genuine Motives in Ministry (2:1-6)

"You know, brothers and sisters, that our visit to you was not without results. We had previously suffered and been treated outrageously in Philippi, as you know, but with the help of our God we dared to tell you his gospel in the face of strong opposition.

For the appeal we make does not spring from error or impure motives, nor are we trying to trick you. On the contrary, we speak as those approved by God to be entrusted with the gospel. We are not trying to please people but God, who tests our hearts.

You know we never used flattery, nor did we put on a mask to cover up greed - God is our witness. We were not looking for praise from people, not from you or anyone else, even though as apostles of Christ we could have asserted our authority."
(1 Thessalonians 2:1-6)

Paul begins by reminding the Thessalonians of how he and his companions came to them, not with error or impure motives, but as men approved by God to be entrusted with the gospel. They did not seek praise from people, only from God.

This sets a foundational truth for all ministry: our motive must always be to please God, not people. In a world that often measures success by numbers and accolades, Paul calls us back to the heart of service - a heart that seeks God's approval above all else.

Reflect on your service within the church and community. Are your efforts aimed at gaining approval from others or from God? Let us strive to serve with purity of motive, seeking to please God as those entrusted with the precious gospel of Christ.

The Gentle Care of a Mother (2:7-8)

"Instead, we were like young children among you. Just as a nursing mother cares for her children, so we cared for you. Because we loved you so much, we were delighted to share with you not only the gospel of God but our lives as well."
(1 Thessalonians 2:7-8)

Paul uses the tender image of a nursing mother to describe his approach to ministry among the Thessalonians. This metaphor speaks volumes about the nature of Christian leadership and service. It's not about authority or power but about gentleness, affection, and a willingness to share not only the gospel but our very lives as well.

Application: Consider how you can embody this gentle, caring approach in your interactions and service. In what ways can you share your life more deeply with those you are serving?

Let us remember that genuine ministry involves more than just sharing words; it's about sharing our very selves.

The Diligent Labour of a Father (2:9-12)

"Surely you remember, brothers and sisters, our toil and hardship; we worked night and day in order not to be a burden to anyone while we preached the gospel of God to you. You are witnesses, and so is God, of how holy, righteous and blameless we were among you who believed.

For you know that we dealt with each of you as a father deals with his own children, encouraging, comforting and urging you to live lives worthy of God, who calls you into his kingdom and glory."
(1 Thessalonians 2:9-12)

Shifting metaphors, Paul then compares his ministry to the labour of a normal father, emphasizing hard work, integrity, and the encouragement and admonition that comes from a place of deep love and concern. Paul's exhortation to live lives worthy of God, who calls us into His kingdom and glory, is a powerful reminder of the ultimate goal of all Christian ministry: to guide others toward God's calling and eternal glory.

In your sphere of influence, how might you more effectively encourage and admonish those God has placed in your care, doing so with the integrity and diligence of a loving father? Let us labour diligently, aiming to lead others toward a life worthy of God's calling.

The Thessalonians' Reception of the Word (2:13-16)

"And we also thank God continually because, when you received the word of God, which you heard from us, you accepted it not as a human word, but as it actually is, the word of God, which is indeed at work in you who believe.

For you, brothers and sisters, became imitators of God's churches in Judea, which are in Christ Jesus: You suffered from your own people the same things those churches suffered from the Jews who killed the Lord Jesus and the prophets and also drove us out. They displease God and are hostile to everyone in their effort to keep us from speaking to the Gentiles so that they may be saved. In this way they always heap up their sins to the limit. The wrath of God has come upon them at last." (1 Thessalonians 2:13-16)

Paul celebrates the Thessalonians for receiving the word of God not as a human word, but as it actually is, the word of God. This reception of the word worked effectively in those who believed, demonstrating the transformative power of God's word when received with faith.

How do we receive the word of God? Is it merely as human words, or do we truly embrace it as the living word of God, allowing it to work effectively within us?

Let us approach God's word with reverence and openness, allowing it to transform us from the inside out.

Conclusion

1 Thessalonians Chapter 2 presents us with a beautiful picture of genuine ministry, marked by pure motives, gentle care, diligent labour, and a deep commitment to the word of God. As we go forth, let us embody these principles in our service to one another and to the world.

May our ministry always reflect the love, integrity, and dedication that Paul demonstrated, and may our lives be a testament to the transformative power of the gospel we have been entrusted to share.

~ 1 THESSALONIANS 3 ~

Introduction

This third chapter is rich with the themes of faith, love, and endurance amid adversity. The Apostle Paul, unable to bear the separation from the Thessalonian believers any longer, sends Timothy to strengthen and encourage them in their faith. This chapter is a testament to the deep bond between spiritual leaders and their congregations, and it reveals the critical nature of faith and love as sustenance through trials.

The Sending of Timothy (3:1-5)

"So when we could stand it no longer, we thought it best to be left by ourselves in Athens. We sent Timothy, who is our brother and co-worker in God's service in spreading the gospel of Christ, to strengthen and encourage you in your faith, so that no one would be unsettled by these trials. For you know quite well that we are destined for them. In fact, when we were with you, we kept telling you that we would be persecuted. And it turned out that way, as you well know. For this reason, when I could stand it no longer, I sent to find out about your faith. I was afraid that in some way the tempter had tempted you and that our labours might have been in vain." (1 Thessalonians 3:1-5)

Paul's decision to send Timothy to Thessalonica during a time of distress speaks volumes about the apostle's pastoral heart. Despite his own hardships, Paul is primarily concerned with the spiritual well-being of each of the Thessalonian believers. He understands that faith is not static; it requires nurturing, especially in the face of persecution and trials. Timothy's mission is to strengthen and encourage the Thessalonians in their faith, ensuring that the tempter has not derailed them from their spiritual path.

Reflect on the importance of spiritual mentorship and community support in your own journey of faith. In times of trial, do you isolate, or do you seek the encouragement and strength found in the body of Christ?

Let us be reminded of our need for one another, committing to support, encourage, and pray for our brothers and sisters in Christ.

Encouragement in the Midst of Affliction (3:6-8)

"But Timothy has just now come to us from you and has brought good news about your faith and love. He has told us that you always have pleasant memories of us and that you long to see us, just as we also long to see you. Therefore, brothers and sisters, in all our distress and persecution we were encouraged about you because of your faith. For now we really live, since you are standing firm in the Lord." (1 Thessalonians 3:6-8)

The return of Timothy with good news of the Thessalonians' faith and love is a source of immense comfort to Paul. Despite their afflictions, their steadfastness in faith brings joy and encouragement to Paul, affirming the life-giving connection between believers. This mutual encouragement in the faith highlights the power of the gospel to sustain believers even in the harshest of circumstances.

Consider how your faith journey impacts others. Your steadfastness in trials not only strengthens your own faith but can also encourage and embolden your fellow believers. In the midst of your afflictions, look for opportunities to share your faith and love, becoming a beacon of hope and encouragement in your community.

Prayers of Night and Day (3:9-10)

"How can we thank God enough for you in return for all the joy we have in the presence of our God because of you? Night and day we pray most earnestly that we may see you again and supply what is lacking in your faith." (1 Thessalonians 3:9-10)

Paul's response to the encouraging report is unceasing prayer, thanking God for the Thessalonians and earnestly praying for an opportunity to visit them again. His prayers of night and day underscore the continuous, fervent nature of intercessory prayer.

Paul's desire to supply what is lacking, demonstrates the ongoing process of spiritual growth and the apostle's role in nurturing this growth in other believers.

How does prayer feature in your life, especially in relation to the well-being of others? Are you committed to praying earnestly for the spiritual growth and steadfastness of your church family?

Let Paul's example inspire you to dedicate time to pray for those God has placed in your life, asking for opportunities to serve them and contribute to their journey of faith.

A Prayer for Love and Strengthening of Hearts (3:11-13)

"Now may our God and Father himself and our Lord Jesus clear the way for us to come to you. May the Lord make your love increase and overflow for each other and for everyone else, just as ours does for you. May he strengthen your hearts so that you will be blameless and holy in the presence of our God and Father when our Lord Jesus comes with all his holy ones."
(1 Thessalonians 3:11-13)

Paul concludes the chapter with a beautiful prayer that the Lord would make the way clear for him to visit the Thessalonians, that their love may increase and overflow for each other and for everyone else, and that their hearts would be strengthened.

This prayer encompasses the essence of Christian living: a love that knows no bounds and a heart established in holiness before God. Paul's longing is not only for the Thessalonians' perseverance in faith but for their growth in love and holiness, preparing them for the coming of our Lord Jesus Christ.

Perhaps you could examine your own prayer life. Are you praying for the growth in love and holiness both in your life and in the lives of those around you?

Let us adopt Paul's prayer as our own, asking God to increase our love, strengthen our hearts, and prepare us for the coming of our Lord.

Conclusion

Chapter 3 is a profound reminder of the centrality of faith, the necessity of Christian fellowship, and the power of prayer. As we face trials and tribulations, let us be encouraged by the example of the Thessalonian believers, holding fast to our faith and to each other.

May our prayers echo Paul's, seeking an overflowing love and a steadfast heart, as we await the glorious coming of our Lord Jesus Christ.

~ 1 THESSALONIANS 4 ~

Introduction

In the heart of Paul's first letter to the Thessalonians, Chapter 4 stands as a poignant call to a life that pleases God. This passage challenges us, as believers, to examine the way we live daily in light of God's will for holiness, love, and hope.

Paul transitions from pastoral care to practical instructions, guiding the Thessalonians (and us) on how to walk in a manner worthy of God who calls us into His own kingdom and glory.

A Life of Holiness (4:1-8)

"As for other matters, brothers and sisters, we instructed you how to live in order to please God, as in fact you are living. Now we ask you and urge you in the Lord Jesus to do this more and more. For you know what instructions we gave you by the authority of the Lord Jesus.

It is God's will that you should be sanctified: that you should avoid sexual immorality; that each of you should learn to control your own body in a way that is holy and honourable, not in passionate lust like the pagans, who do not know God; and that in this matter no one should wrong or take advantage of a brother or sister. The Lord will punish all those who commit such sins, as we told you and warned you before. For God did not call us to be impure, but to live a holy life. Therefore, anyone who rejects this instruction does not reject a human being but God, the very God who gives you his Holy Spirit." (1 Thessalonians 4:1-8)

Paul urges the Thessalonians to live in a way that pleases God, specifically exhorting them to abstain from sexual immorality. This call to holiness is not merely a list of dos and don'ts but a fundamental aspect of our identity in Christ. We are called to control our own bodies in holiness and honour, not in the passion of lust like those who do not know God. This distinction between believers and the world is crucial; our call to holiness is a testimony of God's work in our lives.

Reflect on your personal pursuit of holiness. Are there areas of your life where the world's influence has crept in, diluting your testimony? Holiness is not just about avoiding sin; it's about embodying Christ's purity and love in every aspect of our lives. Let us commit to living out this holiness, honouring God with our bodies and our choices.

The Call to Love (4:9-10)

> *"Now about your love for one another we do not need to write to you, for you yourselves have been taught by God to love each other. And in fact, you do love all of God's family throughout Macedonia. Yet we urge you, brothers and sisters, to do so more and more ..."* (1 Thessalonians 4:9-10)

Paul commends the Thessalonian believers for the love they have for one another but encourages them to love even more. This love is not static; it grows and deepens. The call to love more and more is a reminder that our capacity to love is boundless when rooted in Christ. This love is practical and tangible, affecting how we treat one another within the church family and beyond.

Evaluate the depth and breadth of your love for others. Is it growing and extending beyond your comfort zone? Love in action can be as simple as checking on a neighbour, offering encouragement, or providing for someone's needs. Let's seek ways to express God's love more fully in all our interactions and relationships.

The Quiet Life (4:11-12)

> *"... and to make it your ambition to lead a quiet life: You should mind your own business and work with your hands, just as we told you, so that your daily life may win the respect of outsiders and so that you will not be dependent on anybody."*
> (1 Thessalonians 4:11-12)

Paul's instruction to lead a quiet life, to mind our own affairs, and to work with our hands is profoundly counter-cultural.

In a society that often measures worth by noise, busyness, and external success, the call to a quiet life is a radical invitation to find value in simplicity, integrity, and diligent work. This lifestyle fosters respect from outsiders and independence, allowing us to live in a way that always reflects God's peace and provision.

Consider the pace and focus of your life at present. Are you caught in the cycle of busyness and comparison, or are you embracing the simplicity and contentment found in Christ? Let us aspire to live quietly, focusing on what God has called us to do, cultivating a life that is pleasing to Him and attractive to those outside the faith.

The Hope of Resurrection (4:13-18)

"Brothers and sisters, we do not want you to be uninformed about those who sleep in death, so that you do not grieve like the rest of mankind, who have no hope.

For we believe that Jesus died and rose again, and so we believe that God will bring with Jesus those who have fallen asleep in him. According to the Lord's word, we tell you that we who are still alive, who are left until the coming of the Lord, will certainly not precede those who have fallen asleep.

For the Lord himself will come down from heaven, with a loud command, with the voice of the archangel and with the trumpet call of God, and the dead in Christ will rise first. After that, we who are still alive and are left will be caught up together with them in the clouds to meet the Lord in the air. And so we will be with the Lord forever. Therefore encourage one another with these words." (1 Thessalonians 4:13-18)

Paul concludes the chapter with a message of hope concerning the resurrection and the return of the Lord. This passage addresses the Thessalonians' concern for their loved ones who have died in Christ. Paul reassures them that those who have fallen asleep in Jesus will not be forgotten at His coming.

This hope is not wishful thinking but a sure and steadfast anchor for our souls, promising that we will be reunited with our loved ones and will be with the Lord forever.

How does the hope of Christ's return shape your life? Are you living in a way that reflects this blessed hope? The assurance of resurrection and eternal life with Christ should infuse our daily living with joy, purpose, and anticipation. Let this hope comfort us in times of grief and motivate us to share the gospel with others.

Conclusion

1 Thessalonians Chapter 4 calls us to a life that is radically different - a life that pleases God through holiness, love, hard work, and the hope of Christ's return.

As we strive to live out these instructions, let us be encouraged by the power of the Holy Spirit within us, transforming us day by day into the likeness of Christ.

Introduction

As we reach the concluding chapter of Paul's first letter to the Thessalonians, we find ourselves immersed in a rich tapestry of exhortation and encouragement, all under the overarching theme of the imminent return of our Lord Jesus Christ.

This chapter serves not only as a reminder of this fundamental Christian hope but also as a practical guide for living in anticipation of that day. Let us explore how Paul's words to the Thessalonians speak directly into our lives today, urging us to live as children of light in a dark world.

The Day of the Lord (5:1-11)

"Now, brothers and sisters, about times and dates we do not need to write to you, for you know very well that the day of the Lord will come like a thief in the night. While people are saying, "Peace and safety," destruction will come on them suddenly, as labour pains on a pregnant woman, and they will not escape.

But you, brothers and sisters, are not in darkness so that this day should surprise you like a thief. You are all children of the light and children of the day. We do not belong to the night or to the darkness. So then, let us not be like others, who are asleep, but let us be awake and sober. For those who sleep, sleep at night, and those who get drunk, get drunk at night.

But since we belong to the day, let us be sober, putting on faith and love as a breastplate, and the hope of salvation as a helmet. For God did not appoint us to suffer wrath but to receive salvation through our Lord Jesus Christ.

He died for us so that, whether we are awake or asleep, we may live together with him. Therefore encourage one another and build each other up, just as in fact you are doing."
(1 Thessalonians 5:1-11)

Paul begins this chapter by addressing the timing of the Lord's return, emphasizing that it will come unexpectedly, *"like a thief in the night."* This metaphor is a powerful reminder of the vigilance and preparedness required of us as believers.

We are not to be caught off guard but to live in a state of readiness, fully clothed in faith and love, and wearing the hope of salvation as a helmet.

Reflect on your own spiritual readiness. Are you living each day in anticipation of Christ's return, or have the cares and distractions of this world lulled you into complacency? Let us awaken from spiritual slumber and live alert, sober lives, fully invested in our relationship with God and our mission as His ambassadors.

Living as Children of Light (5:12-22)

> *"Now we ask you, brothers and sisters, to acknowledge those who work hard among you, who care for you in the Lord and who admonish you. Hold them in the highest regard in love because of their work. Live in peace with each other.*
>
> *And we urge you, brothers and sisters, warn those who are idle and disruptive, encourage the disheartened, help the weak, be patient with everyone. Make sure that nobody pays back wrong for wrong, but always strive to do what is good for each other and for everyone else. Rejoice always, pray continually, give thanks in all circumstances; for this is God's will for you in Christ Jesus.*
>
> *Do not quench the Spirit. Do not treat prophecies with contempt but test them all; hold on to what is good, reject every kind of evil." (1 Thessalonians 5:12-22)*

Paul transitions to practical instructions on how to live as children of the day. He urges respect and love for those who labour among us, admonishes us to live in peace with one another, and calls us to encourage the disheartened, help the weak, and be patient with everyone.

Importantly, Paul calls us to rejoice always, pray continually, give thanks in all circumstances, recognizing these as God's will for us in Christ Jesus. This blueprint for Christian living is as relevant today as it was for the Thessalonians, providing a framework for a life that pleases God and shines His light into the darkness.

How does this call to live as children of light manifest in your daily life? Are you actively seeking to embody the love, joy, peace, and patience of Christ in your interactions with others? Let's strive to embrace Paul's instructions, not out of obligation, but as a joyful response to the love we have received from God.

The Call to Holiness (5:23-24)

"May God himself, the God of peace, sanctify you through and through. May your whole spirit, soul and body be kept blameless at the coming of our Lord Jesus Christ. The one who calls you is faithful, and he will do it." (1 Thessalonians 5:23-24)

Paul's prayer for the Thessalonians' sanctification encapsulates his desire for their (and our) wholeness and holiness in every aspect of being. He prays that God Himself, the God of peace, would sanctify us through and through, preserving us blameless at the coming of our Lord Jesus Christ. This prayer highlights the transformative power of God's grace, capable of moulding us into the likeness of His Son.

Consider the areas of your life in need of God's sanctifying work. Are there habits, thoughts, or attitudes that hinder your growth in holiness? Let us approach God with open hearts, trusting in His faithfulness to complete the good work He has begun in us.

Personal Requests and Blessings (5:25-28)

"Brothers and sisters, pray for us. Greet all God's people with a holy kiss. I charge you before the Lord to have this letter read to all the brothers and sisters. The grace of our Lord Jesus Christ be with you." (1 Thessalonians 5:25-28)

Paul concludes his letter by asking the Thessalonians to pray for him and his companions, underscoring the mutual dependence within the body of Christ. Then, he urges them to greet all the brothers and sisters with a holy kiss, signifying the unity and affection that should characterize the Christian community.

Paul asks that his letter be read to all the believers, emphasizing the great importance of shared instruction and encouragement. Finally, he concludes with a benediction, invoking the grace of the Lord Jesus Christ to be with them, reinforcing the centrality of grace in the Christian faith and life. These verses reflect Paul's deep pastoral care and his desire for the spiritual well-being and unity of the church.

Conclusion

1 Thessalonians Chapter 5 provides us with a profound yet very practical guide for living in the light of Christ's return. Paul's words encourage us to remain vigilant, to embody the characteristics of children of light, and to pursue holiness with the assurance of God's faithfulness.

As we await our Lord's return, let us be found faithful, living in such a way that reflects the hope and love we have received through Christ.

~ 2 THESSALONIANS ~

Introduction

The book of 2 Thessalonians, a letter from the Apostle Paul (along with Silvanus and Timothy) to the church in Thessalonica, serves as a sequel to 1 Thessalonians. Written in the first century A.D., this epistle addresses ongoing concerns within the Thessalonian community, including persecution, the return of the Lord Jesus Christ, and idleness among its members.

Through its three chapters, Paul provides encouragement, correction, and instruction to the young church. Allow me to offer a brief overview of each chapter.

Chapter 1:

Chapter 1 opens with Paul expressing gratitude for the Thessalonians' growing faith and steadfast love in the face of persecution and trials. He reassures them that their endurance in faith is evidence of God's righteous judgment and their worthiness for the kingdom of God, for which they are suffering.

The Justice of God (1:5-10): Paul introduces the theme of divine retribution and comfort. He assures the Thessalonians that God will repay with affliction those who afflict them and grant relief to the afflicted. This eschatological justice is centred on the revelation of the Lord Jesus from heaven with mighty angels, bringing vengeance on those who do not know God. This passage highlights God's ultimate authority and the vindication of His people.

Prayer for Worthiness (1:11-12): Paul concludes the chapter with a prayer for the Thessalonians, that God may make them worthy of His calling and fulfill every resolve for good and every work of faith by His power. Paul's prayer underscores the interconnectedness of God's enablement and our responsiveness to His calling, culminating in the glorification of Jesus Christ through the believers.

Chapter 2:

Paul addresses concerns regarding the "Day of the Lord," correcting misunderstandings that it had already come. He describes the apostasy and the revelation of the "man of lawlessness" as events that must precede the Day of the Lord.

The Apostasy and the Man of Lawlessness (2:1-12): This section contains one of the New Testament's most enigmatic prophecies. Paul speaks of a "rebellion" (apostasy) and a figure known as the "man of lawlessness" or "son of destruction," who opposes God and exalts himself above every deity. This lawless one, whose coming is associated with Satan's activity, will deceive those who are perishing.

Paul reassures the Thessalonians that the lawless one will be overthrown by Jesus at His coming. This passage has been interpreted in various ways throughout Christian history, often viewed through the lens of eschatological speculation about end-time figures.

Stand Firm (2:13-17): In contrast to the doom awaiting the lawless one and his followers, Paul expresses thanksgiving for the Thessalonian believers' election by God. He exhorts them to stand firm and hold to the teachings passed on to them, either by word of mouth or by letter from Paul. This exhortation is coupled with a prayer for their encouragement and strengthening in every good deed and word.

Chapter 3:

The final chapter shifts focus to practical instructions regarding idleness within the community. Paul commands the church to keep away from believers living in idleness and not according to the tradition received from the apostles.

Warning Against Idleness (3:6-12): Paul addresses the issue of believers who are not working but are busybodies. This concern likely stems from misunderstandings about the imminence of the Day of the Lord, leading some to abandon many of their daily responsibilities.

Paul invokes his own example of labour and self-sufficiency as a model for the community, urging the idle to work quietly and earn their own living.

Final Instructions and Benediction (3:13-18): Despite the stern warning against idleness, Paul encourages the church not to grow weary in doing good. He concludes the letter with a benediction, praying for the Lord's peace and presence to be with all the believers. The personal greeting with Paul's own hand serves as a mark of authenticity for the letter.

Conclusion

2 Thessalonians provides a profound insight into early Christian eschatology, community ethics, and pastoral care. Paul's letter balances the theological with the practical, offering hope and instruction for living faithfully in anticipation of Christ's return.

For contemporary readers, this epistle encourages perseverance in the face of persecution, caution against idleness, and vigilance in doctrine and life as we await the fulfillment of God's ultimate justice and redemption.

Now I will unpack each of the three chapters in more detail as we explore this letter in more detail.

Introduction

In the opening chapter of his second letter to the Thessalonian church, the Apostle Paul greets the community with grace and peace, immediately diving into words of encouragement and praise for their growing faith and love in the midst of persecution and trials. Today, as we unpack this profound passage, we are reminded of the timeless truth that in every age, followers of Christ are called to a life marked by faith, love, endurance, and the hope of divine justice.

Growing Faith and Increasing Love (2:1-3)

"Paul, Silas and Timothy, to the church of the Thessalonians in God our Father and the Lord Jesus Christ: Grace and peace to you from God the Father and the Lord Jesus Christ.

We ought always to thank God for you, brothers and sisters, and rightly so, because your faith is growing more and more, and the love all of you have for one another is increasing."
(2 Thessalonians 1:1-3)

Paul is expressing his gratitude to God for the Thessalonians, noting specifically their "growing faith" and "increasing love." This isn't just a passive acknowledgment; it is a vibrant, living testament to the work of the Spirit in their community.

In a world that often breeds isolation and selfishness, the Thessalonians are a model of spiritual growth and communal love. Their faith wasn't stagnant but increasing in the face of harsh persecution.

Let's pause and reflect on our own journey. Is our faith growing? Is our love for one another increasing? These aren't just ideals to aspire to; they're evidence of God's active presence in our lives. Like the Thessalonians, let us commit to nurturing our faith and allowing God's love to overflow from us to others, especially those within our faith community.

Endurance in Persecution (1:4-5)

"Therefore, among God's churches we boast about your perseverance and faith in all the persecutions and trials you are enduring. All this is evidence that God's judgment is right, and as a result you will be counted worthy of the kingdom of God, for which you are suffering." (2 Thessalonians 1:4-5)

The Thessalonians' faith and love were not grown in a vacuum but in the harsh soil of constant persecution. Paul speaks of their "perseverance and faith in all the persecutions and trials" they are enduring. This endurance is not a grim, teeth-clenched stoicism but a living hope in the kingdom of God for which they are suffering. Their steadfastness in the face of opposition is a clear sign of God's righteous judgment, affirming their calling and election by God. We, too, may face various trials and opposition, whether from within our own circles or from the society at large. In these moments, let us draw strength from the Thessalonians' example, remembering that our endurance under trial is a testimony to our faith.

The Righteous Judgment of God (1:6-10)

"God is just: He will pay back trouble to those who trouble you and give relief to you who are troubled, and to us as well. This will happen when the Lord Jesus is revealed from heaven in blazing fire with his powerful angels. He will punish those who do not know God and do not obey the gospel of our Lord Jesus. They will be punished with everlasting destruction and shut out from the presence of the Lord and from the glory of his might on the day he comes to be glorified in his holy people and to be marvelled at among all those who have believed. This includes you because you believed our testimony to you."(2 Thessalonians 1:6-10)

Paul assures the Thessalonians that God's justice will prevail. The Lord will repay trouble to those who trouble them and give relief to the afflicted. This divine retribution will be revealed when Jesus Christ is unveiled from heaven in blazing fire with His powerful angels. For those who have rejected the Gospel, this will be a day of reckoning. But for those who have believed, it will be a day of salvation and glory.

The promise of God's righteous judgment offers both a warning and a comfort. It warns us against complacency and complicity in injustice, reminding us that God will not overlook evil. But it also comforts us, knowing that our suffering and perseverance are not in vain. Injustice and persecution will not have the last word. Let us then live with a sober awareness of God's ultimate justice, letting it shape our actions and attitudes.

Paul's Prayer (1:11-12)

> *"With this in mind, we constantly pray for you, that our God may make you worthy of his calling, and that by his power he may bring to fruition your every desire for goodness and your every deed prompted by faith. We pray this so that the name of our Lord Jesus may be glorified in you, and you in him, according to the grace of our God and the Lord Jesus Christ."*
> *(2 Thessalonians 1:11-12)*

Paul concludes the chapter with a prayer that the Thessalonians might be "counted worthy of God's calling" and that God might "fulfill every resolve for good and every work of faith by his power." This prayer encapsulates the heart of the Christian journey: to live a life worthy of the calling we have received, fully reliant on God's power to bring it to fruition.

As we reflect on Paul's prayer, let us also make it our own. May we live lives worthy of the calling we have received, serving others in love, enduring trials with faith, and always leaning on God's mighty power to work in and through us for His glory.

Conclusion

In the midst of our own trials and tribulations, the message of this chapter speaks to us with fresh urgency. It calls us to grow in faith, to abound in love, to endure in hope, and to live in the light of God's righteous judgment. Let us take heart from the example of the Thessalonian church, knowing that our labour in the Lord is not in vain, and let us look forward to the day of His coming with joy and anticipation.

~ 2 THESSALONIANS 2 ~

Introduction

In this chapter, the Apostle Paul addresses a critical concern within the Thessalonian church: the confusion regarding the Day of the Lord.

In the midst of the turmoil and the deception that had infiltrated the community, Paul provides a clarion call to understanding, vigilance, and steadfastness.

As we explore this profound passage, we are invited to reflect on the themes of discernment, faithfulness, and the importance of standing firm in the truth of the Gospel.

The Day of the Lord (2:1-2)

"Concerning the coming of our Lord Jesus Christ and our being gathered to him, we ask you, brothers and sisters, not to become easily unsettled or alarmed by the teaching allegedly from us - whether by a prophecy or by word of mouth or by letter - asserting that the day of the Lord has already come."
(2 Thessalonians 2:1-2)

Paul opens this chapter with an appeal for calm and clarity concerning the return of Christ. The Thessalonians were unsettled by false teachings suggesting that the Day of the Lord had already come.

This misinformation had caused distress and confusion, detracting from their faith and daily living. Paul's words serve as a reminder that our understanding of God's timing must be anchored in Scripture, not swayed by rumours or false teachings.

In our present time, just as in Thessalonica, false teachings and misconceptions about the end times can lead to fear, confusion, and distraction from our mission. Let us be diligent in seeking the truth, grounding our understanding in the Word of God, and relying on the Holy Spirit for discernment.

The Rebellion and the Man of Lawlessness (2:3-12)

"Don't let anyone deceive you in any way, for that day will not come until the rebellion occurs and the man of lawlessness is revealed, the man doomed to destruction. He will oppose and will exalt himself over everything that is called God or is worshiped, so that he sets himself up in God's temple, proclaiming himself to be God.

Don't you remember that when I was with you, I used to tell you these things? And now you know what is holding him back, so that he may be revealed at the proper time. For the secret power of lawlessness is already at work; but the one who now holds it back will continue to do so till he is taken out of the way. And then the lawless one will be revealed, whom the Lord Jesus will overthrow with the breath of his mouth and destroy by the splendour of his coming.

The coming of the lawless one will be in accordance with how Satan works. He will use all sorts of displays of power through signs and wonders that serve the lie, and all the ways that wickedness deceives those who are perishing. They perish because they refused to love the truth and so be saved.

For this reason, God sends them a powerful delusion so that they will believe the lie and so that all will be condemned who have not believed the truth but have delighted in wickedness."
(2 Thessalonians 2:3-12)

Paul introduces two significant events that must precede the Day of the Lord: the rebellion (apostasy) and the revelation of the man of lawlessness. This "man of lawlessness" symbolizes the epitome of rebellion against God, exalting himself above all that is called God.

His coming is marked by satanic power, deception, and counterfeit miracles, leading those who are perishing to believe the lie. This passage highlights the spiritual battle at play, emphasizing the need for vigilance and faithfulness amidst deception.

The warning against apostasy and the deception of the lawless one challenges us to examine the foundations of our faith. Are we being led astray by the allure of sin or the promise of false miracles?

Therefore, let us hold fast to the truth of the Gospel, which saves and sanctifies us, resisting the temptation to compromise or capitulate to the lies of the enemy.

Standing Firm (2:13-17)

> *"But we ought always to thank God for you, brothers and sisters loved by the Lord, because God chose you as first fruits to be saved through the sanctifying work of the Spirit and through belief in the truth. He called you to this through our gospel, that you might share in the glory of our Lord Jesus Christ. So then, brothers and sisters, stand firm and hold fast to the teachings we passed on to you, whether by word of mouth or by letter.*
>
> *May our Lord Jesus Christ himself and God our Father, who loved us and by his grace gave us eternal encouragement and good hope, encourage your hearts and strengthen you in every good deed and word." (2 Thessalonians 2:13-17)*

In contrast to the grim fate of those deceived by the lawless one, Paul turns to thanksgiving for the Thessalonian believers, chosen by God for salvation through sanctification by the Spirit and belief in the truth. He exhorts them to stand firm and hold to the teachings passed on to them. This exhortation to steadfastness is not just a call to intellectual assent but to a living, active faith that works itself out in love, hope, and endurance.

Standing firm in the faith requires more than just a passive resistance to falsehood; it involves an active commitment to living out the Gospel in every area of life. Are we anchored in the teachings of Christ, allowing them to shape our thoughts, actions, and relationships? Let us be a people so deeply rooted in the truth that we are immovable in the face of deception and apostasy.

Conclusion:

2 Thessalonians Chapter 2 presents us with a vivid depiction of the spiritual battle that rages until the return of Christ. In the midst of confusion, deception, and apostasy, Paul's message to the Thessalonians - and to us - is clear: stand firm in the truth.

As we await the coming of our Lord, may we too be vigilant, discerning, and faithful, holding fast to the truth of the Gospel, which is the power of God for salvation to everyone who believes.

Introduction

This final chapter speaks volumes about the Christian life, work ethic, and community responsibility. Although brief, it is packed with instructions, prayers, and commands that are as relevant today as they were when the Apostle Paul first penned them.

The Thessalonian church was a young but vibrant community facing persecution, confusion about the Day of the Lord, and issues related to idleness among its members. In response, Paul writes to correct, encourage, and instruct them on how to live in anticipation of Christ's return.

Prayer for the Spread of the Gospel and Protection (1:1-5)

"As for other matters, brothers and sisters, pray for us that the message of the Lord may spread rapidly and be honoured, just as it was with you. And pray that we may be delivered from wicked and evil people, for not everyone has faith.

But the Lord is faithful, and he will strengthen you and protect you from the evil one. We have confidence in the Lord that you are doing and will continue to do the things we command. May the Lord direct your hearts into God's love and Christ's perseverance." (2 Thessalonians 1:1-5)

Paul begins by requesting prayers for himself and his fellow workers. He asks that the message of the Lord may spread rapidly and be honoured, just as it was with the Thessalonians. Paul also seeks prayer for protection against wicked and evil people, acknowledging that not everyone has faith. This introduction sets a tone of dependence on God for success in ministry and protection from adversaries.

Like Paul, we should recognize the importance of prayer in our lives, especially when facing opposition or hardship. Let us be diligent in praying for the advancement of the Gospel and for protection against the forces that would oppose it.

Warning Against Idleness (1:6-15)

"In the name of the Lord Jesus Christ, we command you, brothers and sisters, to keep away from every believer who is idle and disruptive and does not live according to the teaching you received from us. For you yourselves know how you ought to follow our example. We were not idle when we were with you, nor did we eat anyone's food without paying for it. On the contrary, we worked night and day, labouring and toiling so that we would not be a burden to any of you.

We did this, not because we do not have the right to such help, but in order to offer ourselves as a model for you to imitate. For even when we were with you, we gave you this rule: "The one who is unwilling to work shall not eat."

We hear that some among you are idle and disruptive. They are not busy; they are busybodies. Such people we command and urge in the Lord Jesus Christ to settle down and earn the food they eat. And as for you, brothers and sisters, never tire of doing what is good.

Take special note of anyone who does not obey our instruction in this letter. Do not associate with them, in order that they may feel ashamed. Yet do not regard them as an enemy but warn them as you would a fellow believer." (2 Thessalonians 1:6-15)

Paul then addresses a specific issue within the Thessalonian community: idleness. Some members were not working and were instead becoming busybodies. Paul commands them in the name of the Lord Jesus Christ to settle down and earn the food they eat. He reminds them of his own example, working night and day not to be a burden to anyone.

This passage is not just about physical work; it's a call to responsibility and active participation in the community's life. Paul emphasizes that those who do not work should not eat, highlighting the principle of contributing to the community as one is able.

In our communities, we should be encouraging a spirit of responsibility, where each person contributes according to their abilities. Let's also remember to approach those who are struggling with a spirit of gentleness, aiming to restore rather than to condemn.

Benediction (1:16-18)

> *"Now may the Lord of peace himself give you peace at all times and in every way. The Lord be with all of you. I, Paul, write this greeting in my own hand, which is the distinguishing mark in all my letters. This is how I write. The grace of our Lord Jesus Christ be with you all." (2 Thessalonians 1:16-18)*

Paul concludes with a prayer for peace from the Lord at all times and in every way. He affirms his authorship with his own hand, which is a sign of authenticity, and ends with a grace-filled blessing for all the Thessalonians.

Peace and grace are gifts from the Lord that sustain us in our daily lives and ministries. Let us be channels of God's peace in our communities, showing grace to one another as we await the Lord's return.

Conclusion

2 Thessalonians Chapter 3 challenges us to consider our work ethic, our involvement in the community, and our reliance on prayer. It reminds us that as we await Christ's return, we are to live responsibly, contribute to the well-being of our community, and support one another in love and good deeds.

Let's take to heart Paul's instructions and his example, striving to live in a manner worthy of the calling we have received. As we go forth this week, let us pray for one another, work diligently, and seek to embody the peace and grace of our Lord Jesus Christ in every aspect of our lives.

~ 1 TIMOTHY ~

Introduction

Paul's first Epistle to Timothy, is a pivotal pastoral letter that provides guidance on church leadership, doctrine, and Christian living. Addressed to Timothy, a young leader in the early church, this letter is rich with advice that spans theological instruction, practical church management, and personal conduct. Allow me to offer you a brief overview of each of the six chapters.

Chapter 1:

Paul begins with a caution against false teachings and the misuse of the law, highlighting the importance of sound doctrine rooted in faith and love. He contrasts this with his own story of redemption, emphasizing God's grace in his life as a foremost example of Christ's patience and mercy.

False Teachings: Paul identifies the problem of false doctrines, emphasizing that the goal of the commandment is love from a pure heart, a good conscience, and sincere faith. This serves as a reminder that true teaching leads to godliness and love.

Paul's Testimony: Paul shares his testimony, acknowledging his former life of blasphemy and persecution of the church. His story underscores the depth of God's mercy and the transformative power of the gospel, serving as an encouragement for all believers to embrace God's grace.

Chapter 2:

Paul addresses the conduct of public worship, emphasizing prayer for all people, including those in authority. He also outlines the roles of men and women in worship settings, stressing orderliness and modesty.

Prayer for All: The call to pray for all people reflects the universal scope of the gospel's offer of salvation and the desire for a peaceful and godly life for the Christian community.

Role of Women: The instructions regarding women in worship have been widely debated among scholars. Paul's emphasis on learning in quietness and submission, and the reference to Eve's deception, highlight the importance of order and authority in worship.

These instructions must be understood in their cultural and historical context and interpreted in light of the whole counsel of Scripture regarding women's roles in the church.

It is really important that all of these texts about women in ministry are viewed through the clear 'window' of Galatians 3:28, which so clearly states that within God's kingdom, there is *"neither male nor female"* and that must always be our starting point in interpreting these problematic texts.

Chapter 3:

Paul lists the qualifications for overseers (elders) and deacons, emphasizing character, ability to teach, and manage their households well. This chapter underscores the high standard expected of those in church leadership.

Overseers and Deacons: The qualities listed—above reproach, faithful to his wife, sober-minded, self-controlled, respectable, hospitable, able to teach, not a drunkard, not violent but gentle, not quarrelsome, not a lover of money—emphasize moral integrity, spiritual maturity, and relational skills.

Church as the Pillar of Truth: The chapter concludes by highlighting the church's role as the "pillar and buttress of the truth," signifying the importance of leadership in maintaining the integrity and purity of the gospel message.

Chapter 4:

Paul warns against false ascetic teachings that deviate from the truth, advocating instead for godliness and personal discipline as means of spiritual growth.

Warning Against False Asceticism: Paul predicts the rise of teachings that forbid marriage and require abstinence from foods, describing them as demonic influences that promote unnecessary self-denial.

Discipline for Godliness: Paul encourages Timothy to train himself for godliness, valuing it as holding promise for both the present life and the life to come. This reflects the holistic view of salvation that impacts all areas of life.

Chapter 5:

Paul gives specific instructions on how to treat various groups within the church - older men, younger men, older women, younger women, an widows—highlighting the importance of familial respect, purity, and care for those in need.

Care for Widows: The detailed instructions regarding the support of widows underscore the early church's commitment to social welfare and the prioritization of those truly in need.

Respect and Purity: Paul's guidance stresses the importance of treating all members of the church with respect and purity, fostering a community marked by godliness and mutual care.

Chapter 6:

Paul concludes the letter by addressing the dangers of false teaching and the love of money. He contrasts this with the pursuit of righteousness, godliness, faith, love, steadfastness, and gentleness, culminating in a charge to Timothy to guard the faith against error.

Dangers of Love of Money: Paul famously notes that the love of money is a root of all kinds of evils, warning against the temptation to stray from faith in pursuit of material gain.

The Good Fight of Faith: The final exhortation to Timothy to fight the good fight of faith and keep the commandment unstained until the appearing of our Lord Jesus Christ encapsulates the pastoral concern of the entire letter: to remain steadfast in faith and doctrine amid external pressures and internal temptations.

Summary

This first letter of Paul's to his much-loved brother in the Lord, Timothy, presents a comprehensive guide for church leadership, addressing doctrinal integrity, worship practices, leadership qualifications, and personal conduct.

Its enduring message challenges us all as believers to pursue godliness, uphold sound teaching, and fulfill their calling within the body of Christ with integrity and love.

Now I will unpack each of the six chapters in more detail as we explore this letter in more detail.

~ 1 TIMOTHY 1 ~

Introduction

In the first chapter of 1 Timothy, the Apostle Paul pens a heartfelt and instructive letter to Timothy, his true son in the faith, laying a foundation for godly leadership and sound teaching within the church. This passage confronts false teachings, upholds the proper use of the law, and showcases the transformative power of the Gospel through Paul's personal testimony.

Greeting (1:1-2)

"Paul, an apostle of Christ Jesus by the command of God our Saviour and of Christ Jesus our hope, to Timothy my true son in the faith: Grace, mercy and peace from God the Father and Christ Jesus our Lord." (1 Timothy 1:1-2)

Paul's opening words to Timothy, underscore Paul's role as an apostle *"by the command of God"* and highlighting the intimate mentor-disciple relationship between Paul and Timothy, whom he calls "my true son in the faith." This opening sets a tone of authority and affection, framing the letter as both a personal communication and an authoritative instruction. Paul extends a blessing of "grace, mercy, and peace," foundational elements of the Christian faith, from God and Christ Jesus.

The Charge Against False Teachings (1:3-7)

As I urged you when I went into Macedonia, stay there in Ephesus so that you may command certain people not to teach false doctrines any longer or to devote themselves to myths and endless genealogies. Such things promote controversial speculations rather than advancing God's work — which is by faith. The goal of this command is love, which comes from a pure heart and a good conscience and a sincere faith. Some have departed from these and have turned to meaningless talk. They want to be teachers of the law, but they do not know what they are talking about or what they so confidently affirm. "
(1 Timothy 1:3-7)

Paul urges Timothy to stay in Ephesus to combat false teachings and myths that were leading believers astray. These false teachers, obsessed with myths and endless genealogies, were promoting controversies rather than God's work. Paul's strong admonition reminds us of the ever-present danger of false doctrines that can subtly infiltrate the church, emphasizing the need for vigilance and adherence to sound doctrine. In a world flooded with information and varying interpretations of Scripture, how do we ensure that we are not led astray? The key lies in grounding ourselves in the truth of God's Word, being discerning listeners, and seeking the guidance of the Holy Spirit.

The Purpose of the Law (1:8-11)

"We know that the law is good if one uses it properly. We also know that the law is made not for the righteous but for lawbreakers and rebels, the ungodly and sinful, the unholy and irreligious, for those who kill their fathers or mothers, for murderers, for the sexually immoral, for those practicing homosexuality, for slave traders and liars and perjurers - and for whatever else is contrary to the sound doctrine that conforms to the gospel concerning the glory of the blessed God, which he entrusted to me." (1 Timothy 1:8-11)

Paul clarifies the proper use of the law, stating it is good if used lawfully, understanding that it is not meant for the righteous but for lawbreakers and rebels. The law serves as a mirror, reflecting our sinfulness and our need for a Saviour. It points us to Christ, in whom we find grace and redemption. How do we view God's commands? Are we tempted to view them as mere guidelines or, conversely, as a means to earn our salvation? Let us recognize the law's role in leading us to the end of ourselves and the foot of the cross, where grace abounds.

Paul's Testimony: A Display of God's Mercy (1:12-17)

"I thank Christ Jesus our Lord, who has given me strength, that he considered me trustworthy, appointing me to his service. Even though I was once a blasphemer and a persecutor and a violent man, I was shown mercy because I acted in ignorance and unbelief."

> *"The grace of our Lord was poured out on me abundantly, along with the faith and love that are in Christ Jesus. Here is a trustworthy saying that deserves full acceptance: Christ Jesus came into the world to save sinners - of whom I am the worst.*
>
> *But for that very reason I was shown mercy so that in me, the worst of sinners, Christ Jesus might display his immense patience as an example for those who would believe in him and receive eternal life. Now to the King eternal, immortal, invisible, the only God, be honour and glory for ever and ever. Amen."*
> *(1 Timothy 1:12-17)*

In a moving testament to God's grace, Paul shares his story, from being a blasphemer and persecutor of the church to becoming a recipient of Christ's limitless mercy.

Paul's transformation showcases the Gospel's power to change the most hardened heart. This testimony is a beacon of hope for all, affirming that no one is beyond the reach of God's grace.

Paul's story encourages us to reflect on our own testimonies. How has the grace of God transformed your life? Let us be bold in sharing our stories, not as trophies of our goodness, but as testimonies of God's mercy and grace.

May our lives be living epistles, known and read by all, pointing others to the hope we have in Christ.

Upholding Faith and a Good Conscience (1:18-20)

> *"Timothy, my son, I am giving you this command in keeping with the prophecies once made about you, so that by recalling them you may fight the battle well, holding on to faith and a good conscience, which some have rejected and so have suffered shipwreck with regard to the faith. Among them are Hymenaeus and Alexander, whom I have handed over to Satan to be taught not to blaspheme." (1 Timothy 1:18-20)*

Paul concludes the chapter by charging Timothy to wage the good warfare, holding onto faith and a good conscience.

This exhortation to steadfastness in the faith, coupled with the warning against shipwrecking one's faith, serves as a sobering reminder of the necessity of perseverance and integrity in our walk with God.

In the battles we face, both externally and internally, are we holding fast to faith and maintaining a good conscience? Let us be diligent in prayer, rooted in Scripture, and accountable within the community of believers.

As we navigate through trials and temptations, may our anchor hold firm in the truths of God's Word and the hope of the Gospel.

Conclusion

1 Timothy Chapter 1 challenges us to stand firm against false teachings, to understand and appreciate the purpose of the law, and to be transformed and motivated by the grace of God as demonstrated in Paul's life. As we uphold faith and a good conscience, may we be vessels of God's grace, proclaiming the truth of the Gospel with our words and our lives.

~ 1 TIMOTHY 2 ~

Introduction

In the heart of Paul's first letter to Timothy, the second chapter stands as a clarion call for the church to engage deeply in a life marked by prayer, peace, and godly order. This chapter, rich with instruction and insight, not only outlines the priorities for communal worship but also addresses the roles within the church, underpinning all actions with the motivation of leading peaceful and quiet lives that are pleasing to God. Let's explore the depths of this text now and uncover how its teachings apply to our lives and our worship.

Prayer for All People (2:1-4)

"I urge, then, first of all, that petitions, prayers, intercession and thanksgiving be made for all people - for kings and all those in authority, that we may live peaceful and quiet lives in all godliness and holiness. This is good, and pleases God our Saviour, who wants all people to be saved and to come to a knowledge of the truth." (1 Timothy 2:1-4)

Paul begins by urging that *"...petitions, prayers, intercession and thanksgiving be made for all people.."* highlighting the importance of a prayerful life that extends beyond our immediate circles to include all humanity, especially those who are in authority. This universal approach to prayer emphasizes God's desire for all to be saved and to come to the knowledge of the truth.

In our divided and often contentious world, the call to pray for all, including those with whom we disagree or those in leadership positions, is both radical and transformative. It challenges us to see beyond political, ethnic, or social divides, recognizing the value of every person in God's eyes. Are we committed to praying for our leaders, for peace, and for the salvation of all? Let us be faithful in prayer, remembering that it is a powerful tool in the Kingdom of God for bringing about change and drawing all people to Him.

One Mediator Between God and Mankind (2:5-7)

"For there is one God and one mediator between God and mankind, the man Christ Jesus, who gave himself as a ransom for all people. This has now been witnessed to at the proper time. And for this purpose, I was appointed a herald and an apostle - I am telling the truth, I am not lying - and a true and faithful teacher of the Gentiles." (1 Timothy 2:5-7)

Paul reinforces the foundational Christian doctrine that there is one God and one mediator between God and mankind, Jesus Christ, who gave Himself as a ransom for all. This truth underpins the reason for our prayers for everyone: Christ's sacrificial love and His unique role as the mediator who bridges the gap between a holy God and sinful humanity.

The exclusivity of Christ as the mediator is a cornerstone of our faith. It calls us to a renewed appreciation for the Gospel and its message of reconciliation. In a culture that often promotes a plurality of ways to God, how are we upholding and sharing the truth of Christ's unique role? Let our lives and our words consistently point to Jesus as the only way to the Father, motivated by a desire for all to know Him.

Instructions on Worship and Roles within the Church (2:8-15)

"Therefore, I want the men everywhere to pray, lifting up holy hands without anger or disputing. I also want the women to dress modestly, with decency and propriety, adorning themselves, not with elaborate hairstyles or gold or pearls or expensive clothes, but with good deeds, appropriate for women who profess to worship God.

A woman should learn in quietness and full submission. I do not permit a woman to teach or to assume authority over a man; she must be quiet. For Adam was formed first, then Eve. And Adam was not the one deceived; it was the woman who was deceived and became a sinner. But women will be saved through childbearing - if they continue in faith, love and holiness with propriety." (1 Timothy 2:8-15)

Paul provides specific instructions for men and women in the context of worship at that time, emphasizing the importance of order, modesty, and godly conduct. For men, Paul calls for prayers without anger or quarrelling. For women, the focus is on modesty and good deeds, as fitting for those who are professing godliness.

As I have already stressed a number of times in this study, we should view these difficult, culturally-anchored passages through the lense of Galatians 3:28 – where we are told by Paul in the clearest possible language, that within the kingdom of God, there is neither male nor female. So to take very specific, culturally conditioned instructions about women and apply them across the board to all women inside and outside the church, is both reckless and a fundamental interpretation error.

These verses often spark debate concerning the roles of men and women in the church today. Regardless of all the various interpretations, the underlying principles of peace, order, and godliness are clear.

The underlying principles in this passage are clear: in our gatherings, are we fostering an environment of peace and encouragement? Are our actions and attire reflective of a heart devoted to God? Let's seek to embody these virtues in our worship and in our daily lives, contributing to a community that glorifies God in all things.

Conclusion

1 Timothy Chapter 2 lays out a vision for a praying church that intercedes for all people, recognizes the central truth of Christ as our mediator, and conducts itself according to principles of peace, order, and godliness.

As we reflect on this chapter, let us be motivated to deepen our commitment to prayer, to cherish the unique role of Christ in our salvation, and to always pursue peace and order within our own communities of faith.

~ 1 TIMOTHY 3 ~

Introduction

In the third chapter of his first letter to Timothy, the Apostle Paul lays out a detailed blueprint for leadership within the church. This chapter, rich in wisdom and guidance, delineates the qualifications for overseers (bishops) and deacons, emphasizing character over charisma, integrity over influence, and godliness over mere ability.

As we delve into these inspired guidelines, we're invited to reflect not only on the structure and health of the church but also on our individual walks with Christ, for every believer is called to embody these virtues in their life.

The Call to Overseership (3:1-7)

"Here is a trustworthy saying: Whoever aspires to be an overseer desires a noble task. Now the overseer is to be above reproach, faithful to his wife, temperate, self-controlled, respectable, hospitable, able to teach, not given to drunkenness, not violent but gentle, not quarrelsome, not a lover of money.

He must manage his own family well and see that his children obey him, and he must do so in a manner worthy of full respect. (If anyone does not know how to manage his own family, how can he take care of God's church?)

He must not be a recent convert, or he may become conceited and fall under the same judgment as the devil. He must also have a good reputation with outsiders, so that he will not fall into disgrace and into the devil's trap." (1 Timothy 3:1-7)

Paul begins with a profound statement: *"Whoever aspires to be an overseer desires a noble task."* This desire for leadership within the church is not to be taken lightly; it's a calling that demands a life marked by exemplary character.

It is important to note that list of qualifications that follows is not merely a checklist but a portrait of Christlikeness.

An overseer must be above reproach, faithful to his spouse, sober-minded, self-controlled, respectable, hospitable, able to teach, not a drunkard, not violent but gentle, not quarrelsome, not a lover of money, managing his own household well, and not a recent convert. These qualities highlight the importance of moral integrity, spiritual maturity, and relational wisdom in church leadership.

How do these qualifications for overseers challenge us in our personal and communal lives? While not all are called to the office of overseer, we are all called to pursue godliness and integrity.

Let us examine our lives in light of these standards, asking God to reveal areas where we need growth and grace. For those in leadership, this is a sober reminder of the high calling you've received; for those who are not, it's a call to support, pray for, and encourage your leaders, recognizing the weighty task they carry.

The Role of Deacons (3:8-13)

"In the same way, deacons are to be worthy of respect, sincere, not indulging in much wine, and not pursuing dishonest gain. They must keep hold of the deep truths of the faith with a clear conscience. They must first be tested; and then if there is nothing against them, let them serve as deacons. In the same way, the women are to be worthy of respect, not malicious talkers but temperate and trustworthy in everything.

A deacon must be faithful to his wife and must manage his children and his household well. Those who have served well gain an excellent standing and great assurance in their faith in Christ Jesus." (1 Timothy 3:8-13)

Deacons, much like overseers, are called to a standard of character that reflects the transformative power of the gospel. They must be dignified, not double-tongued, not addicted to much wine, not greedy for dishonest gain, holding the mystery of the faith with a clear conscience, and always managing their households well.

Their wives, too, are called to be dignified, not slanderers, but sober-minded and faithful in all things. The role of a deacon is one of service, embodying the servant-hearted nature of Christ Himself. The calling of a deacon is a powerful reminder that leadership in the kingdom of God is characterized by service and sacrifice. In what ways are we serving within our church and community? Are we pursuing the virtues outlined for deacons in our own lives, regardless of our official roles? Let this passage inspire us to serve one another with humility, integrity, and a clear conscience before God.

The gender issue: Once again, we are confronted with the reality of the male-dominated reality of life in the ancient world. Paul addresses his teaching male deacons only because there were no female deacons at that time.

The liberation of all women in Christ did not flow through into the day-to-day life of the Church for many generations to come. In fact, in some churches today, there is still no room for women to become deacons and even less room for them to be pastors and teachers. Once again, we must allow Paul's clear words in Galatians 3:28 to echo through the hallowed halls of every church in the modern world: *"There is neither Jew nor Gentile, neither slave nor free, nor is there male and female, for you are all one in Christ Jesus."*

I've been blessed and enriched over the years to work alongside many women deacons and I have sat under the teaching of a number of women Pastors. It has been a great blessing in my personal walk with God.

The sad reality is that those who insist on taking these culturally anchored directives out of their context and applying them to our life now, only do so in part. Many churches today insist that women cannot be in a leadership role within the church, and yet they don't insist they cover their heads remain quiet in gatherings! This inconsistency only highlights the selective interpretation of scripture – to suit long-held prejudices which never came from God.

The Church: The Pillar and Ground of the Truth (3:14-16)

"Although I hope to come to you soon, I am writing you these instructions so that, if I am delayed, you will know how people ought to conduct themselves in God's household, which is the church of the living God, the pillar and foundation of the truth.

Beyond all question, the mystery from which true godliness springs is great: He appeared in the flesh, was vindicated by the Spirit, was seen by angels, was preached among the nations, was believed on in the world, was taken up in glory. "
(1 Timothy 3:14-16)

Paul concludes this chapter by expressing his hope to come to Timothy soon but also acknowledges that delays might occur. Hence, he provides these instructions so that Timothy, and indeed all who read this letter, might know how to conduct themselves in the household of God, which is the church of the living God, the pillar and ground of the truth. This high calling of the church underscores the importance of leadership that upholds and embodies the truth of the gospel. The mystery of godliness, encapsulated in the confession of Christ's incarnation, vindication, and ascension, is the foundation upon which the church stands.

As members of the household of God, how are we contributing to the upholding of truth within our community? Are our lives, both individually and corporately, a reflection of the mystery of godliness revealed in Christ? Let us strive to be a church that, through its leadership and its members, serves as a pillar and ground of the truth in a world desperately in need of the gospel.

Conclusion

This chapter challenges us to reflect on the quality of leadership and the character of our lives in light of God's holy standards. Whether called to be overseers, deacons, or faithful members of the body of Christ, we are all called to pursue a life of integrity, service, and godliness. May we, as the church, be a beacon of truth, love, faithfully embodying the mystery of godliness that has been entrusted to us.

~ 1 TIMOTHY 4 ~

Introduction

The Apostle Paul now provides Timothy, and by extension all believers, with some profound guidance on how to live as faithful servants of Christ in the midst of a world filled with deceit and temptation.

This chapter is a clarion call to godliness, underpinned by a life dedicated to the Word of God and the nurturing of one's spiritual gifts. As we explore this passage, we are invited to consider our own commitment to living out our faith, fostering personal holiness, and being vigilant against false teachings.

The Challenge of Apostasy (4:1-5)

"The Spirit clearly says that in later times some will abandon the faith and follow deceiving spirits and things taught by demons. Such teachings come through hypocritical liars, whose consciences have been seared as with a hot iron. They forbid people to marry and order them to abstain from certain foods, which God created to be received with thanksgiving by those who believe and who know the truth.

For everything God created is good, and nothing is to be rejected if it is received with thanksgiving, because it is consecrated by the word of God and prayer." (1 Timothy 4:1-5)

Paul gives us a stark warning about the latter times, indicating that some will depart from the faith, seduced by deceitful spirits and teachings of demons. This apostasy is characterized by restrictions on marriage and foods, which God created to be received with thanksgiving. Here, the Apostle emphasizes that everything created by God is good, and nothing is to be rejected if it is received with thanksgiving.

The warning against apostasy serves as a timely reminder of the constant need for discernment in our spiritual lives. Are we grounded in Scripture, able to discern truth from error?

Do we recognize the freedom we have in Christ, a freedom that calls us not to legalism but to gratitude for God's good gifts? Let us be vigilant, always returning to the truth of God's Word as our standard and guide.

The Discipline of Godliness (4:6-10)

"If you point these things out to the brothers and sisters, you will be a good minister of Christ Jesus, nourished on the truths of the faith and of the good teaching that you have followed.

Have nothing to do with godless myths and old wives' tales; rather, train yourself to be godly. For physical training is of some value, but godliness has value for all things, holding promise for both the present life and the life to come.

This is a trustworthy saying that deserves full acceptance. That is why we labour and strive, because we have put our hope in the living God, who is the Saviour of all people, and especially of those who believe."(1 Timothy 4:6-10)

Paul instructs Timothy to be a good servant of Christ Jesus, nourished on the truths of the faith and avoiding irreverent, silly myths. Instead, Timothy, and by extension all believers, is to train himself for godliness.

Paul contrasts physical training, which is of some value, with godliness, which holds promise for both the present life and the life to come. This pursuit of godliness is grounded in the living God, who is the Saviour of all people, especially of those who believe.

How are we training ourselves for godliness? Like any discipline, godliness requires intentional effort - engagement with Scripture, prayer, and the cultivation of spiritual disciplines.

As we navigate our daily lives, let us prioritize our spiritual health, recognizing its eternal value. May our lives reflect a deep commitment to living out the truths of our faith, displaying the transformative power of the gospel.

A Model of Faithful Service (4:11-16)

> *"Command and teach these things. Don't let anyone look down on you because you are young, but set an example for the believers in speech, in conduct, in love, in faith and in purity. Until I come, devote yourself to the public reading of Scripture, to preaching and to teaching. Do not neglect your gift, which was given you through prophecy when the body of elders laid their hands on you. Be diligent in these matters; give yourself wholly to them, so that everyone may see your progress. Watch your life and doctrine closely. Persevere in them, because if you do, you will save both yourself and your hearers."*
> *(1 Timothy 4:11-16)*

Paul encourages Timothy to set an example for the believers in speech, in conduct, in love, in faith, in purity. He is to devote himself to the public reading of Scripture, to exhortation, to teaching, and not to neglect the gift he received. Paul's admonition to keep a close watch on himself and on the teaching highlights the importance of personal holiness and doctrinal integrity in Christian leadership. Each of us, regardless of our role within the church, is called to be an example of faithfulness in our sphere of influence. How does your life reflect the transformative power of the gospel?

Are you nurturing the spiritual gifts God has given you for the edification of the church and the advancement of His kingdom? Let us each take seriously the call to be models of faithfulness, always aware of the impact our lives have on those around us.

Conclusion

1 Timothy Chapter 4 challenges us to stand firm in the faith, to diligently pursue godliness, and to live out our calling as good servants of Christ Jesus. In a world where truth is often distorted, and godliness is undervalued, let us be beacons of truth, love, and purity. May our commitment to the Lord be evident in all we do, as we train ourselves for godliness, set an example for others, and faithfully steward the gifts God has entrusted to us.

~ 1 TIMOTHY 5 ~

Introduction

Chapter 5 presents us with the Apostle Paul's wisdom on how to conduct ourselves within the Christian community, emphasizing the treatment of widows, elders, and each other.

This passage offers profound insights into the responsibilities we bear towards one another, underlining the values of respect, honour, and purity that should characterize our interactions. As we delve into these instructions, let's consider how they challenge and guide us to live out our faith in community.

Respect and Care for Widows (5:1-16)

"Do not rebuke an older man harshly but exhort him as if he were your father. Treat younger men as brothers, older women as mothers, and younger women as sisters, with absolute purity.

Give proper recognition to those widows who are really in need. But if a widow has children or grandchildren, these should learn first of all to put their religion into practice by caring for their own family and so repaying their parents and grandparents, for this is pleasing to God. The widow who is really in need and left all alone puts her hope in God and continues night and day to pray and to ask God for help. But the widow who lives for pleasure is dead even while she lives.

Give the people these instructions, so that no one may be open to blame. Anyone who does not provide for their relatives, and especially for their own household, has denied the faith and is worse than an unbeliever.

No widow may be put on the list of widows unless she is over sixty, has been faithful to her husband, and is well known for her good deeds, such as bringing up children, showing hospitality, washing the feet of the Lord's people, helping those in trouble and devoting herself to all kinds of good deeds"

"As for younger widows, do not put them on such a list. For when their sensual desires overcome their dedication to Christ, they want to marry. Thus, they bring judgment on themselves because they have broken their first pledge. Besides, they get into the habit of being idle and going about from house to house. And not only do they become idlers, but also busybodies who talk nonsense, saying things they ought not to. So, I counsel younger widows to marry, to have children, to manage their homes and to give the enemy no opportunity for slander. Some have in fact already turned away to follow Satan.

If any woman who is a believer has widows in her care, she should continue to help them and not let the church be burdened with them, so that the church can help those widows who are really in need." (1 Timothy 5:1-16)

Paul begins the chapter with guidelines for caring for widows, a matter of great importance in the early church. The instructions reflect a deep concern for social justice and the well-being of vulnerable community members. He distinguishes between widows who are truly in need and those who have family members to care for them, urging the church to support the former. This prioritization ensures that the church's resources are used wisely, providing for those most in need.

The church today continues to be a place where the vulnerable should find support and care. How are we identifying and addressing the needs within our community and beyond? Are we, as individuals or as a church, actively seeking to support those who are truly in need, while also encouraging families to fulfill their responsibilities towards their own members? Let our community be marked by genuine compassion and practical support for the vulnerable among us.

Honouring Church Leaders (5:17-21)

"The elders who direct the affairs of the church well are worthy of double honour, especially those whose work is preaching and teaching. For Scripture says, "Do not muzzle an ox while it is treading out the grain," and "The worker deserves his wages."

"Do not entertain an accusation against an elder unless it is brought by two or three witnesses. But those elders who are sinning you are to reprove before everyone, so that the others may take warning. I charge you, in the sight of God and Christ Jesus and the elect angels, to keep these instructions without partiality, and to do nothing out of favouritism." (1 Timothy 5:17-21)

Paul shifts his focus to the elders of the church, emphasizing that those who lead well, especially in preaching and teaching, are worthy of double honour. This acknowledgment extends beyond respect to practical matters, including financial remuneration. Yet, with honour comes accountability; Paul also addresses the issue of disciplining elders who sin, advocating for a process that is both just and respectful.

Our attitude towards leadership within the church reflects our understanding of God's order and provision. Are we honouring those who labour among us in word and doctrine? At the same time, are we maintaining a standard of accountability that safeguards the integrity of the church? Let us be committed to both honouring and holding our leaders accountable, doing so with grace and truth.

Purity and Personal Conduct (5:22-24)

"Do not be hasty in the laying on of hands, and do not share in the sins of others. Keep yourself pure. Stop drinking only water and use a little wine because of your stomach and your frequent illnesses. The sins of some are obvious, reaching the place of judgment ahead of them; the sins of others trail behind them. In the same way, good deeds are obvious, and even those that are not obvious cannot remain hidden forever." (1 Timothy 5:22-24)

Paul concludes the chapter with personal advice to Timothy, warning him against hasty ordination, sharing in others' sins, and neglecting his health. These instructions, while personal, carry broader implications for our conduct. The emphasis on not being hasty in laying on hands speaks to the importance of discernment and wisdom in leadership decisions.

Paul's caution about purity and his concern for Timothy's health remind us of the holistic nature of our faith, which encompasses both spiritual and physical well-being.

How are we exercising discernment and wisdom in all our decisions, both personally and corporately? Are we maintaining purity, not just in our actions, but in our associations and responsibilities? Furthermore, are we caring for our physical well-being, recognizing that our bodies are temples of the Holy Spirit? Let us strive for a balanced approach to our faith, one that honours God in body, mind, and spirit.

Conclusion

1 Timothy Chapter 5 presents a compelling vision for Christian community, one marked by compassion, honour, accountability, and personal integrity. As we reflect on Paul's instructions, let us consider how we might better embody these principles in our interactions within the church and our wider community.

May our lives reflect the love, purity, and respect that Paul advocates, bearing witness to the transforming power of the gospel in our relationships.

~ 1 TIMOTHY 6 ~

Introduction

As we turn our attention to the final chapter of Paul's first letter to Timothy, we find ourselves confronted with a rich tapestry of guidance that speaks to the heart of Christian living. This is a compelling call to pursue godliness with contentment, to guard against the love of money, and to fight the good fight of faith. Through Paul's instructions to Timothy, we are invited to reflect on our own values, attitudes, and commitments, examining what it truly means to live a life that honours God.

The Christian and Service (6:1-2)

"All who are under the yoke of slavery should consider their masters worthy of full respect, so that God's name and our teaching may not be slandered. Those who have believing masters, should not show them disrespect just because they are fellow believers. Instead, they should serve them even better because their masters are dear to them as fellow believers and are devoted to the welfare of their slaves. These are the things you are to teach and insist on." (1 Timothy 6:1-2)

Paul begins by addressing those within the Christian community who are under the yoke of servitude, urging them to regard their masters as worthy of all honour. This instruction is not an endorsement of the servitude system but a call to live in such a way that God's name and the teaching are not blasphemed. For those who have believing masters, they are not to be disrespectful but are rather to serve all the more diligently because their masters are brothers in the faith.

While the direct context might differ from any of our modern experiences, the principle of working with integrity and respect applies universally. How do we conduct ourselves in our workplaces, schools, or homes? Are we living in such a way that our actions speak well of our faith, showing respect and diligence in all we do?

Let us strive to be exemplary in our conduct, honouring God through our service to others, regardless of our position.

Contentment versus the Love of Money (6:3-10)

> "If anyone teaches otherwise and does not agree to the sound instruction of our Lord Jesus Christ and to godly teaching, they are conceited and understand nothing. They have an unhealthy interest in controversies and quarrels about words that result in envy, strife, malicious talk, evil suspicions and constant friction between people of corrupt mind, who have been robbed of the truth and who think that godliness is a means to financial gain.
>
> But godliness with contentment is great gain. For we brought nothing into the world, and we can take nothing out of it. But if we have food and clothing, we will be content with that. Those who want to get rich fall into temptation and a trap and into many foolish and harmful desires that plunge people into ruin and destruction.
>
> For the love of money is a root of all kinds of evil. Some people, eager for money, have wandered from the faith and pierced themselves with many griefs." (1 Timothy 6:3-10)

Paul warns Timothy about those who view godliness as a means to financial gain, contrasting this with true godliness coupled with contentment, which he declares is great gain. He reminds us that we brought nothing into the world and can take nothing out of it, highlighting the futility of placing our hope in material wealth. The love of money is identified as a root of all kinds of evil, leading many away from the faith.

In a culture that often equates success with financial prosperity, how do we guard our hearts against the love of money? Are we seeking contentment in our relationship with God, or are we caught in the endless pursuit of material gain?

Let us remember that our true treasure is found in Christ, and in Him, we have everything we need. Let contentment and godliness be our pursuit, recognizing that these bring true and lasting fulfillment.

The Good Fight of Faith (6:11-16)

"But you, man of God, flee from all this, and pursue righteousness, godliness, faith, love, endurance and gentleness. Fight the good fight of the faith. Take hold of the eternal life to which you were called when you made your good confession in the presence of many witnesses.

In the sight of God, who gives life to everything, and of Christ Jesus, who while testifying before Pontius Pilate made the good confession, I charge you to keep this command without spot or blame until the appearing of our Lord Jesus Christ, which God will bring about in his own time - God, the blessed and only Ruler, the King of kings and Lord of lords, who alone is immortal and who lives in unapproachable light, whom no one has seen or can see. To him be honour and might forever. Amen."
(1 Timothy 6:11-16)

Paul exhorts Timothy to flee from the things of this world and pursue righteousness, godliness, faith, love, steadfastness, and gentleness. He is called to fight the good fight of faith, to take hold of eternal life, and to keep the commandment unstained and free from reproach until the appearing of our Lord Jesus Christ. This passage is a powerful reminder of the Christian's calling to live a life that is markedly different from the world's values, actively pursuing the things of God.

does it mean for us to fight the good fight of faith in our daily lives? Are we actively pursuing righteousness and godliness, or are we complacent in our spiritual journey? Let us be encouraged to live with purpose and determination, seeking first the kingdom of God and His righteousness, and striving to fulfill our calling with honour and integrity.

Final Exhortations and Conclusion (6:17-21)

"Command those who are rich in this present world not to be arrogant nor to put their hope in wealth, which is so uncertain, but to put their hope in God, who richly provides us with everything for our enjoyment."

"Command them to do good, to be rich in good deeds, and to be generous and willing to share. In this way they will lay up treasure for themselves as a firm foundation for the coming age, so that they may take hold of the life that is truly life.

Timothy, guard what has been entrusted to your care. Turn away from godless chatter and the opposing ideas of what is falsely called knowledge, which some have professed and in so doing have departed from the faith."(1 Timothy 6:17-21)

Paul closes the chapter with instructions for the rich, urging them not to be haughty nor to set their hopes on the uncertainty of riches, but on God who richly provides us with everything to enjoy. He encourages generosity and good works, storing up treasure for themselves as a good foundation for the future. Timothy is reminded to guard what has been entrusted to him, avoiding irreverent babble and contradictions of what is falsely called "knowledge."

How are we stewarding the resources God has entrusted to us? Are we generous, willing to share, and investing in the work of the kingdom? Moreover, are we guarding the truth of the gospel, ensuring that our beliefs and teachings are rooted in Scripture? Let us be mindful of the responsibility we have to use our resources for God's glory and to remain steadfast in the truth of the gospel.

Conclusion

1 Timothy Chapter 6 challenges us to evaluate our priorities, to pursue godliness with contentment, to resist the lure of materialism, and to live in a manner worthy of our calling. A

s we seek to apply these truths to our lives, may we be reminded of the profound joy and peace that come from living in alignment with God's will, fighting the good fight of faith, and setting our hope on the eternal riches found in Christ Jesus.

~ 2 TIMOTHY ~

Introduction

The book of 2 Timothy is traditionally understood as the Apostle Paul's final letter, written from a Roman prison and addressed to his beloved protégé, Timothy, who is leading the church in Ephesus. This epistle is both personal and profound, filled with Paul's reflections on his life of service, his impending death, and his final instructions and encouragements to Timothy. By way of introduction, I have provided a brief overview of each of the four chapters in this epistle.

Chapter 1:

Paul opens with a warm greeting, expressing his longing to see Timothy and recalling Timothy's sincere faith. He encourages Timothy to *"fan into flame the gift of God"* (v.6) and not to be ashamed of testifying about the Lord or of Paul, a prisoner for the Lord's sake. Instead, Timothy is to join Paul in suffering for the gospel, empowered by God.

Spiritual Heritage and Gift: Paul reminds Timothy of his spiritual heritage and the gift imparted through the laying on of hands, highlighting the importance of spiritual mentorship and the continuation of faith across generations.

A Call to Courage: The emphasis on not being ashamed and being willing to suffer for the gospel underlines the theme of courage and steadfastness in the face of persecution, a theme that resonates throughout the letter.

Chapter 2:

Paul uses three metaphors to describe the Christian life: a soldier, an athlete, and a farmer, each illustrating aspects of dedication, discipline, and hard work. He emphasizes the importance of remaining faithful to the teachings of Jesus and avoiding quarrels that lead nowhere. Paul also highlights the importance of godly living for effective ministry.

Endurance and Faithfulness: The call to endure hardship as a good soldier of Christ Jesus (v.3) speaks to the commitment required in serving the gospel, akin to the discipline seen in soldiers, athletes, and farmers.

Correct Handling of the Word: The instruction to correctly handle the word of truth (v.15) stresses the importance of sound doctrine and the dangers of false teachings, which can lead to quarrels and divisions within the church.

Chapter 3:

Paul describes the challenges of the "last days," characterized by people's love for themselves, money, and pleasure rather than love for God. He warns Timothy about the dangers of false teachers who will lead people astray. Paul contrasts this by urging Timothy to continue in what he has learned, emphasizing the sacredness and utility of Scripture for teaching, rebuking, correcting, and training in righteousness.

Moral Decay and False Teaching: The vivid description of moral decay and false teaching in the last days serves as both a warning and a call to vigilance for Timothy and the church at large.

The Role of Scripture: Paul's affirmation of the inspiration and purpose of Scripture reinforces its central role in the believer's life and ministry, providing guidance, correction, and training to equip the servant of God for every good work.

Chapter 4:

In this final chapter, Paul charges Timothy to preach the word, to be prepared in season and out of season, and to correct, rebuke, and encourage with great patience and careful instruction.

Paul warns of a time when people will not put up with sound doctrine but instead, to suit their own desires, will gather around them a great number of teachers to say what their itching ears want to hear.

Paul reflects on his life as being "poured out like a drink offering" and expresses confidence in his reward from the Lord. He concludes with personal remarks and greetings.

Urgency of Preaching the Word: The solemn charge to preach the word (v.2) underscores the urgency and centrality of proclaiming the gospel, especially in the face of increasing opposition to sound doctrine.

Paul's Farewell: Paul's reflection on his life and ministry (v.6-8) is both poignant and powerful, offering a model of faithfulness and hope in the face of death. His confidence in the "crown of righteousness" awaiting him speaks to the assurance of eternal reward for those who have faithfully served Christ.

Final Instructions and Greetings: The personal notes and final greetings (v.9-22) reveal the communal aspect of ministry and the importance of support and fellowship among believers.

Conclusion

2 Timothy stands as a testament to the enduring power of faith, the importance of sound teaching, and the necessity of perseverance in the face of hardship. Paul's final letter to Timothy serves as a poignant reminder of the cost and reward of discipleship, calling all believers to faithfulness, diligence, and the relentless proclamation of the gospel.

Through his words, we are encouraged to stand firm in our faith, to uphold the truth of Scripture, and to finish the race set before us with our eyes fixed on Jesus, the author and perfecter of our faith.

Now I will unpack each of the four chapters in more detail as we explore this letter in more detail.

~ 2 TIMOTHY 1 ~

Introduction

In the shadow of his impending martyrdom, the Apostle Paul pens a deeply personal and powerful letter to Timothy, his beloved son in the faith. The opening chapter of 2 Timothy is not merely a greeting; it is a clarion call to courage, faithfulness, and the stewardship of the gospel amid hardship.

As we explore this poignant chapter, let us listen closely to Paul's heart and find encouragement for our own journey of faith.

The Gift of Heritage and Faith (1:1-5)

> *"Paul, an apostle of Christ Jesus by the will of God, in keeping with the promise of life that is in Christ Jesus, to Timothy, my dear son: Grace, mercy and peace from God the Father and Christ Jesus our Lord.*
>
> *I thank God, whom I serve, as my ancestors did, with a clear conscience, as night and day I constantly remember you in my prayers. Recalling your tears, I long to see you, so that I may be filled with joy. I am reminded of your sincere faith, which first lived in your grandmother Lois and in your mother Eunice and, I am persuaded, now lives in you also." (2 Timothy 1:1-5)*

Paul begins by grounding Timothy in the faithfulness of his heritage - a faith first lived out by his grandmother Lois and his mother Eunice. This reminder serves not only to affirm Timothy but also to remind all believers of the spiritual legacy they either have received or are called to pass on. The genuine faith that dwelt in Timothy is a testament to the power of godly influence and the importance of nurturing faith within the family and community.

Reflect on your own spiritual heritage. Whether you come from a long line of believers or are the first in your family to follow Christ, you are part of a greater story - God's redemptive work through generations.

Consider how you are contributing to this legacy. Are you nurturing faith in those God has placed in your life, modelling genuine faith that inspires others?

Fan into Flame the Gift of God (1:6-7)

> *"For this reason, I remind you to fan into flame the gift of God, which is in you through the laying on of my hands. For the Spirit God gave us does not make us timid, but gives us power, love and self-discipline." (2 Timothy 1:6-7)*

Paul exhorts Timothy to *"fan into flame the gift of God,"* a vivid metaphor reminding Timothy (and us) of the need to actively cultivate the spiritual gifts God has bestowed upon the church. The spirit God has given us is not one of fear but of power, love, and self-discipline. In the face of intimidation or suffering for the gospel, believers are empowered by the Holy Spirit to stand firm with courage and conviction.

Consider the gifts God has entrusted to you. Are you actively seeking to develop and use these gifts in service to the Lord and His people? Let us reject fear, embracing instead the power, love, and self-discipline that the Holy Spirit provides, to boldly live out our calling.

Do Not Be Ashamed (1:8-12)

> *"So do not be ashamed of the testimony about our Lord or of me his prisoner. Rather, join with me in suffering for the gospel, by the power of God. He has saved us and called us to a holy life — not because of anything we have done but because of his own purpose and grace. This grace was given us in Christ Jesus before the beginning of time, but it has now been revealed through the appearing of our Saviour, Christ Jesus, who has destroyed death and has brought life and immortality to light through the gospel. And of this gospel I was appointed a herald and an apostle and a teacher. That is why I am suffering as I am. Yet this is no cause for shame, because I know whom I have believed, and am convinced that he is able to guard what I have entrusted to him until that day." (2 Timothy 1:8-12)*

Paul's charge to Timothy to not be ashamed of the testimony about our Lord or of Paul himself is a powerful reminder of the cost of discipleship. Paul, imprisoned and facing death for the gospel, embodies the call to suffer for the sake of Christ. Yet, in his suffering, Paul's confidence remains unshaken, grounded in his knowledge of Whom he has believed and convinced of God's ability to guard what has been entrusted to him.

Are there areas in your life where fear of shame or rejection has silenced your testimony or hindered your obedience? Paul's example challenges us to look beyond our present circumstances, fixing our eyes on the eternal God we serve, who is faithful to sustain and empower us.

Guard the Good Deposit (1:13-14)

> *"What you heard from me, keep as the pattern of sound teaching, with faith and love in Christ Jesus. Guard the good deposit that was entrusted to you - guard it with the help of the Holy Spirit who lives in us." (2 Timothy 1:13-14)*

Paul closes this chapter by urging Timothy to hold fast to the sound teaching he has received and to guard the good deposit of faith with the help of the Holy Spirit. This exhortation serves as a strong reminder of the preciousness of the gospel and the responsibility of every believer to preserve and proclaim it.

How are we guarding the gospel in our own lives and ensuring its faithful transmission to others? In a world of shifting truths and moral ambiguity, let us commit to being people of the Word, deeply rooted in the truth of Scripture, and reliant on the Holy Spirit to guide and empower us.

Conclusion

The first chapter of 2 Timothy stands as a testament to the power of faith, the importance of spiritual heritage, and the call to courageous faithfulness in the face of adversity. As Paul encouraged Timothy, so too are we encouraged to fan into flame the gift of God within us, to live unashamed of the gospel, and to guard the precious truth entrusted to us.

Introduction

This chapter is a very rich tapestry of guidance, exhortation, and profound theology, aimed not just at Timothy, a young leader in the early church, but at all believers, calling us to endurance, faithfulness, and diligent pursuit of truth.

As we unpack this chapter, let's reflect on its relevance to our lives today, encouraging us to stand firm in our faith and engage in the work God has called us to.

The Call to Endurance (2:1-13)

"You then, my son, be strong in the grace that is in Christ Jesus. And the things you have heard me say in the presence of many witnesses entrust to reliable people who will also be qualified to teach others. Join with me in suffering, like a good soldier of Christ Jesus. No one serving as a soldier gets entangled in civilian affairs, but rather tries to please his commanding officer.

Similarly, anyone who competes as an athlete does not receive the victor's crown except by competing according to the rules. The hardworking farmer should be the first to receive a share of the crops. Reflect on what I am saying, for the Lord will give you insight into all this.

Remember Jesus Christ, raised from the dead, descended from David. This is my gospel, for which I am suffering even to the point of being chained like a criminal. But God's word is not chained. Therefore, I endure everything for the sake of the elect, that they too may obtain the salvation that is in Christ Jesus, with eternal glory.

Here is a trustworthy saying: If we died with him, we will also live with him; if we endure, we will also reign with him. If we disown him, he will also disown us; if we are faithless, he remains faithful, for he cannot disown himself." (2 Timothy 2:1-13)

Paul is urging Timothy to be strong in the grace that is in Christ Jesus. The strength Paul refers to isn't physical; it's a spiritual fortitude that comes from a deep relationship with Christ.

He uses three metaphors to describe the Christian life: a soldier, an athlete, and a farmer, each highlighting aspects of discipline, adherence to rules, and hard work that leads to reward.

Like Timothy, we are called to endure hardships for the sake of the Gospel. This means staying focused on our mission, obeying God's commands, and patiently working towards the Kingdom, even when the going gets tough. The question for us is, are we willing to endure hardship for the Gospel's sake?

Handling the Word of Truth (2:14-19)

> *"Keep reminding God's people of these things. Warn them before God against quarrelling about words; it is of no value, and only ruins those who listen. Do your best to present yourself to God as one approved, a worker who does not need to be ashamed and who correctly handles the word of truth.*
>
> *Avoid godless chatter, because those who indulge in it will become more and more ungodly. Their teaching will spread like gangrene. Among them are Hymenaeus and Philetus, who have departed from the truth. They say that the resurrection has already taken place, and they destroy the faith of some.*
>
> *Nevertheless, God's solid foundation stands firm, sealed with this inscription: "The Lord knows those who are his," and, "Everyone who confesses the name of the Lord must turn away from wickedness." (2 Timothy 2:14-19)*

Paul warns Timothy about quarrelling over words and godless chatter, which only lead to ruin. Instead, Timothy is to rightly handle the word of truth, steering clear of falsehoods that can erode faith. This section is a stark reminder of the responsibility that comes with teaching and living out the Gospel. In our era of information overload, discerning truth from falsehood is more crucial than ever.

We are tasked with diligently studying and accurately teaching God's Word, ensuring that our lives and teachings reflect His truth.

Instruments for Special Purposes (2:20-26)

> *"Flee the evil desires of youth and pursue righteousness, faith, love and peace, along with those who call on the Lord out of a pure heart.*
>
> *Don't have anything to do with foolish and stupid arguments because you know they produce quarrels. And the Lord's servant must not be quarrelsome but must be kind to everyone, able to teach, not resentful.*
>
> *Opponents must be gently instructed, in the hope that God will grant them repentance leading them to a knowledge of the truth, and that they will come to their senses and escape from the trap of the devil, who has taken them captive to do his will."*
> *(2 Timothy 2:20-26)*

Paul uses the analogy of a large house to describe the church, filled with vessels which have varying materials and purposes. He encourages Timothy to cleanse himself to be an instrument for noble purposes. This purification process involves fleeing from youthful passions and pursuing righteousness, faith, love, and peace.

We must examine our lives and rid ourselves of anything that hinders our effectiveness for God's work. This means letting go of sinful desires and instead, pursuing virtues that draw us closer to God and make us more like Christ.

Conclusion

2 Timothy Chapter 2 presents a compelling call to perseverance, faithfulness, and purity in our Christian walk. Paul's instructions to Timothy echo across the centuries to us, urging us to withstand hardship, engage diligently with the truth of God's Word, and purify ourselves for His service.

Let's take these words to heart, allowing them to spur us on in our faith journey. May we be strong in the grace of Christ Jesus, handling the word of truth with care, and striving to be vessels of honour, ready for every good work God calls us to.

As we close, let us remember Paul's assurance: If we die with Him, we will also live with Him; if we endure, we will also reign with Him. Let this promise inspire us to faithful endurance, knowing that our labour in the Lord is not in vain.

Introduction

This chapter paints a very vivid picture of the challenges faced by believers due to the moral and spiritual decay in our society.

Paul's words to Timothy serve as a sobering reminder that the journey of faith is navigated through tumultuous waters, but also as a beacon of light and hope, and a guide for living faithfully in challenging times.

The Perilous Times (3:1-9)

"But mark this: There will be terrible times in the last days. People will be lovers of themselves, lovers of money, boastful, proud, abusive, disobedient to their parents, ungrateful, unholy, without love, unforgiving, slanderous, without self-control, brutal, not lovers of the good, treacherous, rash, conceited, lovers of pleasure rather than lovers of God - having a form of godliness but denying its power. Have nothing to do with such people.

They are the kind who worm their way into homes and gain control over gullible women, who are loaded down with sins and are swayed by all kinds of evil desires, always learning but never able to come to a knowledge of the truth.

Just as Jannes and Jambres opposed Moses, so also these teachers oppose the truth. They are men of depraved minds, who, as far as the faith is concerned, are rejected. But they will not get very far because, as in the case of those men, their folly will be clear to everyone." (2 Timothy 3:1-9)

Paul begins by warning Timothy of the perilous times to come in the "last days," characterized by people who are lovers of themselves, lovers of money, boastful, proud, abusive, and having a form of godliness but denying its power. These descriptors are not just ancient observations; they are a mirror reflecting our own society today.

The challenge for us is to recognize these attitudes within ourselves and our society, and to respond not with despair but with discernment and faithfulness. As believers, we are called to stand in contrast to these behaviours, embodying Christ's love, humility, and truth in our words and actions.

Holding to the Truth (3:10-17)

"You, however, know all about my teaching, my way of life, my purpose, faith, patience, love, endurance, persecutions, sufferings - what kinds of things happened to me in Antioch, Iconium and Lystra, the persecutions I endured. Yet the Lord rescued me from all of them. In fact, everyone who wants to live a godly life in Christ Jesus will be persecuted, while evildoers and impostors will go from bad to worse, deceiving and being deceived.

But as for you, continue in what you have learned and have become convinced of, because you know those from whom you learned it, and how from infancy you have known the Holy Scriptures, which are able to make you wise for salvation through faith in Christ Jesus. All Scripture is God-breathed and is useful for teaching, rebuking, correcting and training in righteousness, so that the servant of God may be thoroughly equipped for every good work." (2 Timothy 3:10-17)

In contrast to the grim picture painted earlier, Paul then focuses on the importance of holding to the truth of the Gospel. He reminds Timothy of his own example in teaching, in conduct, in purpose, in faith, in patience, in love, and in endurance amidst persecutions and sufferings. Paul emphasizes that all who desire to live a godly life in Christ Jesus will be persecuted, yet they are not without hope.

Paul also underscores the importance of Scripture, stating that *"All Scripture is God-breathed and is useful for teaching, rebuking, correcting and training in righteousness."* This powerful affirmation reminds us that the Bible is not just a historical document or a collection of moral tales, but the living word of God, essential for our formation as followers of Christ.

We are urged to immerse ourselves in the Scriptures, allowing God's word to shape us, guide us, and equip us for every good work. In an age of relative truth and scepticism, holding fast to the biblical truth is our anchor and guide.

Paul concludes with a powerful statement on the purpose and utility of Scripture: to equip the believer for every good work. This equipping is comprehensive, addressing every aspect of our being and calling us to a life of service, righteousness, and godliness.

This passage challenges us to ask ourselves if we are truly allowing Scripture to equip us. Are we engaging with the Word in a way that transforms us, prepares us, and compels us to action? Our engagement with Scripture is not meant to be passive but active, shaping us to be agents of God's love, truth, and justice in the world.

Conclusion

Chapter 3 offers us both a warning and a guide. It warns us of the challenges and opposition we will face as believers in a world that often runs counter to the values of the Kingdom of God. Yet, it also guides us on how to live faithfully amidst these challenges - by holding fast to the truth of the Gospel, allowing ourselves to be shaped by Scripture, and living out our calling with perseverance and love.

As we go forth this week, let us reflect on how we can embody the teachings of this chapter in our own lives. May we be lights in the darkness, truth-speakers in a world of deception, and beacons of hope for those seeking the way.

Let us hold firmly to the Word of God, allowing it to equip us for every good work, that we might live out our faith boldly and courageously.

Introduction

We come now to the closing chapter of Paul's second letter to Timothy, 2 Timothy Chapter 4. This passage stands as a solemn charge, a poignant farewell from Paul, and a timeless beacon for all who seek to faithfully follow Christ.

Paul, aware that his earthly journey is nearing its end, imparts wisdom, encouragement, and instructions not only to Timothy but to all believers, urging us to remain steadfast in our faith and diligent in our service to the Lord.

The Charge to Preach the Word (4:1-5)

"In the presence of God and of Christ Jesus, who will judge the living and the dead, and in view of his appearing and his kingdom, I give you this charge: Preach the word; be prepared in season and out of season; correct, rebuke and encourage - with great patience and careful instruction.

For the time will come when people will not put up with sound doctrine. Instead, to suit their own desires, they will gather around them a great number of teachers to say what their itching ears want to hear. They will turn their ears away from the truth and turn aside to myths. But you, keep your head in all situations, endure hardship, do the work of an evangelist, discharge all the duties of your ministry." (2 Timothy 4:1-5)

Paul begins with a solemn charge to Timothy, urging him to preach the Word in season and out of season, to correct, rebuke, and encourage with great patience and careful instruction. This charge is set against the backdrop of a time when people will not put up with sound doctrine but will gather teachers who say what their itching ears want to hear.

This exhortation remains critically relevant for us today. In an era of relativism and the dilution of truth, the call to preach the Gospel faithfully and to stand firm on the teachings of Scripture challenges every believer.

We must be prepared to speak God's truth, even when it is unpopular or inconvenient, doing so with love, patience, and integrity.

Paul's Farewell (4:6-8)

"For I am already being poured out like a drink offering, and the time for my departure is near. I have fought the good fight, I have finished the race, I have kept the faith. Now there is in store for me the crown of righteousness, which the Lord, the righteous Judge, will award to me on that day - and not only to me, but also to all who have longed for his appearing." (2 Timothy 4:6-8)

Paul reflects on his life and ministry with the metaphor of being poured out like a drink offering, signalling the imminent end of his earthly life. He declares, "*I have fought the good fight, I have finished the race, I have kept the faith.*" Paul's words are not just a farewell; they are a testament to a life lived in faithful service to Jesus Christ.

Paul's reflection invites us to consider our own spiritual journey. Are we living in such a way that, at the end of our days, we can also declare we have fought the good fight and kept the faith? Let this be a call to perseverance and faithfulness in our Christian walk.

The Call to Endurance (4:9-18)

"Do your best to come to me quickly, for Demas, because he loved this world, has deserted me and has gone to Thessalonica. Crescens has gone to Galatia, and Titus to Dalmatia. Only Luke is with me.

Get Mark and bring him with you, because he is helpful to me in my ministry. I sent Tychicus to Ephesus. When you come, bring the cloak that I left with Carpus at Troas, and my scrolls, especially the parchments.

Alexander the metalworker did me a great deal of harm. The Lord will repay him for what he has done. You too should be on your guard against him, because he strongly opposed our message."

"At my first defence, no one came to my support, but everyone deserted me. May it not be held against them. But the Lord stood at my side and gave me strength, so that through me the message might be fully proclaimed and all the Gentiles might hear it. And I was delivered from the lion's mouth.

The Lord will rescue me from every evil attack and will bring me safely to his heavenly kingdom. To him be glory for ever and ever. Amen." (2 Timothy 4:9-18)

Paul expresses some personal sentiments, requesting Timothy's presence and sharing about his current circumstances, including the desertion by Demas and the support from Luke and others.

Despite all the hardships and loneliness, Paul affirms the Lord's presence and deliverance in his life, showcasing his unwavering trust in God.

Like Paul, we may face loneliness, hardships, and even betrayal in our journey. Yet, the call to endurance reminds us that God's presence is constant. We are never truly alone. In our trials, let us lean into God's enduring presence and faithfulness.

Final Greetings and Benediction (4:19-22)

"Greet Priscilla and Aquila and the household of Onesiphorus. Erastus stayed in Corinth, and I left Trophimus sick in Miletus. Do your best to get here before winter. Eubulus greets you, and so do Pudens, Linus, Claudia and all the brothers and sisters. The Lord be with your spirit. Grace be with you all."
(2 Timothy 4:19-22)

Paul concludes his final letter with personal greetings and a benediction, extending grace to Timothy and all who are in Christ Jesus.

These closing words, though personal, encapsulate the heart of Paul's message throughout the letter — a message of grace, community, and perseverance in faith.

As we close this chapter and letter, let us reflect on the grace that has been extended to us in Christ Jesus. May we also extend grace to those around us, fostering a community of faith that supports, encourages, and builds up one another in love.

Conclusion

2 Timothy Chapter 4 stands as a powerful reminder of the call to faithfulness, the reality of hardship, and the promise of God's enduring presence.

As we go forth, may we take to heart Paul's charge to preach the Word, to fight the good fight of faith, and to finish the race set before us with perseverance and joy.

~ TITUS ~

Introduction

The book of Titus is a pastoral epistle written by the Apostle Paul to his fellow worker, Titus, who was overseeing the church on the island of Crete. This letter provides instructions on church organization, leadership, and Christian living, emphasizing good works as evidence of true faith. Through its three chapters, Paul articulates a vision for a healthy church, marked by sound teaching, godly leadership, and a community living out the transformative power of the Gospel. Let's look at an overview of these three chapters.

Chapter 1:

Paul begins by affirming the reason for leaving Titus in Crete: to appoint elders in every town according to the qualifications laid out by Paul. These qualifications focus on character, family life, hospitality, love for what is good, self-control, and holiness. The chapter also addresses the issue of false teachers, highlighting their disruptive influence and the necessity for rebuke to promote sound faith.

Leadership Qualifications: A detailed criteria for elders underscore the importance of integrity, both in personal and public life, reflecting the character of God Himself. Leadership in the church is not merely about capability but godliness.

Confronting False Teachers: The presence of false teachers in Crete presented a significant challenge, promoting Jewish myths and legalistic practices. Paul's directive to Titus to rebuke them sharply illustrates the importance of protecting the integrity of the Gospel and ensuring that the church remains rooted in the truth of Scripture.

Chapter 2:

Paul outlines the behaviours expected of various demographic groups within the church - older men, older women, young women, young men, and slaves - emphasizing that their conduct should reflect the transforming power of the Gospel.

Titus himself is called to be a model of good works, showing integrity and sound speech. The chapter culminates in a profound theological statement about the grace of God that brings salvation and trains us to live righteously while we await Christ's return.

Roles Within the Church: The specific instructions to different groups highlight the communal aspect of sanctification. Each member, regardless of age or social status, plays a crucial role in manifesting the kingdom of God on earth.

Theological Foundation: Paul roots ethical exhortations in the theological truth of Christ's redeeming work and impending return. This ensures that ethical behaviour is not pursued as a means of earning salvation but as a response to the grace already received.

Chapter 3:

The final chapter reinforces the importance of submission to authorities and readiness to perform good works, warning again against divisiveness and quarrelling.

Paul reminds Titus and the Cretan believers of their past condition, the transformative work of the Holy Spirit in salvation, and the basis of justification by grace. This theological grounding leads to a practical exhortation for believers to devote themselves to good works, meeting urgent needs and avoiding unprofitable controversies.

Christian Witness in Society: Paul's emphasis on good works and peaceful living in society serves as a witness to the transformative power of the Gospel. By living in contrast to the prevailing culture, Christians demonstrate the reality of God's kingdom.

Salvation and Good Works: The reminder of the believers' past and the grace of God in their lives serves to motivate godly living. Good works are framed not as the basis of salvation but as its natural and necessary fruit, showcasing the integral relationship between faith and works in the Christian life.

Conclusion

The book of Titus offers a compelling blueprint for church health and Christian living that balances doctrinal integrity with ethical conduct. Paul's instructions to Titus underscore the necessity of godly leadership, sound teaching, and a life marked by good works as evidence of genuine faith.

In doing so, Paul paints a picture of the church as a community that reflects the grace and goodness of God to a watching world. Through Titus, we are reminded that the Gospel not only saves us but also summons us to a life of purposeful engagement with the world, grounded in the hope of Christ's return and the ultimate renewal of all things.

Now I will unpack each of the three chapters in more detail as we explore this letter in more detail.

~ TITUS 1 ~

Introduction

In the pastoral letter to Titus, one of his trusted companions, the Apostle Paul addresses the critical theme of leadership within the church. Situated in Crete, a society known for its moral challenges, Titus faced the formidable task of establishing order and godliness. Chapter 1 of this letter provides not only the qualifications for church leaders but also underscores the spiritual warfare against false teachings that threaten the integrity of the Gospel. As we delve into this chapter, let's explore the profound principles of godly leadership and their application in our lives and churches today.

The Charge to Titus (1:1-5)

> *"Paul, a servant of God and an apostle of Jesus Christ to further the faith of God's elect and their knowledge of the truth that leads to godliness - in the hope of eternal life, which God, who does not lie, promised before the beginning of time, and which now at his appointed season he has brought to light through the preaching entrusted to me by the command of God our Saviour to Titus, my true son in our common faith: Grace and peace from God the Father and Christ Jesus our Saviour*
>
> *The reason I left you in Crete was that you might put in order what was left unfinished and appoint[a] elders in every town, as I directed you." (Titus 1:1-5)*

Paul begins by establishing his apostolic authority and then his mission of promoting faith and knowledge among God's elect. The greeting sets the stage for the entire letter, highlighting the themes of truth, godliness, and the hope of eternal life.

Paul's specific charge to Titus was to appoint elders in every town, a task of critical importance for the young church in Crete. This mandate reveals the necessity of structured leadership in the flourishing of the church community.

Like Titus, we are called to be stewards of God's truth in our communities. The task of building up the church will require discernment, courage, and a deep commitment to God's clearly stated standards. How are we contributing to the establishment and strengthening of godly leadership within our spheres of influence?

Qualifications for Elders (1:6-9)

"An elder must be blameless, faithful to his wife, a man whose children believe and are not open to the charge of being wild and disobedient. Since an overseer manages God's household, he must be blameless - not overbearing, not quick-tempered, not given to drunkenness, not violent, not pursuing dishonest gain. Rather, he must be hospitable, one who loves what is good, who is self-controlled, upright, holy and disciplined. He must hold firmly to the trustworthy message as it has been taught, so that he can encourage others by sound doctrine and refute those who oppose it." (Titus 1:6-9)

The criteria laid out for elders (overseers) are stringent, focusing on character, family life, and doctrinal integrity. We should understand by now that the culture within which Paul ministered would not have considered a woman for such roles which is why the text only addresses men.

There are many female elders serving across the Church today and so the underlying principles Paul outlines are applicable to women elders also.

An elder must be blameless, faithful in marriage, and his/her children must be believers not accused of debauchery or rebellion. Additionally, an elder must be hospitable, self-controlled, upright, holy, disciplined, able to teach, not a drunkard, not violent, gentle, not quarrelsome, and not greedy.

These qualifications transcend mere skill sets or charisma, highlighting the importance of a transformed life that reflects the character of Christ.

The call to leadership is a call to holiness. For those in leadership, these qualifications serve as a mirror for self-examination and growth. For the wider church, they provide a guideline for recognizing and affirming godly leaders. Let us strive for such character in our lives, knowing that we all influence others, whether we hold official titles of leadership or not.

The Threat of False Teachers (1:10-16)

"For there are many rebellious people, full of meaningless talk and deception, especially those of the circumcision group. They must be silenced, because they are disrupting whole households by teaching things they ought not to teach - and that for the sake of dishonest gain.

One of Crete's own prophets has said it: "Cretans are always liars, evil brutes, lazy gluttons." This saying is true. Therefore, rebuke them sharply, so that they will be sound in the faith and will pay no attention to Jewish myths or to the merely human commands of those who reject the truth.

To the pure, all things are pure, but to those who are corrupted and do not believe, nothing is pure. In fact, both their minds and consciences are corrupted. They claim to know God, but by their actions they deny him. They are detestable, disobedient and unfit for doing anything good." (Titus 1:10-16)

Paul warns of false teachers, especially those of the circumcision party, who were disrupting the church by teaching for shameful gain what they ought not to teach. These individuals were leading others astray, prioritizing tradition and legalism over the transformative power of the Gospel. Paul's instructions to rebuke them sharply underscore the necessity of protecting the flock from doctrines that lead away from the truth of the Gospel.

The church today is certainly not immune to the influence of false teachings. How are we guarding ourselves and our communities against such dangers? Are we grounded in Scripture, able to discern truth from error?

Let us be committed to studying God's Word, fostering a love for truth, and courageously standing against any teaching that distorts the Gospel.

Conclusion

Titus Chapter 1 lays a solid foundation for understanding godly leadership and the vigilance required to maintain the integrity of the church's teaching.

As we reflect on these principles, let us pray for wisdom and strength to apply them in our lives, aspiring to the character of the leaders described here, and actively participating in the life of our church communities with discernment and grace.

May we be leaders who reflect the heart of our Lord Jesus Christ, leading others to Him through our words and our lives.

Introduction

Paul's letter to Titus, specifically the second chapter, provides a blueprint for Christian living that transcends time and culture. It outlines how believers of various demographics within the church - older men, older women, young women, young men, and workers - should conduct themselves. At its core, Titus 2 challenges us to reflect the transforming power of the Gospel not just in our beliefs, but in our daily actions and relationships. Today, we will explore how these instructions apply to our lives, urging us to live out the Gospel in a way that adorns the doctrine of God our Saviour.

Teaching Sound Doctrine (2:1)

"You, however, must teach what is appropriate to sound doctrine." (Titus 2:1)

Paul begins with a simple yet profound exhortation to Titus: "But as for you, teach what accords with sound doctrine." This call sets the stage for the practical advice that follows, underscoring the importance of our lives reflecting the truth of the Gospel we profess.

Are we committed to learning and living out sound doctrine in our daily lives? Sound doctrine isn't merely about correct theology; it's about letting that theology shape our lives, our decisions, and our relationships. Let us be people who not only know the Word but live it, demonstrating the beauty and truth of the Gospel in every aspect of our lives.

Living Examples in the Church (2:2-10)

"Teach the older men to be temperate, worthy of respect, self-controlled, and sound in faith, in love and in endurance.
Likewise, teach the older women to be reverent in the way they live, not to be slanderers or addicted to much wine, but to teach what is good."

"Then they can urge the younger women to love their husbands and children, to be self-controlled and pure, to be busy at home, to be kind, and to be subject to their husbands, so that no one will malign the word of God.

Similarly, encourage the young men to be self-controlled. In everything set them an example by doing what is good. In your teaching show integrity, seriousness 8 and soundness of speech that cannot be condemned, so that those who oppose you may be ashamed because they have nothing bad to say about us.

Teach slaves to be subject to their masters in everything, to try to please them, not to talk back to them, and not to steal from them, but to show that they can be fully trusted, so that in every way they will make the teaching about God our Saviour attractive."
(Titus 2:2-10)

Paul provides specific instructions for various groups within the church, emphasizing virtues like sober-mindedness, dignity, self-control, purity, and love. These instructions are not arbitrary moral codes but they are designed to show how the Gospel can transform every aspect of our lives, from how we teach and love to how we work and interact with others.

Older Men and Women: They are to be examples of faith, love, and patience, embodying the wisdom and maturity that come from walking with God.

Young Women and Men: They are encouraged to live lives of purity and integrity, setting an example for others in their conduct and devotion to God.

Workers: They are called to show integrity, honesty, and faithfulness in their work, making the teaching about God our Saviour attractive to all.

Regardless of our age or stage in life, we are called to live in a manner worthy of the Gospel. How does your life reflect the transformative power of the Gospel to those around you? Are you an example of godliness in your family, workplace, and community? Let's strive to be people whose lives make the Gospel attractive to others.

The Grace of God That Brings Salvation (2:11-15)

"For the grace of God has appeared that offers salvation to all people. It teaches us to say "No" to ungodliness and worldly passions, and to live self-controlled, upright and godly lives in this present age, while we wait for the blessed hope - the appearing of the glory of our great God and Saviour, Jesus Christ, who gave himself for us to redeem us from all wickedness and to purify for himself a people that are his very own, eager to do what is good.

These, then, are the things you should teach. Encourage and rebuke with all authority. Do not let anyone despise you." *(Titus 2:11-15)*

In these verses, Paul presents the theological foundation for the ethical exhortations given earlier. The grace of God has appeared, bringing salvation for all people, training us to renounce ungodliness and worldly passions and to live self-controlled, upright, and godly lives in the present age. This passage reminds us that our motivation for godly living is not to earn God's favour but to respond to the grace we have already received in Christ Jesus.

Are we allowing the grace of God to train us in godliness? The Christian life is not a static achievement but a dynamic process of being shaped and moulded by God's grace. Let this grace fuel your desire for holiness, knowing that you are empowered by the Holy Spirit to live a life that pleases God.

Paul concludes with a reminder of our ultimate hope - the glorious appearing of our great God and Saviour, Jesus Christ. This future hope has present implications, motivating us to live godly lives as we await Christ's return. How does the hope of Christ's return impact your daily living? Are you living in a way that anticipates His coming?

Let the hope of the Gospel not only comfort you in trials but also challenge you to live each day for the glory of God.

Paul finishes this chapter with verse 15 which emphasises the importance of teaching, encouragement, and rebuke in Christian leadership, all carried out with God-given authority.

Paul instructs Titus to assertively guide the believers, ensuring his teachings align with sound doctrine and are delivered with confidence. This verse underlines the important balance between encouragement and correction in fostering a godly community, highlighting the leader's role in promoting spiritual growth and integrity.

Conclusion

Titus Chapter 2 calls us to a life that beautifully reflects the Gospel. As individuals and as a church, let's commit to living in a way that honours God, serves others, and points a watching world to the hope we have in Christ.

May our lives be so marked by the grace of God that those around us are drawn to the Saviour we love and serve.

~ TITUS 3 ~

Introduction

In the final chapter of Paul's letter to Titus, we are presented with a rather powerful juxtaposition of the life we once lived, the transformative work of Christ on our behalf, and the resultant call to engage in good works. This chapter not only encapsulates the essence of the Christian faith but also propels us toward living out that faith in practical, everyday expressions of kindness, generosity, and godliness.

As we explore chapter 3, let us be reminded of the depth of God's mercy towards us and the high calling we have to reflect His love to the world around us.

A Reminder of Our Past and Present (3:1-3)

> *"Remind the people to be subject to rulers and authorities, to be obedient, to be ready to do whatever is good, to slander no one, to be peaceable and considerate, and always to be gentle toward everyone. At one time we too were foolish, disobedient, deceived and enslaved by all kinds of passions and pleasures. We lived in malice and envy, being hated and hating one another."*
> *(Titus 3:1-3)*

Paul begins by instructing Titus to remind the believers in Crete to be submissive to rulers and authorities, to be obedient, and to be ready for every good work. This call to submission and readiness for good works is set against the backdrop of our former way of life - characterized by foolishness, disobedience, and enslavement to various passions and pleasures. This stark contrast serves as a humbling reminder of where we have come from and the transformative power of the Gospel in our lives.

Reflect on your own life before encountering Christ and the changes He has made in you. In light of this transformation, how are we living out our new identity in Christ? Are we engaging in good works, not out of a desire to earn God's favour, but as a natural outflow of the grace we have received?

The Foundation of Our Salvation (3:4-7)

"But when the kindness and love of God our Saviour appeared, he saved us, not because of righteous things we had done, but because of his mercy. He saved us through the washing of rebirth and renewal by the Holy Spirit, whom he poured out on us generously through Jesus Christ our Saviour, so that, having been justified by his grace, we might become heirs having the hope of eternal life." (Titus 3:4-7)

The heart of this chapter, and indeed the entire letter, is found in these verses, where Paul beautifully articulates the basis of our salvation. It is not because of righteous things we had done, but because of God's mercy, through the washing of rebirth and renewal by the Holy Spirit.

This salvation, poured out generously through Jesus Christ our Saviour, justifies us by His grace and makes us heirs of eternal life. This passage is a profound declaration of the Gospel - our salvation is entirely the work of God's grace, from start to finish.

How does this understanding of salvation by grace through faith in Jesus Christ impact the way you live? Are you resting in the assurance of God's grace, or are you still striving to earn His approval? Let us rejoice in the freedom of our salvation, which empowers us to serve God and others with joy and peace.

The Call to Good Works and Godly Living (3:8-15)

"This is a trustworthy saying. And I want you to stress these things, so that those who have trusted in God may be careful to devote themselves to doing what is good. These things are excellent and profitable for everyone.

But avoid foolish controversies and genealogies and arguments and quarrels about the law, because these are unprofitable and useless. Warn a divisive person once, and then warn them a second time. After that, have nothing to do with them. You may be sure that such people are warped and sinful; they are self-condemned."

"As soon as I send Artemas or Tychicus to you, do your best to come to me at Nicopolis, because I have decided to winter there. Do everything you can to help Zenas the lawyer and Apollos on their way and see that they have everything they need. Our people must learn to devote themselves to doing what is good, in order to provide for urgent needs and not live unproductive lives.

Everyone with me sends you greetings. Greet those who love us in the faith." (Titus 3:8-15)

Paul wraps up this letter by emphasizing the great importance of believers engaging in good works, which are profitable for everyone. This exhortation to maintain good deeds is not a supplementary aspect of our faith but a crucial element of our witness to the world. Paul also addresses the need for discipline within the church, instructing Titus to warn divisive individuals and, if necessary, to have nothing more to do with them, highlighting the importance of unity and purity within the body of Christ.

In what ways are you actively participating in good works within your community? Are you contributing to the unity and purity of the church, or are you sowing seeds of division and strife? Let us be diligent in pursuing good works, eager to help cases of urgent need, and avoid unprofitable controversies, thus reflecting the character of Christ in our actions and relationships.

Conclusion

Titus Chapter 3 calls us to remember the depths from which we have been lifted by the grace of God, to rejoice in the salvation we have received purely as a gift through Jesus Christ, and to respond by living lives marked by good works and godliness.

This is the essence of the Christian life - a life transformed by grace, lived out in gratitude, and characterized by love and good deeds toward all.

~ PHILEMON ~

Introduction

This New Testament book is a personal letter written by the Apostle Paul to Philemon, a wealthy Christian and church living in Colossae. This epistle, while brief, is rich in themes of forgiveness, reconciliation, and the transformative power of the Gospel in social relationships.

Through Paul's appeal for Onesimus, a runaway slave who had become a Christian, the letter beautifully illustrates how the Gospel breaks down social barriers and creates new, godly relationships within the body of Christ. Let's explore a detailed commentary and analysis of this profound letter.

Background and Context:

Philemon owned Onesimus, who had run away, possibly after having stolen from his master. Onesimus fled to Rome, where he encountered Paul and converted to Christianity.

Paul, imprisoned at the time, grew fond of Onesimus and saw his spiritual potential. Instead of keeping Onesimus with him, Paul decided to send him back to Philemon with this letter, appealing for Onesimus's forgiveness and acceptance not as a slave but as a brother in Christ.

Overview:

Opening (Verses 1-3): Paul begins with a warm greeting, not only to Philemon but also to Apphia, Archippus, and the church that meets in Philemon's home, indicating the communal nature of the letter's contents and implications. The inclusion of others in the greeting suggests that the matters discussed, while personal, have broader community relevance and impact.

Thanksgiving and Prayer (Verses 4-7): Paul expresses his gratitude for Philemon's love and faith towards Jesus and all the saints, highlighting Philemon's personal reputation for generosity and encouragement.

This sets a positive tone for the appeal that follows, reminding Philemon of the Christian virtues he is known for and subtly preparing him to act accordingly in the situation with Onesimus.

Paul's Appeal for Onesimus (Verses 8-21): In the heart of the letter, Paul makes a tactful and heartfelt appeal for Onesimus. He cleverly avoids direct commands, instead opting for persuasive and brotherly appeal, stressing the transformation in Onesimus's life. Paul emphasizes that Onesimus, whose name means "useful," has lived up to his name, not in the way he had previously as a slave but now more significantly as a brother in Christ.

Paul's request challenges the social norms of the time, elevating the relationship between slave and master to one of equality in Christ. He offers to repay any wrong or debt Onesimus owes, highlighting the theme of substitutionary atonement, though subtly implying that Philemon also owes Paul a "debt" for his own spiritual life. Paul expresses his desire for Onesimus to be welcomed as he would welcome Paul, blurring the lines between slave and free, and showing the radical implications of the Gospel on social structures.

Closing Remarks and Greetings (Verses 22-25): Paul concludes with a request for lodging, expressing his hope for release and anticipation of visiting Philemon, further strengthening the personal connection and mutual respect between them. He sends greetings from fellow workers and a final grace benediction, which seals the letter with a reminder of the grace that underpins the entire appeal and the Christian life.

Themes and Application:

Forgiveness and Reconciliation: Philemon stands as a powerful testament to the Gospel's call for forgiveness and reconciliation. Paul's appeal to Philemon to forgive Onesimus and welcome him back not as a slave but as a brother illustrates the radical nature of Christian forgiveness, which transcends social norms and legal rights.

The Transformative Power of the Gospel: The letter showcases the transformative impact of the Gospel on individual lives and relationships. Onesimus's conversion and subsequent change in status from slave to beloved brother exemplify how faith in Christ brings about deep internal transformation that has significant external implications.

Christian Equality: Philemon highlights the essential equality of all believers in Christ, regardless of social status. In the Kingdom of God, there is no slave or free, only brothers and sisters in Christ. This principle challenges us to examine and dismantle any remaining barriers of discrimination or inequality within the Christian community.

Summary:

The book of Philemon, while brief, delivers a potent message on the power of Christian love, forgiveness, and the radical social implications of the Gospel. It challenges us to embody the same spirit of reconciliation and mutual respect in our relationships, reflecting the unity and equality we share in Christ.

As we navigate our diverse and often divided world, may the timeless truths of Philemon inspire us to be agents of grace, reconciliation, and transformation in the communities God has placed us in.

Now let's have a closer look at this short, but important epistle.

Introduction

In the very heart of the New Testament, nestled between letters to churches and grand theological treatises, we find the personal, powerful letter of Paul to Philemon. This brief letter, though comprising only one chapter, unfolds the beauty of forgiveness, the challenge of reconciliation, and the radical nature of Gospel transformation. Let's examine this profound letter, exploring the story of Onesimus and Philemon, and uncovering the timeless truths that speak to the heart of Christian living.

Philemon, a wealthy Christian and church leader in Colossae, faces a personal and spiritual dilemma brought to his doorstep in the form of Onesimus, a runaway slave who has wronged him. Onesimus finds Paul in prison, becomes a Christian, and is now sent back to Philemon with this letter. Paul appeals to Philemon not on the basis of authority but love, asking him to forgive Onesimus and welcome him as a brother in Christ.

The Appeal of Love (1-21)

"Paul, a prisoner of Christ Jesus, and Timothy our brother, to Philemon our dear friend and fellow worker - also to Apphia our sister and Archippus our fellow soldier - and to the church that meets in your home: Grace and peace to you from God our Father and the Lord Jesus Christ.

I always thank my God as I remember you in my prayers, because I hear about your love for all his holy people and your faith in the Lord Jesus. I pray that your partnership with us in the faith may be effective in deepening your understanding of every good thing we share for the sake of Christ. Your love has given me great joy and encouragement, because you, brother, have refreshed the hearts of the Lord's people.

Therefore, although in Christ I could be bold and order you to do what you ought to do, yet I prefer to appeal to you on the basis of love."

~ THE IMPACT OF ONE MAN ~

The Apostle Paul, once a fervent and somewhat brutal persecutor of all Christians, experienced a very dramatic and profound transformation that redirected the course of his life and, subsequently, the Christian faith and the world at large.

His conversion on the road to Damascus stands as one of the most pivotal moments in religious history, embodying the transformative power of divine grace. As a result, Paul became one of Christianity's most ardent apostles, spreading the teachings of Jesus Christ across the Roman Empire.

Paul's extensive travels and missionary efforts played a crucial role in establishing early Christian communities throughout the Mediterranean region. His commitment to spreading the gospel across cultural and geographical boundaries laid the foundation for Christianity's expansion beyond its Jewish origins into a global religion. Paul's approach to evangelism, characterized by adaptability and deep theological insight, set a precedent for missionary work that continues to influence Christian missions today.

Beyond the establishment of churches and the direct conversion of individuals, Paul's impact is profoundly felt in the rich theological legacy he left behind. His letters to the early Christian communities, which make up a significant portion of the New Testament, address a wide array of theological, ethical, and practical issues.

These writings have shaped Christian doctrine on topics such as salvation, grace, the nature of the church, and the end times. Paul's articulation of justification by grace through faith has been particularly influential, underpinning so many other key theological developments and reform movements throughout church history. Moreover, Paul's teachings have transcended religious boundaries, influencing Western philosophy, legal thought, and cultural norms.

His nuanced views on issues such as law, authority, and social ethics have contributed to discussions on governance, justice, and human rights. The principles he espoused, particularly those related to love, equality, and freedom in Christ, have challenged societal structures and inspired movements for social change.

In addition to his theological and missionary achievements, Paul's life and work have had a profound impact on the cultural and intellectual development of the Western world. His epistles have influenced a wide range of literature, art, and philosophical thought, shaping the moral and ethical framework of Western civilization.

His emphasis on community, unity, and love continues to resonate across denominations and traditions, fostering efforts toward reconciliation and mutual understanding.

In summary, the Apostle Paul's contributions to the Christian faith and the broader world are immense and enduring. His life's work facilitated the spread of Christianity beyond its early confines, shaped so many foundational Christian doctrines, and influenced moral and ethical thought across centuries.

Through his writings and example, Paul continues to inspire, challenge, and guide believers and non-believers alike, leaving an indelible mark on the tapestry of human history.

I hope and pray that you have been as blessed reading this somewhat lengthy treatise as I have been writing it over the past twelve months. May God continue to challenge, inspire and bless you through the timeless letters from the heart of the great Apostle Paul.